Ma
Tel:

Forced Marriage

About the Editors

Dr Aisha K. Gill is a Senior Lecturer in Criminology at Roehampton University. She has been involved in addressing the problem of Violence Against Women (VAW) at the grassroots and activist levels for the past thirteen years. She is currently an active member of the 'End Violence Against Women' Coalition (EVAW), an invited advisor to the Independent Police Complaints Commission (IPCC) strategic support group on investigations and complaints involving gendered forms of violence against women in the UK, and a member of Kurdish Women's Rights Watch.

Dr Sundari Anitha is a Lecturer in Criminology at the School of Social Sciences, University of Lincoln. She previously worked as a manager in a Women's Aid refuge, is currently a trustee of a specialist refuge, Asha Projects, and is active in campaigning and policy making on violence against women.

Forced Marriage

Introducing a social justice and human rights perspective

Edited by

AISHA K. GILL and SUNDARI ANITHA

Zed Books

LONDON & NEW YORK

Forced Marriage: Introducing a social justice and human rights perspective was first published in 2011 by Zed Books Ltd, 7 Cynthia Street, London N1 9JF, UK and Room 400, 175 Fifth Avenue, New York, NY 10010, USA

www.zedbooks.co.uk

Designed and typeset in Garamond by Kate Kirkwood
Index by John Barker
Cover designed by www.alice-marwick.co.uk
Printed in the UK by Mimeo Ltd, Huntingdon, Cambridgeshire PE29 6XX

MIX
Paper from
responsible sources
FSC
www.fsc.org   FSC® C019549

Distributed in the USA exclusively by Palgrave Macmillan, a division of St Martin's Press, LLC, 175 Fifth Avenue, New York, NY 10010, USA

A catalogue record for this book is available from the British Library
Library of Congress Cataloging in Publication Data available

ISBN 978 1 84813 462 1 hb
ISBN 978 1 84813 463 8 pb

Dedication

Aisha – For Monique and Renée Gill, with love

Sundari – For Ma

Contents

Acknowledgements   ix
Foreword by Professor Yakin Ertürk   xi

Introduction: framing forced marriage as a form of violence   1
against women
Aisha K. Gill and Sundari Anitha

Part 1: Definitions, contexts and theoretical concepts

1   Understanding forced marriage: definitions and realities   25
     *Geetanjali Gangoli, Khatidja Chantler, Marianne Hester and
     Ann Singleton*

2   Reconceptualising consent and coercion within an   46
     intersectional understanding of forced marriage
     Sundari Anitha and Aisha K. Gill

3   Forced marriage: the European Convention on Human   67
     Rights and the Human Rights Act 1998
     Shazia Choudhry

4   Border control to prevent forced marriages: choosing   90
     between protecting women and protecting the nation
     Anja Bredal

5   The social construction of forced marriage and its 'victim'   112
     in media coverage and crime policy discourses
     Sundari Anitha and Aisha K. Gill

Part 2: Policy and practice

6   Forced marriage legislation in the UK: a critique   137
     Aisha K. Gill and Sundari Anitha

7   The law, the courts and their effectiveness   158
     Teertha Gupta and Khatun Sapnara

8   The practice of law making and the problem of forced marriage: 177
     what is the role of the Muslim Arbitration Tribunal?
     Samia Bano

9   Constructing victims, construing credibility: forced marriage,   200
     Pakistani women and the UK asylum process
     Marzia Balzani

10   'Wayward girls and well-wisher parents': habeas corpus,   221
     women's rights to personal liberty, consent to marriage and
     the Bangladeshi courts
     Sara Hossain

About the contributors   241
Index   246

Acknowledgements

Various people have helped us, in different ways, in putting this book together. While it is not possible to thank everyone by name, we would like to single out a number of people who believed in this project and provided logistical support. We both wish to thank the wonderful staff of Zed Books for their help, support and attention to detail. We especially wish to thank Tamsine O'Riordan, Senior Commissioning Editor, for her enthusiasm and for providing the platform that allowed this unique collection of papers to be published as a single volume. This book was made possible by the generous support of all the contributors: we offer them our thanks and our gratitude for their readiness to work to the project's tight deadlines.

Aisha K. Gill and Sundari Anitha

I am incredibly blessed to have so many people to thank: my fellow editor and I have been extremely fortunate to receive help, assistance and support from many sources during the evolution of this project. You know who you are and how critical you have been to the success of my journey. I thank you all for your encouragement, support, insight and laughter: you mean the world to me and I couldn't have done it without you. Special mention and heartfelt thanks are due to the many friends and colleagues who commented on the book and provided valuable ideas: I would especially like to thank Suki Dhanda, Paminder Parbha-Bal, Alexia Casale, Pathik Pathak and Floya Anthias. I would also like to thank Rowena Macaulay and Tabitha Freeman for their friendship, their assistance in accessing various key journal articles, and their brilliant cover design for the book. My deepest gratitude goes to all the courageous women who have shared their stories of violence and forced marriage with me over the years: your courage continues to inspire me.

Aisha K. Gill

ACKNOWLEDGEMENTS

I would like to thank friends at the Asha Projects in London, Ila Patel, Prafulla Vadagama and the very many more women who cannot be named, but whose struggles and courage have been a reminder of how far we have come and how much further we have to go. I would also like to thank colleagues at the School of Social Sciences, University of Lincoln, in whose company work has been a pleasure. And finally, my gratitude is to my family for their support, especially to my mother, Sundari Joshi, who has been a source of strength and inspiration over the years.

Sundari Anitha

Foreword

Professor Yakin Ertürk

Middle East Technical University, Ankara, Turkey

It is with great pleasure and honour that I write this foreword to *Forced Marriage: Introducing a social justice and human rights perspective*. This represents the first collective endeavour to address the phenomenon of forced marriage, which is increasingly an issue in the media, public debates, policy concerns and research projects in different parts of the world. In particular, reports of immigrant girls in Western European countries who are taken to their country of origin to be forcibly married have provoked significant public reaction and become yet another site of control for immigration from the South to the North.

The chapters in this volume aim to challenge simplistic and essentialist perceptions of forced marriage and move the debate to a level of dialogue that problematises the construction of 'difference' as a form of survival, control and regulation in the context of power relations within and between communities. In the process, the authors raise a number of pertinent issues confronting both feminist and human rights paradigms and praxis. In this sense, the book makes a significant addition to the global women's rights movement, which has in turn made fundamental contributions not only to feminist research but also to the new theorising about the role of human rights in state formation, sovereignty, territoriality, bounded society, multiculturalism, diversity, and the terms of social contract in the emerging world order.

The diversification of the global women's rights movement and its interaction with international jurisprudence have made it one of the most *effective* transnational movements in stimulating change, both nationally and internationally. In this respect, the 1993 Vienna Conference on Human Rights, where violence against women was officially recognised as a human rights issue, marked a turning point in women's activism and feminist scholarship as well as the mainstream human rights discourse. Despite the differences among women, the recognition of shared and interlinked conditions of discrimination and sub-ordination, emanating from institutionalised structures of power and systems of inequality, has connected resistance at local and national levels, consolidating these struggles into one of the most *inclusive* global social movements.

Contrary to the previous gender equality agendas (for example 'women in development'), the human rights movement, with violence against women as its primary entry point, has exposed the patriarchal power governing private life and its intersections with other systems of inequality and hegemonic structures that create multiple and diverse layers of oppression for different women's groups. This feature of the women's human rights agenda has been a source both of controversy and backlash as well as promoting the potential for transformation.

The engagement of the global women's movement with the international human rights system has been particularly noteworthy in confronting not only the historically rooted norms and customs that have normalised women's differential subordination around the world, but also the normative blindness – at both national and international levels – of the particularities in which violations of women's rights are manifested in different legal and cultural traditions.

However, the multifaceted and often rough journey women must embark upon both individually and collectively to achieve a more sexually egalitarian and just world has been a dialectical one; while uncovering and demystifying gendered hierarchies it has also unleashed new traps and challenges. The wish to respond to forced marriage as a particular form of patriarchal control over women is illustrative of this challenge as it involves a similar dilemma. Women of the Global South who confront specific marriage practices that infringe on their rights often find themselves entangled within a cultural debate that imposes on women a choice between enduring oppression in silence or siding with imperialist/ethnocentric projects. This dilemma is rooted in the colonial experience which selectively targeted certain gender-related norms and institutions to promote the imperialists' 'civilising' agenda. While some of these colonial initiatives complemented local women's concerns, in other instances they contradicted them and undermined women's agency. As a result, women's rights issues became instrumentalised into anti-colonial struggles and nationalist narratives.

With such contradictory trends in mind, writing this foreword provides me with a moment to reflect and offer a critical overview of the achieve-ments, risks and challenges facing the global agenda on violence against women. While serving for six years as the UN Special Rapporteur on Violence Against Women, I promoted and monitored women's human rights globally, through embarking on fact-finding visits to seventeen countries, representing diverse geographies and socio-historical experiences, communicating with governments on the basis of individual complaints received from all parts of the world, and preparing annual thematic reports on pertinent issues. The work undertaken in this context was naturally grounded in and guided by universal human rights principles and standards inherent in the Universal Declaration of Human Rights, conventions, declarations and resolutions adopted within the context of multilateral dialogue.

The consolidation of local women's struggles in a global movement and the creation of the UN has facilitated the emergence of an international women's rights and equality regime. The UN provided women with an international platform from which to voice their demands, and the women's movement transformed the organisation as well as the essence of international relations, the site of 'high politics'. Given the unwillingness of most national governments to respond to women's demands, the international arena offered a viable environment to push for gender-sensitive standards. Once negotiated and adopted by governments, these consensus documents became a reservoir of globally available norms for legitimate claim-making, and set the standards against which the human rights performance and accountability of states can be measured.

While the *founding mothers*, present at the creation of the UN (and of the League of Nations before it), made significant contributions to 'engendering' the UN language and institutions, the main breakthrough in the human rights arena came with the recognition of violence against women as a human rights issue at the 1993 Vienna Human Rights Conference. This paved the way for gender-inclusive standards in human rights protection, partially correcting the male-biased language of mainstream international human rights law. In this regard, the adoption of the Declaration on the Elimination of Violence against Women by the United Nations General Assembly the same year, and the creation of the post of Special Rapporteur on Violence against Women (SRVAW) in 1994, are most relevant, as they opened up – for the first time – patriarchal relations in private life to public scrutiny.

The 1990s also saw sexual violence and rape used as a deliberate war strategy in the conflicts in the former Yugoslavia and Rwanda. The public outcry against these activities gave them visibility in conflict analysis and integrated them into the mandates of international tribunals created to prosecute the perpetrators of war crimes. Today, rape is accepted both as a war crime and as a crime against humanity by the Rome Statute of the International Criminal Court.

Gender-aware normative instruments and mechanisms adopted in the course of the past decade also recognise women's varied role in war, including their potential to contribute to peace. Among the most significant developments in this regard are the Security Council Resolutions 1325 (2000) and 1820 (2008), and the most recent resolutions 1888 (2009) and 1889 (2009) on women, peace and security. In accordance with Resolution 1888, the UN Secretary-General has recently appointed a Special Representative in charge of monitoring sexual crimes in conflict zones.

The development of the new standards and treaties that allow prosecutions to be brought for crimes against women in conflicts, as well as the criminalisation of domestic and other forms of violence against women, reveals a significant shift from impunity to accountability with respect to crimes specifically targeting women (Chinkin 2004, 118).

The global women's movement thrives on diversity; as the movement became more inclusive, so did the demands for new standards, allowing the agenda to move beyond formal equality and 'women-only' interventions. While some women used international law as their main bargaining tool, others have strategised from within their own cultural and religious traditions to argue for justice, thus enriching the debate and broadening the feminist agenda. Liz Kelly (2010), in paying tribute to South Asian women's activism and its contributions to British feminism, has eloquently demonstrated how black and minority ethnic groups working on violence against women have increased 'space for action' for women whose agency has largely been denied.

The achievements in transcending the boundaries of rights, as suggested above, have not been problem-free. The focus on violence against women, which resulted in cataloguing specific forms of unjust practices previously not recognised as human rights violations and enhanced women's access to justice and redress, has also resulted in the *essentialising* of certain cultures as the source of the problem (Ertürk 2007, 13). Gill and Mitra-Kahn have argued that forced marriage in the British context, for example, has been characterised 'as something that stems from an *Othered* (or foreign non-British) culture', which has resulted in government adoption of stricter immigration controls (Gill and Mitra-Kahn 2010, 136).

Female genital mutilation and so called 'honour crimes', among others, are forms of assault on women that are treated as categories of crime uniquely

embedded in the cultures of certain countries or immigrant/minority groups.
Such associations became particularly pronounced after 9/11, as the *women
issue* became hostage to the 'clash of civilisations' rhetoric, and international
relations became fundamentally altered, arranged around divisive cultural
and religious lines (Ertürk 2009, 63).

Thus, one of the unintended outcomes of universal claims for the rights
of Third World and immigrant/minority women has been to play into the
hands of orientalist narratives that define these women as victims of deviant
and essentially misogynous cultures. This has created a new front of struggle
for women of the Global South in particular and poses an urgent challenge
to the feminist human rights paradigm to tackle the universalist/relativist
debate in order to strategise towards a common and gender-competent
response to manifestations of all forms of patriarchal transgressions on
women while avoiding cultural reductionist traps.

One critical implication of these developments for Western women
activists is that stereotyping of non-Western cultures as the ultimate cause of
violence against women tends to normalise the patriarchal structures that
constrain Western women. It also has the effect of overlooking the minority/
majority tensions, state-level policy and neoliberal economic environment
that perpetuate gendered/racial /class hierarchies.

All the contributions to *Forced Marriage: Introducing a social justice and
human rights perspective* navigate the different contours of this very challenge.
They show how the criminal justice system, immigration and asylum policies
in the UK respond to notions of coercion and consent in instrumentalising
marriage as a means of border control; at the same time, the chapters probe
critically into the conditions within which consent is constructed and
negotiated by women in minority and majority communities. In this sense,
the authors go beyond the prevailing understandings, laws and policies
regarding forced marriage, and link culture, politics and state action.

Forced Marriage: Introducing a social justice and human rights perspective
will no doubt make a major contribution to the future direction of the debate
on forced marriage and the culturally coded transgressions on women in
general. In the final analysis, the impact of the arguments made by the
contributors will essentially be measured by the degree to which they can
stimulate a new dialogue between majority and minority communities and
context-specific research on gender and human rights, and guide state policy
and action beyond mere regulatory concerns and abstract universalism.
Without recognition of the heterogeneity and diversity in women's experiences

and their varied struggles for equality, state intervention in forced marriage will only compound the problem, while burdening women with a choice between their rights and their communities.

References

Chinkin, C. (2004) 'Gender-related Crimes: A Feminist Perspective', in R. Thakur and P. Malcontent (eds.) *From Sovereign Impunity to International Accountability: A Search for Justice in a World of States*, UN University Press, Tokyo.

Ertürk, Y. (2007) 'Intersections between Culture and Violence against Women: Annual Report to the Human Rights Council' (A/HRC/4/34).

Ertürk, Y. (2009) 'Towards a Post-Patriarchal Gender Order: Confronting the Universality and the Particularity of Violence against Women', *Sociologisk forskning* (Swedish national sociological review), vol. 46, no. 4, 61–70.

Gill, A. K. and Mitra-Kahn, T. (2010) 'Moving towards "Multiculturalism without Culture"', in R. K. Thiara and A. K. Gill (eds.), *Violence against Women in South Asian Communities*, Jessica Kingsley Publishers, London.

Kelly, L. (2010) 'Foreword', in R. K. Thiara and A. K. Gill (eds.), *Violence against Women in South Asian Communities*, London, Jessica Kingsley Publishers.

Introduction
Framing forced marriage as a form of violence against women

Aisha K. Gill and Sundari Anitha

Theoretical debates about the relationship between violence against women and forced marriage provide a framework for examining the challenges of tackling violence against black and minority ethnic women in a manner that takes account of the continuities between different forms of gender-based violence while also addressing the specificity of particular forms of violence against women. The aim of this interdisciplinary collection of essays is to promote a more nuanced understanding of forced marriage that addresses these commonalities and particularities. This is achieved by locating forced marriage within the discourses on human rights, social justice, multiculturalism and assimilative models that shape particular understandings of forced marriage, and also policy approaches to this problem, both national and international. This understanding of forced marriage provides the foundation for an intersectional approach that allows for effective examination of the dominant paradigms that reduce violence against women to a cultural problem; it also offers a method for reviewing existing research and presenting new evidence in a theoretically informed, practice-orientated manner.

Whilst there is a considerable amount of literature, across a range of disciplines, on various manifestations of violence against women, little attention has been paid to the specific problem of forced marriage, and scholarship that addresses the issue from a multidisciplinary perspective is even rarer. One possible reason for this lacuna is the fact that the recent foregrounding of forced marriage in media and policy discourses has taken place through the lens of cultural essentialism; thus, the fact that forced marriage often results from the intersection of a range of causal factors has been largely occluded. This collection unites work from academics and practitioners who seek to address this gap in the literature by challenging both the dominant perspectives on forced marriage and the institutions, structures and ideologies that underpin this form of violence against women.

A note on terminology

The linguistic labelling of social phenomena is never straightforward. Language carries the weight of past imaginings into present meanings and the designation of terms (Glynos 2001). Language produces and is produced in social contexts: it is the vehicle through which meaning is ascribed and experience and reality are conjured (Glynos 2001). The question 'What is violence?' seems straightforward. However, given the power of language, perhaps the question should be 'What do we mean when we use the word violence?' or even 'What meanings and power relations are associated with terms such as violence, violence against women, domestic violence and forced marriage?'

Violence is a key force in the production, maintenance, intensification and legitimation of domination and subordination. The harm produced through violence need not be intentional; indeed, it is often a by-product of the establishment or pursuit of domination of other persons or groups. For example, colonial violence provides the context for genocide, sexual violence, war and territorial occupation. Violence is always played out against a backdrop of different types of violence: colonial, neocolonial, gendered and/or racial. Each type is associated with specific tactics and methods of subjugation, such as rape, threats or intimidation. However, different forms of violence are often interrelated, co-constitutive and intersecting, mutually reinforcing one another. Violence emerges from, through and within the social landscape. Thus, women often experience multiple forms of violence at the state, institutional and individual levels (Erez, Adelman and Gregory 2009; Yuval-Davis 2006; Verloo 2006).

Etymologically, the term 'violence' refers to the Latin word for 'forced': the verb derived from the noun translates as 'to violate', which speaks to the breaking of dignity (Oxford English Dictionary 2009). However, defining violence against women is more challenging: the United Nations (UN) definition of violence against women does not talk simply of 'violence' committed 'against women', but allows for exploration of the interrelatedness and the situatedness of different manifestations of violence against women. According to Article 1 of the UN Declaration on the Elimination of Violence Against Women, violence against women comprises

2

any act of gender-based violence that results in, or is likely to result in, physical, sexual or psychological harm or suffering to women, including threats of such acts, coercion or arbitrary deprivation of liberty, whether occurring in public or private life.

Thus, the terms 'violence against women', 'gendered violence' and 'gender-based violence' are used interchangeably by the contributors to this volume.

In the UK, debates on domestic violence have resulted in violence against women becoming the focus of significant political, media and policy attention. Although it is common for the terms to be used interchangeably, feminists have pushed, in recent years, for the adoption of the term 'violence against women' (Horvath and Kelly 2007) to focus attention on the gendered nature of many forms of domestic violence (Walby and Allen 2004) and the fact that these exist within a complex continuum of violence constituted by multiple forms of inequality, including gender, race and class. Violence against women is perpetrated by men not just against female partners but also against female family members: it is often used to assert and maintain power over women for the purpose of regulating and controlling their behaviour and compelling them to comply with patriarchal norms. The part of the violence against women continuum associated with such patterns of coercive control forms the focus of this book as a whole (Anderson 2009; Stark 2007).

Feminists and human rights activists have increasingly used international laws and covenants to hold governments accountable in individual cases of violence against women, drawing attention to states' multifaceted obligations to protect women from violence and to ensure the full and free exercise of their fundamental human rights (Sen, Humphreys and Kelly 2003). Some of the secrecy that previously shrouded the issue has been dissipated by these efforts and, as a result, public and professional awareness and understanding of violence against women has been enhanced. This is a major success, though the supposedly private nature of violence against women, and the shame and silence that continue to surround the issue, means that many women still decide not to report incidents of abuse.

Estimates of the extent of violence against women vary because of this under-reporting. Indeed, variations in how domestic violence is defined make it difficult to obtain accurate statistics about all forms of violence against women: for instance, the prevalence of forced marriage and of murders committed in the name of family honour has been heavily contested. However, the British Crime Survey statistics suggest that nearly 1 million women experience at least one incident of domestic abuse each year; close to 10,000 women are sexually assaulted every week (Kershaw et al. 2008), and at least 750,000 children witness domestic violence every year (Department of Health 2002). Analysis of statistics concerning the extent of violence against women reveals that no class or ethnic group is exempt from gendered forms of violence; this finding has long served to emphasise the commonalities in women's experience of gendered violence and make the case for feminist solidarity. At the same time, the importance of the diversity of women's experiences of gender-based violence is increasingly being recognised by academics, practitioners and policy makers as comprising a vital part of intersectional understandings of violence against women that do not privilege gender as the sole explanation for such violence.

Feminists have been instrumental in bringing the problem of violence against women to light, arguing that men's use of violence against women should be understood as part of a broader pattern of domination and control of women by men (Anderson 2009; Dasgupta 2002; Stark 2007). Changes in mainstream understandings of the 'normal' make-up of families, and the power relations within them, have also had a major impact on efforts to tackle violence against women. Recently, scholars have begun questioning assumptions about domestic violence by exploring not only male-on-female patterns of abuse, but also incidents in which women perpetrate, or are complicit in, domestic violence (Hester et al. 2008). Violence within the family is increasingly coming to be understood in the context of violence outside the family as a result of research which examines the multiple inequalities that shape violence against women and women's agency in responding to it (Anitha, forthcoming; Sokoloff 2008). In pursing a broader understanding of violence against women, domestic violence scholars have also worked to raise awareness of the extent of the problem in different communities: the literature on intersectionality, in particular, has afforded significant insights into why particular forms of violence against women occur more or less frequently in different contexts (Anthias 2009; Crenshaw 1992; Thiara and Gill 2010). These issues are addressed by a number of contributors to this volume.

What is forced marriage?

No marriage shall be legally entered into without the full and free consent of both parties, such consent to be expressed by them in person after due publicity and in the presence of the authority competent to solemnize the marriage and of witnesses, as prescribed by law.

Minimum Age for Marriage and Registration of Marriages Act 1964, Article 1(1)

Forced marriage, which is generally viewed as encompassing child marriage because minors are deemed incapable of giving informed consent, is specifically recognised as an abuse of human rights in a number of UN treaties and other international instruments. However, different instruments employ different definitions of the term 'forced marriage'. The 2005 Council of Europe study *Forced Marriages in Council of Europe Member States* uses a broad definition according to which forced marriage constitutes an

> umbrella term covering marriage as slavery, arranged marriage, traditional marriage, marriage for reasons of custom, expediency or perceived respectability, child marriage, early marriage, fictitious, bogus or shame marriage, marriage of convenience, unconsummated marriage, putative marriage, marriage to acquire nationality and undesirable marriage – in all of which the concept of consent to marriage is at issue[.]

Although no official data on the incidence of forced marriage across European Union (EU) member states exists, there is some evidence that the incidence varies from country to country (Rude-Antoine 2005). It is unclear how these variations relate to the fact that in some states forced marriage has garnered significant media attention in recent years, while in others there has been little or no public debate about the issue. These differences have played a significant role in determining which EU member states have attempted to collect data on forced marriage, though the lack of a generally accepted definition of forced marriage is a complicating factor. However, research conducted by various non-governmental organisations (NGOs) in Europe suggests that the problem is more common in some migrant communities and that individual cases of forced marriage often involve other forms of gender-based violence.

To date, the issue of forced marriage has received little attention in Canada and the United States, despite the presence of indigenous communities with traditions of early marriage and forced marriage, and immigrant communities within which the prevalence of forced marriage has been documented in other contexts. However, anecdotal reports from women's organisations, and newspaper reports documenting survivors' stories (see, for example, Aulakh 2009), indicate that forced marriage is not unknown in the region. The low profile of forced marriage in Canada may soon change as the Department of Justice recently published an exploratory study on forced marriage, taking stock of the policies that a variety of countries have adopted to address the problem (Dostrovsky et al. 2007), with a view to assessing the possible responses to this problem in Canada. Given the general lack of research on, and media and political attention to, forced marriage in non-European Western countries, the focus of this volume is on the situation in Europe, where significant strides have been made in tackling forced marriage, though some contributors also explore the situation in South Asia.

Forced marriage violates the fundamental right to freely consent to marriage that is enshrined in numerous international human rights instruments, including the Universal Declaration of Human Rights (1948),[1] the International Covenant on Civil and Political Rights (1966),[2] and the International Covenant on Economic, Social, and Cultural Rights (1966):[3] these instruments are collectively known as the International Bill of Human Rights. Article 16(2) of the Universal Declaration of Human Rights affirms that 'Marriage shall be entered into only with the free and full consent of the intending spouses.' Article 23 of the International Convention on Civil and Political Rights and Article 10(1) of the International Convention on Economic, Social, and Cultural Rights use similar wording to reiterate this right. Forced marriage also violates Article 12 of the Universal Declaration of Human Rights, which declares that 'Men and women of marriageable age have the right to marry and to found a family, according to the national laws governing the exercise of that right.' This also includes the right *not* to marry. Thus, the article demands that intending spouses give their free and full consent to marriage according to the declaration's underlying principles of self-determination and human dignity.

Various other international treaties specifically condemn and prohibit forced marriage. For instance, early marriage cases, in which one or both parties to a marriage are below the age of legal consent, are addressed in Article 1 of the Convention on the Rights of the Child,[4] which recommends that all States Parties establish 18 as the minimum age for consent in matters of marriage. Article 16(1)(b) of the Convention on the Elimination of All Forms of Discrimination against Women (CEDAW) also explicitly forbids forced marriage:[5]

> States Parties shall take all appropriate measures to eliminate discrimination against women in all matters relating to marriage and family relations and in particular shall ensure, on a basis of equality of men and women: ...

(b) The same right freely to choose a spouse and to enter into marriage only with their free and full consent[.]

Moreover, Article 2 of the CEDAW calls upon States Parties to ensure that 'All appropriate measures [are] taken to abolish existing laws, customs, regulations and practices which are discriminatory against women, and to establish adequate legal protection for equal rights of men and women.' As the CEDAW has been ratified by all EU member states, Article 16 is reflected in states' domestic legislation. In 1994, the Committee on the Elimination of Discrimination against Women issued recommendations regarding the implementation of states' obligations under the CEDAW, especially as regards establishing equality in marriage and family relations; the recommendations pointed to the fact that in many States Parties, although national legislation is largely CEDAW-compliant, discriminatory customs and traditions, and also failures to enforce these laws, constitute violations of CEDAW.

Forced marriage also breaches the right to bodily integrity guaranteed by a range of international human rights instruments and, in some respects, international customary law. For instance, the practice of forced marriage would contravene Article 3 of the European Convention for Human Rights, which aims to prohibit torture and inhumane or degrading treatment. The European Court of Human Rights has provided legal guidelines for determining whether Article 3 has been breached, stressing that the prohibition on torture applies to all mental and physical suffering that exceeds a minimum level of severity. Forced marriage may also involve the deprivation of liberty, primarily via the arbitrary detention of victims by family members, which also comprises a violation of human rights. Moreover, international law indicates that forced marriage constitutes a practice similar to slavery, which is prohibited by customary international law and a range of human rights treaties.[6]

International tribunals have also considered forced marriage a specific gendered harm. The Special Court for Sierra Leone (SCSL) was set up by the Government of Sierra Leone and the UN to try those responsible for violations of law in the territory of Sierra Leone since 30 November 1996; on 25 February 2009, the SCSL convicted three former leaders of the Revolutionary United Front of forced marriage. This was the first time convictions on the specific charge of forced marriage were obtained under international law (Thomas 2009, 17). As legislation and policy usually conceptualise forced marriage as a problem affecting individuals, until this case it was not recognised that forced marriage could also comprise a form of widespread gendered attack on a civilian population. This represents an advance on the stance taken by the International Criminal Tribunal for Rwanda (ICTR), which was set up in 1994 by the UN Security Council to prosecute persons responsible for serious violations of international humanitarian law committed in the territory of Rwanda between 1 January 1994 and 31 December 1994. The ICTR's failure to consider forced marriage a specific crime relevant to its mandate was criticised for sending the message that acts of sexual violence performed within the confines of marriage are acceptable (Kalra, 2001; Park, 2006).

While a number of international human rights instruments provide ways in which to frame forced marriage, and thus tackle it, the practical efficacy of the individual complaints procedures that several of these instruments offer remains uncertain. Moreover, rights that focus on addressing harms that primarily afflict women need to be identified and developed; in particular, it will be important to challenge the fact that many human rights instruments focus on harms and abuses committed in the public sphere in terms of holding states accountable for violations. However, many harms and abuses that particularly affect women occur in the private sphere: excluding such harms from human rights instruments limits the protections and avenues for redress open to victims. However, much of the focus to date has been on how these instruments can be utilised to ensure that states do not violate their obligations, rather than on the measures that states could and should take in order proactively to fulfil their obligations.

Forced marriage and domestic legislation

Forcing someone into marriage is a distinct criminal offence in a number of EU states, including Austria, Cyprus and Germany. Since July 2006, under Austrian criminal law, forcing somebody to marry has constituted grievous compulsion (*schwere Nötigung*). In Germany, both the criminal and civil codes were changed to introduce a specific forced marriage offence. Forced marriage is also a specific crime in a number of non-EU states, including Norway, Serbia and Albania (Enright 2009; Razack 2004; Wikan 2004). In Macedonia, forced marriage is categorised as a crime in specific circum-stances. Looking further afield, Australia has adopted an innovative approach to criminalising forced marriage: through focusing on child victims of forced marriage, Australia has defined forced marriage as akin to the existing crime of human trafficking. However, the assumption that immigration is always involved in cases of forced marriage may lead to a myopic approach that focuses on immigration policy rather than on how forced marriage relates to other forms of violence against women (Ministry of Justice 2005; Harris 2005).

In countries that do not have specific offences associated with forced marriage, it is (at least theoretically) still punishable under general provisions, primarily those concerning coercion. The criminal offences that are frequently associated with, or concurrently committed in the commission of, forced marriage offences vary depending on the specific circumstances of individual cases. Although there is no specific criminal offence relating to 'forcing someone to marry' in England and Wales, criminal offences may nevertheless be committed in the process of carrying out a forced marriage (Foreign Commonwealth Office/Home Office 2005): for instance, perpetrators of forced marriage – usually parents or family members – have been prosecuted for threatening behaviour, assault, kidnapping, abduction, imprisonment and murder. However, the UK has recently amended existing legislation to introduce a civil law (the Forced Marriage Civil Protection Act 2007) aimed at preventing forced marriage.

There is ongoing debate in many European countries, including Sweden and the UK, about whether a specific offence associated with forcing someone into marriage should be created or whether it would be better to strengthen the existing criminal code (Bredal 2005; Rude-Antoine 2005; Tzortzis 2004): for instance, Australia, Denmark and Belgium have amended existing legislation to criminalise activities associated with forced marriage. Some women's and civil liberties groups (e.g. Iranian and Kurdish Women's Rights Organisation, Karma Nirvana) have advocated criminalisation on the basis that a specific criminal offence speaks to the seriousness of the problem and provides to individual victims a number of effective avenues for redress. Supporters of criminalisation have stressed that the development of new criminal law provisions might help to convince resistant sectors of affected communities that forced marriage is wrong, in addition to operating as a mechanism for reconfiguring intra-group power (Belair 2006; Park 2006). In the UK, many activists argue that criminalisation would provide them with a sufficient tactical advantage to prevail against the practice of forced marriage: however, it is not clear whether they believe that legal reform is necessary to allow them to surmount (i) the difficulties inherent in their low status within the affected communities as women and/ or feminists in order to gain the power and influence necessary to effect change, or (ii) the perception within affected communities that their arguments against forced marriage are weak, or (iii) a combination of both these possibilities.

In Afghanistan, sub-Saharan Africa, Iraq and rural China, where bride-price traditions lead many poverty-stricken families to 'marry off' their daughters at a young age, women's groups have supported policies and campaigns discouraging early marriage, and have called for a minimum age for marriage to be established or, where such provisions already exist, for more stringent enforcement of existing laws and policies (Hague and Thiara 2009). Thus, many campaigns and calls for action focus on forced marriages involving children rather than adults. Algeria, Bangladesh, Jordan, Iraq, Malaysia, Morocco, Turkey and France are among the countries that have raised the minimum age for marriage in part to combat forced marriage: in most of these countries, the minimum age is now 18.

However, critics of criminalisation have argued that a change in the law will not necessarily dismantle the structural and institutional contexts that sustain particular forms of gender-based violence. In the UK, many immigrant women who experience domestic abuse, forced marriage and/or 'honour'-based crimes fear that seeking protection from the state will expose their families and partners to a racist criminal justice system (Fekete 2006). Irudayam et al. (2006) have highlighted the increased vulnerability of lower-caste women to domestic violence and public violence in the context of indifference or complicity from state agencies like the police in India; Akpinar (2003) and Mutlu (2009) argue that Kurdish women in Turkey face similar issues. The fact that women from minoritised communities often distrust the legal system, and are thus reluctant to access both the criminal justice system and public support services, becomes another symptom of their exclusion from the protections that citizenship and residency are meant to afford.

Criminalising forced marriage has additional implications in the West, where forced marriage has come to be associated with minority communities. When the criminalisation debate is located within, and contributes to, a context in which the practices of some members of particular communities are deemed so heinous that they warrant the development of specific legal provisions, feminists have argued that criminalisation may serve to reinforce essentialist stereotypes about minority cultural practices. Moreover, there is a danger that criminalisation may reinforce the notion that, in contrast to minority communities, mainstream British society is enlightened, liberated and law-abiding (Gedalof 2007; Razack 2004).

10

Feminist scholars argue that legal measures remain an essential but insufficient route to gender justice both because of the historic inability of the law to capture the multiple ways in which women exercise agency within (and despite) constraints and because the law's preoccupation with the victim-subject often results in protectionist responses that erode women's rights and reinforce gendered stereotypes within legal discourses (Menon 2004; Kapur 2005). For instance, although many countries, including Canada, Australia, the UK and, more recently, the US (see Chapter 9 in this volume, and also Cronin and Badger 2006; Dauvergne and Millbank 2010; Oxford 2006), recognise particular forms of gender-based persecution, including forced marriage, as grounds for claiming asylum, Oxford (2006) argues that to maximise their chances of success women's representatives in asylum cases must shape their clients' claims to fit adjudicators' assumptions about black and minority ethnic women's passivity and victimhood. As women's narratives are reoriented to conform to orientalist tropes, not only does this result in the experiences of individual claimants being ignored, but the very process of seeking asylum may further victimise those making claims on the grounds of forced marriage and other forms of violence against women. Moreover, research indicates that, in practice, decision makers working on applications for refugee status rarely consider an actual or threatened forced marriage to constitute a sufficiently significant harm in and of itself to warrant refugee status being conferred (Dauvergne and Millbank 2010). Therefore, international and domestic legislative measures need to be understood as comprising only part of the solution that is necessary to address and, ultimately, to prevent violence against women.

In the West, in addition to employing responses focused on criminalisation, many states have attempted to address forced marriage through immigration control. In the UK, the Labour government's development of forced marriage policies and initiatives centring on stricter immigration controls was underpinned by the government's conceptualisation of forced marriage as stemming from 'othered' (i.e. foreign) cultures. In this, the UK and France have followed the lead of Denmark and Norway. The Danish amendment to the Aliens Act (2002), which raised the minimum age at which migrant spouses from outside the European Economic Area can obtain a 'reunification' visa to 25, caused considerable furore amongst NGOs in Denmark, especially when the Danish prime minister, Andre Fogh Rasmussen, referred to the amendment as 'firm and fair' (Niessen et al. 2005). Many commentators argued that the new family reunification laws had little to do with ameliorating forced marriage and more to do with tightening up Danish immigration law. According to Nielsen (2005, 8), as a result young women were being

> forced to migrate to other Scandinavian countries where it is not as difficult to obtain family reunification permits. Thus young women are still forced into marriages, but the difference is that now they have to leave their network and families and live in an entirely different country[.]

A number of countries have recently changed their immigration policies to prevent specific categories of people who are assumed to be at risk of, or likely to be involved in, forced marriage from gaining residency, let alone citizenship. These blanket categorisations are discriminatory as they make it substantially more difficult for individuals from particular groups to obtain visas or permits for foreign spouses. Campaigners have argued that this is a disproportionate response to the problem, and constitutes a clear and unwarranted violation of a number of human rights (see articles 8 and 12 of the European Convention of Human Rights), especially when it is noted that these restrictions do not apply to foreign spouses from within the European Economic Area. When viewed in this light, the political agendas at stake in the development of these policies become uncomfortably visible.

Many of the chapters in this volume illustrate how representations of minority communities, diverse and contradictory as they often are, work to enforce a hegemonic unity. For instance, in the UK debates and discourses on forced marriage provide an arena for conflict and contestation not only regarding the values and normative standards associated with marriage, but also over representations and constructions of liberal 'Britishness' versus backward, 'othered' minority groups (Merry 2006; Razack 2007).

These debates and issues are not unique to Europe as they concern the conflict between the perceived interests of dominant social groups and those of minority ethnic groups. Conflict of this kind is rooted, to a certain extent, in the majority society's notion of what is in the best interest of minority groups. While the putative goal of liberalism is to maximise individuals' freedom, many liberal theorists recommend restricting practices that *they* consider illiberal (Kukathas 1998). Often, these recommendations focus on 'harmful traditional practices' associated with cultures that are perceived as being illiberal (Winter et al. 2002). The position that states around the world have taken on forced marriage includes struggling with the dilemma of whether they should support such practices out of a sense of commitment to promoting freedom of culture and religion, or calling for an end to such practices on the basis that they contribute to the violation of other freedoms and fundamental human rights. Thus, in the case of forced marriage, state intervention is often represented in terms of releasing subjugated women from the shackles of their cultures.

Case law, research and anecdotal evidence from campaigners indicates that the spectrum of forced marriage ranges from marriages contracted as a result of physical force or fear of injury or death, to those contracted under the undue imposition of emotional pressure or social expectations (Anitha and Gill 2009; Enright 2009; Gangoli et al. 2009; Park 2006; Razack 2007; Siddiqui 2003). As issues of autonomy and consent lie at the heart of dominant approaches to the problem, any discussion of forced marriage must engage with the difficulty of determining the boundaries between consent and coercion. However, debate is often limited by the binary understandings of women's agency and victimhood that dominate media, legal and policy discourses: many of these discourses assume an absolute distinction between the Western norm of 'marriage for love' and non-Western marriage practices in which suitable partners are often selected by parents or the extended family, rather than the intending couple. However, there is a considerable range of forms of pressure that may be exerted upon, and/or perceived by individuals in the absence of an explicit threat: as such, practitioners who attempt to apply an 'objective' test of coercion may find it difficult to make a definitive determination that one or both of the parties to a marriage were not able to exercise free will. Those who are most at risk of forced marriage tend to experience multiple inequalities on account of their disadvantaged position within disadvantaged communities – a context which shapes their experience of coercion. For this reason, though the question of an 'objective test of coercion' has vexed practitioners, where women's accounts remain central to understandings of volition it is possible to capture the contextual and subjective nature of coercion (see Bredal, in Chapter 4).

Campaigning on specific forms of violence against women, including forced marriage, by women's organisations significantly predates the recent recognition accorded to specific gendered harms by the UN, regional mechanisms and individual countries, including the UK, Turkey and Bangladesh (Ilkkaracan 1998; Hossain and Turner 2001). Responses to the problem have been diverse and so, accordingly, have variously produced successes, failures and limiting factors, as discussed in a number of the chapters in Part 2 of this collection.

Organisation of this book

This volume comprises two parts. The five chapters in Part 1 unpack and interrogate the concept of forced marriage by locating it within theoretical debates on violence against women, human rights, social justice, multiculturalism, and assimilative models. The five chapters in Part 2 focus on particular contexts, policies and aspects of legislation and its implementation to consider both the problems with, and the promise of, current approaches to forced marriage in the UK, Europe and beyond.

In Chapter 1, Gangoli, Chantler, Hester and Singleton discuss their 2006–7 empirical research on forced marriage in the UK as a basis for interrogating current definitions and conceptualisations of forced marriage in order to facilitate a deeper understanding of the complexities of the problem and assess the benefits and limitations of these perspectives. The authors also examine human rights debates, the issues posed by multiculturalism and the violence against women movement, and the feminist framing of forced marriage. They go on to argue that the range of communities and structural conditions in which forced marriage occurs is much wider than generally supposed. In conclusion, Gangoli et al. contrast these assumptions with the lived experiences of their research participants in order to question and destabilise assumptions about the connections between forced marriage and age, gender, nationality, and immigration status.

In Chapter 2, Anitha and Gill examine how existing conceptualisations of coercion shape the binary discourse on forced and arranged marriage, and how this, in turn, impacts on the development of measures to combat forced marriage. They examine the implications of current understandings of coercion for the theory and practice of justice between the genders. The authors make the case for a gendered understanding of forced marriage that takes account of the fact that consent and coercion must be conceptualised as occupying opposing poles on a continuum in order more effectively to capture women's experiences and their location within a matrix of inequalities. The authors conclude with a number of recommendations aimed at improving practical measures and policy initiatives: tackling the problem in a more unified, holistic way, drawing on the theory of intersectionality, would allow for greater recognition of the complexity of forced marriage.

In Chapter 3, Choudhry explores the contribution of human rights discourses to the work of feminist activists, jurists and researchers in the fields of violence against women and forced marriage. The concept of human rights has been enthusiastically adopted by women's movements in developing countries, and has recently gained prominence in the developed world, not least as a result of the UN and the Council of Europe adopting policies on violence against women and forced marriage that are rooted in human rights discourses. However, Choudhry argues that the benefits that human rights discourses may offer in terms of developing more nuanced understandings of forced marriage have hitherto been largely ignored by academics and activists. In this chapter, Choudhry outlines the potential of human rights discourse in arriving at a more nuanced understanding of forced marriage, and in developing and implementing concrete means of legal redress at the national and international levels.

In Chapter 4, Bredal explores how forced marriage is discursively constituted in Europe through immigration law and policy; on this basis, she offers practical suggestions for addressing the difficulties inherent in framing forced marriage as an immigration problem. Bredal's empirical focus on Norway, Denmark and Sweden allows her to compare and contrast Scandinavian public debates on, and policy approaches to, violence against women, forced marriage and honour-related violence, though she also touches on the debates and policies of other European countries.

Finally in Part 1, in Chapter 5 Anitha and Gill consider how forced marriage is constructed in media and policy debates in the UK, and how these constructions define notions of the 'self' and the 'other' in relation to these abuses. The authors examine how the culturalist discourses employed within media and policy debates obscure the gendered nature of the violence enacted against women when this violence occurs within black and minority ethnic communities. Locating the recent hypervisibility of certain forms of violence against black and minority ethnic women in the UK within the context of the shifting debates on multiculturalism, community cohesion, identity and citizenship demonstrates how these abuses have come to be treated as a marker of the difference of black and minority ethnic communities.

Part 2 begins, in Chapter 6, with a discussion by Gill and Anitha of legal responses to forced marriage in the UK, focusing on the background, provisions and implications (for victims, prosecutors and the development of criminal law in general) of the 2007 Forced Marriage (Civil Protection) Act. In exploring the tensions inherent in the creation of civil versus criminal legislation aimed at tackling forced marriage, Gill and Anitha discuss the limits of a legalistic approach to forced marriage and examine the possibilities of extra-legal initiatives.

In Chapter 7, Gupta and Sapnara draw upon their experience as legal practitioners to examine the provisions of the Forced Marriage (Civil Protection) Act and other legislation, including nullity proceedings and special provisions for children, that have been utilised in forced marriage cases. The authors offer a critique of the Forced Marriage (Civil Protection) Act in relation to its aims and ambitions, exploring both its advantages over other avenues of legal redress and its shortcomings from the perspective of barristers and victims.

In Chapter 8, Bano provides a critical reflection on how the problem of forced marriage is tackled by the Muslim Arbitration Tribunal, which, since its establishment in the UK in June 2007, has worked to settle civil disputes in accordance with sharia law. In exploring the experiences of Muslim women who have utilised this dispute resolution process, Bano examines (a) the ways in which Muslim women engage in the practice of law making, (b) the advantages (especially from women's perspectives) of utilising this dialogue-focused, non-adversial system, and (c) whether and to what extent women are able to modify and transform ethno-cultural norms in their communities via engagement with the Muslim Arbitration Tribunal.

In Chapter 9, Balzani draws on cases involving women of Pakistani origin who sought asylum in Britain in the period 2005–10 on the basis of actual or threatened forced marriage: through these case studies, Balzani examines the role that culture plays in the construction of stereotypes of forced marriage victims. Balzani highlights the connections between forced marriage, religious differences, economic advantage and disadvantage, and immigration strategies within family and clan networks, to argue that forced marriages do not take place in isolation from other forms of inequality, and domination and subordination. Indeed, Balzani argues that forced marriage is often employed to curtail women's attempts to exercise agency within this range of con-straints. Through analysis of decision making in relation to applications for refugee status, Balzani demonstrates that women who are perceived as having exercised some degree of agency may be disadvantaged relative to those who conform to the stereotype of the passive victim of gender-based violence.

In Chapter 10, Hossain examines the use of the protective writ of habeas corpus in Bangladesh. Cases typically arise when parents (or other family members) claim that a woman or girl has been the victim of abduction but the 'victim' offers a very different counter-narrative. Judgments in favour of 'release' are littered across the law reports of the courts of Bangladesh, India and Pakistan. However, there has been an increase in the number of cases in which women (or others acting on their behalf) have utilised the writ to assert their right to be free from forced marriage. Hossain examines both how the writ of habeas corpus was utilised in the recent case of Dr Humayra Abedin, and how Dr Abedin pursued legal redress in the British courts under the Forced Marriage (Civil Protection) Act. Hossain argues that this case exemplifies effective cross-border judicial cooperation to secure women's rights and, thus, sets a precedent for future attempts to provide cross-jurisdictional redress for victims.

Given that a range of ideological debates concerning multiculturalism, assimilative models, and immigration control have shaped current understanding of forced marriage in Europe, research in the field is fraught with the dangers of appropriation and misinterpretation. The underlying goal of all the contributors to this volume is to encourage debate and discussion about forced marriage, to shed new light on recent legal, practical and procedural developments, and to explore women's activism on violence against women. However, there are several limitations in the scope and focus of this collection, most of which reflect the limitations in the scope of current research. The experiences of sexual minorities have not been explored in this collection, as, despite increasing recognition that forced marriage impacts the lives of lesbian, gay, bisexual or transgender individuals in specific ways, there has been little research on this subject to date. A nuanced analysis of the role of both gender and sexuality in creating specific constraints and opportunities will be necessary if a holistic understanding of forced marriage is to be developed. Gupta and Sapnara's Chapter 7 in this volume touches on the issue of how forced marriage impacts vulnerable adults, who may not be able to give full, informed consent to any marriage, in specific ways; however, the voices and perspectives of disabled victims deserve more detailed examination.

This collection focuses primarily on the situation in the UK and Europe: this reflects the degree of attention accorded to the issue by policy makers and academics in different regions of the world. To date, campaigning, activism and legal redress in other parts of the world, particularly in Africa and the Middle East, have been examined in only a limited number of studies. The recent developments concerning forced marriage in Canada will bear monitoring, particularly given Canada's record of comparatively progressive immigration law with regard to family reunification.

Women's rights activists across the globe have contributed to the significant advances that have been made in the struggle to end both violence against women in general and forced marriage in particular. Some of this struggle against forced marriage has centred on legislative measures, in terms of civil and criminal codes and international instruments. The international human rights discourse has been vital in reframing gendered harms as human rights abuses so that states, as well as individuals, can be held accountable. However, women's rights groups recognise the limitations not only of domestic legislation, but also of international conventions, treaties and courts. Campaigning by women's rights activists continues to scrutinise and challenge violence against women committed by governments, by peacekeepers and by men in the privacy of the home. Violence against women exists in all states and regions of the world but, although it is not an inevitable feature of life, it is not easily curtailed by scrutiny, surveillance, policies or legislation. However, when women speak out and break the silence that often surrounds violence against women, the resulting visibility of these abuses makes it possible to challenge the norms, values, traditions, practices and attitudes that allow these crimes to continue. However, there is often a lack of accountability at the state, community and individual levels. Only by opening each level up to scrutiny will the elimination of all forms of violence against women be achieved.

Notes

1 Universal Declaration of Human Rights, UN General Assembly Resolution 217A, UN Doc. A/810, 12 December 1948.
2 International Covenant on Civil and Political Rights, UN General Assembly Resolution 2200A (XXI), UN Doc. A/6316, 1966.
3 International Covenant on Economic, Social, and Cultural Rights, UN General Assembly Resolution 2200A (XXI), 1966.
4 See: http://www.endvawnow.org/?legislation&menusub=191&id=1816.
5 UN Convention on the Elimination of All Forms of Discrimination against Women, 18 December 1979.
6 In its 2003 Session, the UN Working Group on Contemporary Forms of Slavery prioritised the issue of contemporary forms of slavery related to and generated by discrimination, in particular gender discrimination, focusing attention on abuses against women and girls, such as forced marriage, early marriage and sale of wives (Sub-Commission on Human Rights resolution 2002/27).

References

Akpinar, A. (2003) 'The Honour/Shame Complex Revisited: Violence Against Women in the Migration Context', *Women's Studies International Forum*, vol. 26, no. 5.

Anderson, K. (2009) 'Gendering Coercive Control', *Violence Against Women,* vol. 15, no. 12, December.

Anitha, S. (forthcoming) 'Legislating Gender Inequalities: The Nature and Patterns of Domestic Violence Experienced by South Asian Women with Insecure Immigration Status in the UK', *Violence Against Women.*

Anitha, S., and Gill, A. (2009) 'Coercion, Consent and the Forced Marriage Debate in the UK', *Feminist Legal Studies,* vol. 17, no. 2.

Anthias, F. (2009) 'Hierarchies, Belongings, Intersectionality: Problems in Theorising Diversity', Professorial Lecture, Roehampton University.

Aulakh, R. (2009) 'Forced to Wed: "They think they're doing what's best for the child"', *The Star,* 14 November. http://www.thestar.com/news/canada/article/725781 (accessed 16 September 2010).

Belair, K. (2006) 'Unearthing the customary law foundations of "forced marriages" during Sierra Leone's civil war: the possible impact of international criminal law customary marriage and women's rights in post-conflict Sierra Leone', *Columbia Journal of Gender and Law,* vol. 15, no. 3, September.

Bredal, A. (2005) 'Arranged Marriages as a Multicultural Battle Field', in Mette Andersson, M., Lithman, Y. and Sernhede, O. (eds.), *Youth, Otherness, and the Plural City: Modes of Belonging and Social Life,* Daidalos, Gothenburg.

Crenshaw, K. (1991) 'Mapping the margins: Intersectionality, identity politics, and violence against women of colour', *Stanford Law Review,* vol. 43, no. 6.

Crenshaw, K. (1992) 'Mapping the Margins: Intersectionality, Identity Politics, and Violence against Women of Colour', *Stanford Law Review,* vol. 43.

Cronin, E., and Badger, E. (2006) 'Refuge for a Bought Bride', *New Jersey Law Journal* (24 April 2006).

Dasgupta, S. (2002) 'A framework for understanding women's use of nonlethal violence in intimate heterosexual relationships', *Violence Against Women,* vol. 8, 1364–89.

Dauvergne, C., and Millbank, J. (2010) 'Forced Marriage as a Harm in Domestic and International Law', *Modern Law Review,* vol. 73, 57–88.

Department of Health (UK) (2002) 'Women's Mental Health: Into the Mainstream – Strategic Development of Mental Health Care for Women'. http://www.dh.gov.uk/assetRoot/04/07/54/87/04075487.pdf (accessed 24 September 2010).

Dostrovsky, N., Cook, R., and Gagon, M. (2007) *Annotated Bibliography on Comparative and International Law Relating to Forced Marriage,* Department for Justice, Canada.

Enright, M. (2009) 'Choice, culture and the politics of belonging: The emerging law of forced and arranged marriage', *Modern Law Review,* vol. 72, no. 3.

Erez, E., Adelman, M. and Gregory, C. (2009) 'Intersections of Immigration and Domestic Violence: Voices of Battered Immigrant Women', *Feminist Criminology,* vol. 4, January.

Fekete, L. (2006) 'Enlightened Fundamentalism? Immigration, Feminism, and the Right', *Race & Class,* vol. 48, no. 2.

Foreign and Commonwealth Office (2005) *Forced Marriage – a Wrong Not a Right,* London: Foreign and Commonwealth Office.

Gangoli, G., McCarry, M. and Razack, A. (2009) 'Child Marriage or Forced Marriage: South Asian Communities in North East England', *Children and Society*, vol. 23, no. 6.

Gedalof, I. (2007) 'Unhomely Homes: Women, Family and Belonging in UK Discourses of Migration and Asylum', *Journal of Ethnic and Migration Studies*, vol. 33, no. 1.

Glynos, J. (2001) 'The Grip of Ideology: A Lacanian approach to the theory of ideology', *Journal of Political Ideologies*, vol. 6, no. 2.

Hague, G. and Thiara, R. (2009) 'Bride-price, Poverty and Domestic Violence in Uganda', *British Academy Review*, 15, March.

Harris, T. (2005) 'Australia: Early and Forced Marriages', *Women Living Under Muslim Laws* (2 August 2005).

Hester, M., Chantler, K. and Gangoli, G. (2008) *Forced Marriage: the Risk Factors and the Effect of Raising the Minimum Age for a Sponsor, and of Leave to Enter the UK as a Spouse or Fiancé(e)*. Bristol: University of Bristol.

Horvath, M. and Kelly, L. (2007) *From the Outset: Why Violence Should Be a Priority for the Commission for Equality and Human Rights*, London: CSWASU.

Hossain, S. and Turner, S. (2001) 'Abduction for Forced Marriage – Rights and Remedies in Bangladesh and Pakistan', *International Family Law* (April): 15–24.

Ilkkaracan, P. (1998) 'Exploring the Context of Women's Sexuality in Eastern Turkey', *Reproductive Health Matters*, vol. 6, no. 12.

Irudayam, A., Mangubhai, J.P. and Lee, J.G. (2006) *Dalit Women Speak Out: Violence against Dalit Women in India*, New Delhi: National Campaign on Dalit Human Rights.

Kalra, M. (2001) 'Forced Marriage: Rwanda's Secret Revealed', *Journal of International Law and Policy*, vol. 197.

Kapur, R. (2005) *Erotic Justice: Law and the New Politics of Post Colonialism*, London: Glass House Press.

Kershaw, C., Nicholas, S., and Walker, A. (eds.), (2008) *Crime in England and Wales 2007/08: Findings from the British Crime Survey and Police Recorded Crime*, Statistical Bulletin 07/08, Home Office, London.

Kukathas, C. (1998) 'Liberalism and Multiculturalism: the Politics of Indifference', *Political Theory*, vol. 26, no. 5.

Menon, N. (2004) *Recovering Subversion: Feminist Politics beyond the Law*, Urbana and Chicago: University of Illinois Press.

Merry, S. (2006) *Human Rights and Gender Violence: Translating International Law into Local Justice*, Chicago: University of Chicago Press, 1–21.

Ministry of Justice, (2005) 'New laws to protect Australian children from forced marriages overseas' (2 August 2005), online: Australian Minister for Justice and Customs, accessed 28 September 2010.

Nielsen, F. (2005) 'Forced and semi-forced marriages in Denmark'. Available: at http://www.etniskkvindeconsult.dk/documents/forced_and_semi_forced_marria ges.pdf (accessed 12 February 2010).

Niessen, J., Schibel, Y., and Thompson, C. (eds.) (2005) *Current Immigration Debates in Europe: A Publication of the European Migration Dialogue*, Migration Policy Group, Danish Institute for Human Rights. http://www.ims.sdu.edu.cn/cms/attachment/080517054754.pdf (accessed 24 September 2010).

Oxford, C. (2006), 'Protectors and victims in the gender regime of asylum', *NWSA Journal*, vol. 17, no. 3, 18–38.

Oxford English Dictionary (2009) http://www.oed.com/ (accessed 5 January 2010).

Park, A. (2006). '"Other inhuman acts": Forced marriage, girl soldiers and the special court for Sierra Leone', *Social & Legal Studies*, vol. 15, no. 3.

Razack, S. (2004) 'Imperilled Muslim Women, Dangerous Muslim Men and Civilised Europeans: Legal and Social Responses to Forced Marriages', *Feminist Legal Studies*, vol. 12.

Razack, S. (2007) *Casting Out: Race and the Eviction of Muslims from Western Law and Politics*, University of Toronto Press.

Rude-Antoine, E. (2005) *Forced Marriages in Council of Europe Member States: a Comparative Study of Legislation and Political Initiatives*. Strasbourg: Council of Europe.

Sen, P., Humphreys, C. and Kelly, L. (2003) *Violence against Women in the UK: Cedaw Thematic Shadow Report*, London, Womankind Worldwide.

Siddiqui, H. (2003) 'It Was Written in Her Kismet: Forced Marriage', in Gupta, R. (ed.), *From Homebreakers to Jailbreakers*, Zed Books, London.

Sokoloff, N. (2008) 'Expanding the Intersectional Paradigm to Better Understand Domestic Violence in Immigrant Communities', *Critical Criminology*, vol. 16, no. 4, December.

Stark, E. (2007) *Coercive Control: How Men Entrap Women in Personal Life*, Oxford University Press, New York.

Thiara, R. and Gill, A. (2010) *Violence against South Asian Women: Issues for Policy and Practice*, London: Jessica Kingsley Publishers.

Thomas, C. (2009) 'Forced and Early Marriage: a Focus on Central and Eastern Europe and Former Soviet Union Countries with Selected Laws from Other Countries', United Nations Conference Centre, 25 to 28 May, Addis Ababa, Ethiopia. http://www.un.org/womenwatch/daw/egm/vaw_legislation_2009/Expert%20Paper%20EGMGPLHP%20_Cheryl%20Thomas%20revised_.pdf (accessed 12 September 2010).

Tzortzis, A. (2004*): Europe Tackles Forced Marriage*, accessed 27 September 2010. http://www.csmonitor.com/2004/0121/p07s01-woeu.html.

Verloo, M. (2006) 'Multiple Inequalities, Intersectionality and the European Union', *European Journal of Women's Studies*, vol. 13, no. 3.

Walby, S. and Allen, J. (2004) *Domestic Violence, Sexual Assault and Stalking: Findings from the British Crime Survey*, Home Office Research Study 276, London: Home Office Research, Development and Statistics Directorate.

Wikan, U. (2008) *In Honor of Fadime: Murder and Shame*. Chicago: University of Chicago Press.

Winter, B., Thompson, D. and Jeffreys, S. (2002) 'The UN Approach to Harmful Traditional Practices', *International Feminist Journal of Politics*, vol. 4, no. 1, April.

Yüksel, M. (2006) 'The Encounter of Kurdish Women with Nationalism in Turkey', *Middle Eastern Studies*, vol. 42, no. 5, 777–802, September.

Yuval-Davis, N. (2006) 'Intersectionality and Feminist Politics', *European Journal of Women's Studies*, vol. 13, no. 3.

Part 1

Definitions, contexts
and theoretical concepts

1
Understanding forced marriage: definitions and realities

Geetanjali Gangoli, Khatidja Chantler, Marianne Hester
and Ann Singleton*

This chapter explores debates around the conceptualisation and definition of forced marriage primarily in the UK, but also at an international level. The reasons for doing so are twofold. First, forced marriage can sometimes, though not always, take place across international borders and, second, international conventions, definitions and understandings of forced marriage have, or at least should have, an impact on British policy and practice. This broader outlook also facilitates a deeper understanding of the complexities of forced marriage, thus helping to resist simplistic explanations of this issue, including the unrepresentative and unfair association of forced marriage with particular ethnic communities and its often wrong conflation with arranged marriage. As the title of the chapter suggests there are often tensions between definitions and the experiences of victims/survivors of forced marriage, a theme we will attempt to explore further here. The chapter draws on key arguments linked to the forced marriage debate and interrogates what each perspective contributes to our understandings of forced marriage. These domains are: (a) the human rights field, (b) the role of multiculturalism, particularly the place of honour, and (c) the violence against women movement and its feminist framing. These

* The research study 'Forced Marriage: The Risk Factors and the Effect of Raising the Minimum Age for a Sponsor, and of Leave to Enter the UK as a Spouse or Fiancé(e)' was commissioned in 2006 and funded by the Home Office. This chapter draws on the study but has substantially developed some of the key issues and locates them within key theoretical frameworks. The views expressed in this chapter are those of the authors, not necessarily those of the Home Office (nor do they reflect government policy). The research team would like to thank all participants for their valuable and insightful contributions. The research team comprised Professor Marianne Hester (Principal Investigator), Dr Khatidja Chantler (co-ordinator, Manchester), Dr Geetanjali Gangoli (co-ordinator, Bristol), Bipasha Ahmed, Jasvinder Devgon, Melanie McCarry, Nicole Westmarland, Sandhya Sharma and Ann Singleton.

three themes are closely interrelated and do not form discrete domains, but each nonetheless offers a useful point of interrogation that is instructive to the formulation of a nuanced and complex definition, whilst also being aware of the exclusions of any definitions one might adopt. We locate the UK debates on forced marriage within these wider discussions to allow for a broader set of issues to be considered in developing a more finely tuned understanding of forced marriage within the UK. This definition will include an understanding of both structural and cultural bases of forced marriage, and allude to the importance of control and consent over both entry and exit into and from marriage to define forced marriage.

Forced marriage as a human rights issue

It has been argued that forced marriage violates a number of international human rights instruments and standards. From a human rights perspective, 'Marriage shall be entered into only with the free and full consent of the intending spouses' (Universal Declaration of Human Rights, Article 16 (2)). This indicates that marriages entered into where there is no free or full consent are considered an abuse of human rights. At face value, this seems perfectly acceptable and indeed forms the cornerstone of the UK definition of forced marriage which is 'a marriage in which one or both spouses do not (or, in the case of some adults with learning disabilities, cannot) consent to the marriage and duress is involved. Duress can include physical, psychological, financial, sexual and emotional pressure' (Foreign and Commonwealth Office 2005, 8). Within both the human rights framework and the UK definition, the issue of consent is central. The UK definition also acknowledges the role of duress and the ways in which this serves to curtail consent. The introduction of duress should also serve to signpost forced marriage as a particular type of violence against women (discussed later). In this section however, we focus on the issue of consent.

A number of writers (e.g. Anitha and Gill 2009; Chantler et al. 2009; Gangoli et al. 2006) have argued that establishing full and free consent in all cases of marriage can be problematic. The issue of consent and its relationship to duress or coercion is discussed very well by Anitha and Gill (2009). Their central argument is that the subject brought to mind in these debates is that of an autonomous, independent, rational being which elides class, gender and racialised positionings, thus extracting consent from the contexts in which it takes place. This position is also presented in Chantler et al.

(2009), where it is argued that women's ability to consent can be mediated by factors such as poverty, for example in the context of bride price, where women are often positioned as conduits for family survival. The notion of consent is further complicated by the definition of forced marriage (Forced Marriage Unit 2008) which counterposes arranged marriages with forced marriage, with arranged marriages, the latter constructed as an acceptable marriage practice in that it requires the consent of both parties. The separation of the two is clearly an attempt at accepting diverse cultural practices, but this dichotomy serves to make invisible some of the more subtle forms of coercion that can sometimes result in a 'slippage' between arranged and forced marriages. Further, the vocabulary of 'forced' marriage is relatively recent, but it is important to note that degrees of coercion have been accepted as the norm within some scholarship on arranged marriages, particularly in the Indian subcontinent (Wadley 1980; Derné 2005). So, whilst we understand the move to extricate forced marriage from arranged marriage practice, we must also be mindful of what the binary that has now emerged occludes.

Another important issue within the consent debate is that of timing. Existing definitions of forced marriage tend to focus on whether one or both spouse had the right or the ability to choose the marriage at the time of entry into the marriage (Samad and Eade 2002). However, as we will see later, women are often unable to exit forced marriages because of continued gender surveillance after marriage, social norms against divorce in some communities, and immigration control in the case of immigrant women.

Importantly, any discussion of marriage whether based on love, arrangement or force presupposes what Hester et al. (2008) recognise as 'compulsory heterosexuality'. This follows from feminists' theorisation on the commonality of women's oppression within marriage, across ethnicity, race and class (Barry 1979; Mackinnon 1987), and Adrienne Rich's (1980) understanding of compulsory heterosexuality. This is the assumption that women and men are innately only and always attracted to each other emotionally and sexually and as such that heterosexuality is both normal and universal. Rich has suggested that compulsory heterosexuality, far from being natural, is a violent political institution making way for the 'male right of physical, economical, and emotional access and marriage' (Rich 1980, 26). Within this understanding, all marriages, indeed all heterosexual relationships, are coerced, and Kathleen Gough, in her elucidation of her comprehensive list of ways that men control women, cites arranged marriage as an example of using women 'as objects in male transactions' (p. 19), along with the sale of women into prostitution. Far from positioning certain cultures as problematic, Rich allows us to understand how different cultures and ethnicities use marriage as a way to control women in varied ways. From this perspective then, it can be argued that all forms of marriage constitute 'force' to varying degrees. Here the hegemonic effect of socio-cultural expectations is that women are schooled to be 'willing victims' of marriage and hence the issue of 'consent' is already compromised.

The other issue raised about compulsory heterosexuality is that it is against lesbian, gay, bisexual and transgender (LGBT) sexualities and relationships, and this is evidenced by the pressure on gay and lesbian communities from all ethnicities to enter into heterosexual relationships and marriages. Forced marriage therefore becomes a way to control non-heterosexual sexuality. Hester argues that control both of sexuality and of the sexualisation of women is central in male control over women through compulsory heterosexuality and within marriage (1992).

Notwithstanding these complications around the notion of consent and the slippage between arranged and forced marriages, thus far we have been discussing forced marriage as an abuse of human rights at an individual level. More recently, there has been another important shift as seen in forced marriage in Sierra Leone where forced marriage was designated as a crime against humanity. In April 2004, the Special Court for Sierra Leone responded to the forced marriages of women to rebel forces during the conflict in Sierra Leone by creating a new crime against humanity, namely the crime of forced marriage. Forced marriage in that context was seen as a systematic and widespread attack on a civilian population. The crime of forced marriage was created using the following four rationales: first, that the international community has already recognised the different acts involved (such as abduction, sexual violence, torture) as crimes against humanity; second, that the international community has a vested interest in protecting marriage and the family, and forced marriage is a perversion of both; third, that a marriage is invalid without the consent of both parties; and finally, that forced marriage is distinct from arranged marriage, as in the latter the intending spouses delegate their rights to choose to their family, while in the former the spouses have no right to choose. With regard to arranged marriage, it is argued that it is not a 'crime against humanity' even where consent may be diluted or imperfect (for example, one of the spouses not being able to consent or object because of a mental illness), because it is not an attack on a civilian population but is done to assist the population, and parents are acting out of benevolent motives, including protecting their children's welfare and perpetuating social and cultural values (Scharf and Mattler 2005). Within this logic, only the specific form of forced marriage that may take place in the context of war or conflict may be defined as a crime against humanity. The human rights discourse in this case does not enter into what has been defined as the slippage between forced and arranged marriage (Gangoli et al. 2006), as the focus is not on individual rights but on community rights. However, it has been argued that the human rights discourses on marriage can also include in some cases the rights of parents, and rights of communities to preserve their identity; therefore there can be a conflict between the rights of young persons and the rights of families (Stobard 2002).

However, many activists argue that all forced marriages violate human rights conventions, as the consent of the intending spouses is crucial. Others argue that human rights violations are most obvious in cases of child marriages, as under international law, children cannot consent and early marriage denies children their human rights under the United Nations Convention on the Rights of the Child (Gangoli et al. 2009; Outtarra et al. 1998).

The issue of forced marriage is also linked to human rights in the context of using immigration to control or reduce forced marriage in the UK and elsewhere in the EU. Hester et al. (2008) investigated the possible impact of increasing the age for sponsorship on a marriage visa from 18 to 21 in the UK, and found that some participants responded to the proposal as an attack on the human rights of minoritised communities, arguing that it would be contentious in relation to race equality and social cohesion, and would deny the right to family life in the UK until both sponsor and incoming spouse reached 21. This finding links to the concerns and evidence from other countries in the EU which suggest that increasing the age has had a disproportionate effect on minoritised communities and has increased racial tension (Phillips and Dustin 2004). The increase in age therefore can be seen as an attack on particular communities, such as South Asian communities, which typically have younger marriage ages than white mainstream communities and where individuals are more likely to marry partners from outside the EU.

While there is clear evidence that forced marriage has many human rights implications, for example in the area of immigration control, child protection or where forced marriage takes place in the context of war or ethnic conflict,

29

there are limitations to using the human rights approach in all cases, as the focus in human rights debates can be on the violation of community rights rather than the rights of individuals. However, the strongest case for individual rights is covered under the requirement for consent, although as argued above consent is not a straightforward concept and cannot be taken at face value.

Forced marriage and multiculturalism

In the UK and elsewhere in Europe, forced marriage is often conceptualised as a form of violence endemic to, or most relevant to, the experiences of particular ethnic communities, religions and cultures. Within these debates, two (largely unhelpful) ideas are particularly persistent: first, 'clash of culture' between first-generation and second-generation immigrants; and, second, forced marriage as a crime of honour. These ideas work to reify specific minority communities in a way that casts forced marriage as a purely cultural issue which is difficult to intervene in to protect victims. Indeed, a purely cultural lens on forced marriage does not even 'see' victims, since women (and men) subject to forced marriage are constructed as (happily) abiding by their cultural norms rather than as victims.

Mike O'Brien, debating in the House of Commons on women's huma. rights in 1999, said, 'Multicultural sensitivity is not an excuse for moral blindness.' This statement assumes that a focus on, and acceptance of, difference between communities could be counterproductive to women's rights; however the critique itself is based on the idea that 'customs' such as forced marriage result from a pathology of some communities, specifically South Asian and/or Muslim communities. Jasvinder Sanghera, a survivor of forced marriage, has written and spoken widely of the inability of her parents to leave their 'culture' behind in India when they moved to the UK in the 1960s; she believes that it is this inability to adapt to 'Western' norms of individual rights that leads to forced marriage (Sanghera 2007, 2009). Within this framing, forced marriage and child marriage are therefore seen as 'harmful cultural' practices (Interights et al. 2000) based on 'traditional laws' and customs (Outtarra et al. 1998). It is worth noting the manner in which issues such as child marriage and forced marriage are represented as 'harmful cultural practices' whilst instances of 'everyday' violence against women, particularly in majority communities, such as domestic violence and marital rape are not cast as such. For example, in majority ethnic white communities, forms of gender-based violence such as date rape or domestic violence are not constructed as culturally sanctioned practices (as forced marriage is) but as individual acts of violence, therefore as cultural anomalies (Chantler and Gangoli, forthcoming). This constructs minoritised cultures as unchanging and unchangeable, and does not for example explore the possibility of how immigration control and structural racism may contribute to the seeming ossification of marriage practices.

The 'culture clash' perspective is also held by the British government and the criminal justice system as illustrated in the following two examples. To some extent, this understanding of the issue is a remnant of a historical imperialistic perception of some communities – often communities that are from former colonies of the UK – as backward, particularly in relation to gender relations. We believe that it also serves a strategic purpose of using unequal gender relations in minoritised communities as legitimising and justifying, for example, immigration control applicable to particular communities as in the recent decision to increase the sponsorship age for spouses outside the EU to 21 years (Chantler et al. 2009). Sir Peter Singer, a High Court judge in the Family Division, London, acknowledges that forced marriage can take place in any country or community, but while speaking of a particular instance of forced marriage perpetuated on a second-generation Sikh woman states that 'The parents came originally from a rural and very traditional family. They maintained their traditions staunchly notwithstanding more than 25 years in England. The children had however received a lifetime of exposure to the advantages and necessarily to the disadvantages of British society' (Singer 2001, 30). Similarly, the Working Group report on forced marriage commissioned by the Home Office suggests that forced marriage is a remnant of cultural practice exported from countries of origin (Samad and Eade 2002). This view persists despite literature arguing that forced marriage is contrary to the tenets of many religions, including Islam (Carroll 1988) and Sikhism (Shan 1991) and that marriage customs in countries of origin are highly variable and subject to class, caste, religion and economic changes (Gangoli et al. 2009; Trawick 1992; Derné 2005). The 'culture clash' approach privileges supposed homogenous and rigid cultural norms over gender, does not recognise culture as dynamic and fluid, associates violence against women in particular communities with culture, and fuels already-circulating negative stereotypes about particular minority communities (cf. Chantler et al. 2001; Patel 2008; Razack 2004).

While it is vital that specific abuses against women in minoritised communities are identified and named, and that appropriate action is taken to protect women, the problem is one of how to name such violations without positioning whole communities as backward and in need of 'modernisation' to a normative Western (supposedly more enlightened and more woman-friendly) model of a progressive or 'good' community. There are many South Asian women's organisations across the UK that have campaigned tirelessly on violence against women within their communities over the past twenty-five to thirty years and have brought new knowledge to understandings of violence against women and to the tension between feminisms and multiculturalism.

While the UK government recognises that forced marriage occurs in a range of communities, its interventions appear to be targeted largely at South Asian communities. This is understandable given that the vast majority of cases that the Forced Marriage Unit deals with are from the Indian sub-continent (Kazimirski et al. 2009). However, these figures need to be unpacked and interrogated rather than accepted at face value. We cannot conclude because most of the cases seen by the Forced Marriage Unit are from South Asian communities that this reflects a higher incidence of forced marriage within these communities compared to others. The reasons it would be erroneous to reach such a conclusion are threefold: (a) South Asian communities constitute the largest ethnic minority group in the UK; (b) because of their longer period of settlement in the UK compared to 'newer' communities (e.g. Somali, Zimbabwean, Congolese), South Asian communities have vibrant community-based organisations, some of which have been actively campaigning on this issue, hence sensitising communities about the problem; and (c) in spite of the recent policy separation of 'arranged' and 'forced' marriage, forced marriage in the UK continues to be associated with South Asian communities where arranged marriages are endemic.

One of the central questions within a feminist frame is to ask the question 'which women' are being reported on, and why? This approach helps to clarify whose experiences are visible and whose experiences are rendered invisible. The emphasis on forced marriage in South Asian communities occludes the experiences of women from other communities (e.g. African, Chinese, ethnic white British aristocratic communities and groups) from being acknowledged and recognised (see Hester et al. 2008). Furthermore, the relatively recent introduction of the term 'honour-based violence' works to strengthen the association of forced marriage with South Asian and Muslim communities and to negate the experiences of women who are not perceived to be influenced by 'honour', thus reinforcing their invisibility within discourse, policy and practice on forced marriage.

In addition, the focus on honour and indeed the question of whether forced marriage should be conceptualised as honour-based violence are matters of contestation. Firstly, we would dispute the assertion that it is only or indeed primarily South Asian or Muslim communities that are bound by codes of honour. In fact, it is difficult to imagine what a community or society without codes of honour would look like or how it would function. Codes of honour stipulate the expected behaviour of members of a community or society, and the sanctions that would be imposed for breaching such codes. It is therefore possible to think of codes of honour as enshrined within the laws of a country: and it is no coincidence that judges in the High Court in the UK are referred to as 'Your Honour' or that Privy Councillors are referred to as 'The Right Honourable'. Clearly, where the concept of honour is accepted by ethnic white British communities, it is seen as a positive trait, and where it is associated with minoritised communities, it has negative connotations. It therefore seems a little perverse to posit that codes of honour only operate in South Asian or Muslim communities when there are many examples from mainstream British society which attest to the importance of honour. Increasingly within the forced marriage debate, 'honour' is seen as a quality of certain minoritised communities, rather than recognised as a more universal facet of society. It would be more accurate to subscribe to the view that all societies operate within codes of honour, but that these differ across the globe. So whilst honour may well be a feature of forced marriage, it is simplistic to characterise forced marriage as only related to honour.

Second, as honour is made visible in relation to minoritised communities but invisible in majority communities, an interrogation is required as to what purpose is served by such differential treatments of the same concept. One interpretation is that the majority views particular understandings of honour as pertaining to 'backward' communities and hence not applicable to itself. This view lends itself well to the culturalist discourse discussed above. Another interpretation is that majority subjects see themselves as autonomous, independent subjects exercising unfettered agency and therefore underplay any prospect of the influence on them of societal expectations. Such a position, in our view, is somewhat naïve given the power of dominant discourses to be internalised and re-presented as one's own (see Rose 1990)

Hester et al. (2008) and Chantler et al. (2009) discuss the importance of taking into account structural factors such as poverty in understanding forced marriage. In particular they draw attention to bride price in many

African communities which, when combined with poverty, reduces 'consent' and induces forced marriage since family survival is dependent on the marriage. Women also reported feeling unable to leave such marriages unless they could reimburse the bride price to the groom's family. Given that the economic position of women worldwide is less favourable than that of men, it is often impossible to repay the 'debt', so that the woman thus becomes trapped in the marriage. The theme of poverty as contributing to early marriages in some parts of the world is discussed by the literature on child marriage. Otoo-Oyertey and Pobi (2003) argue that forced marriage in this context should be conceptualised as a developmental issue. Rather than focusing attention either on the individual (as a 'free' agent able to give consent) or purely on the cultural, a deeper understanding of forced marriage is achieved by unpacking their interaction with structural issues. This method also helps to prevent the pathologising of minoritised communities and the seeing of them as deficient or backward. Multiculturalism as an approach to forced marriage has therefore not been wholly successful. We turn next to consider what can be gained by considering forced marriage as a form of violence against women.

Forced marriage as violence against women

Forced marriage has been examined as gender-based violence, involving an abuse of women's human rights (Uddin and Ahmed 2000; Siddiqui 2002; Hossain, n.d.; Gangoli et al. 2006). In this section, we will explore whether forced marriage can be understood as domestic violence, as a form of gender-based violence or as a part of the continuum of violence against women.

Domestic violence

Documents from the Foreign and Commonwealth Office and the Department of Health perceive forced marriage as a form of domestic violence and as contributing to domestic violence after marriage (Foreign and Commonwealth Office, Home Office and NHS 2007). Forced marriage is also part of the UK government's definition of domestic violence, which states that domestic violence is 'any incident of threatening behaviour, violence or abuse (psychological, physical, sexual, financial or emotional) between adults who are or have been intimate partners or family members, regardless of gender or sexuality' (Home Office, n.d.). There is a further clarification that this definition includes 'issues of concern to black and minority ethnic communities', including forced marriage and honour-related violence. As we will see below, this understanding reflects the success of feminist activism especially from within minoritised communities, who have insisted that the experiences of women from different ethnicities needed to be included within existing definitions of domestic violence, and also may feed into the government's ideas of recognising diversity and multiculturalism.

It is important to note however, that this understanding is relatively new, as the violence against women movement has traditionally viewed domestic violence (and in part continues to do so) as male violence against women in intimate relationships, both past or present (cf. Hague and Malos 2005). Further, the intimate partner definition of domestic violence is closely linked to the Duluth Model of 'power and control' that originated in northern Minnesota in the early 1980s, organised by activists in the battered women's movement. The Duluth Model is based on intimate partner violence, and notes the different ways in which men exercise control over women, including using male privilege, minimising women's experiences of abuse, economic control, coercion and threats, using children as leverage, isolating and intimidating women (Duluth n.d.).

Important as this understanding of domestic violence is, it has been criticised as being limited to the experiences of white, heterosexual women within intimate relationships with men. Women's organisations in the UK working with minoritised women, such as Southall Black Sisters and Imkaan, have pointed out that some communities, including (but not restricted to) South Asian communities, live in extended families, extending over more than one or two generations, and that within that context, domestic violence can and does take place both within and outside the intimate relationships. This domestic violence can include: forced marriage, child marriage, female genital mutilation, mother-in-law violence against daughters-in-law (Talwar Oldenburg 2002; Ahluwalia and Gupta 1997), and perpetrators include not only intimate partners but wider family members of both genders (Kazimirski et al. 2009; Shan 1991; Sanghera 2009).

The use of the domestic violence definition with regard to forced marriage has limitations. First, the definition includes family members, but forced marriage can often include wider community members that are not seen as family in the mainstream British sense, including members of the community – for example, all the families of a particular village may be treated as members of the same wider familial or kin and therefore participate in the surveillance of young people that contributes to forced marriage

35

(Gangoli et al. 2009). Second, the state definition of domestic violence is incident-based, while forced marriage, like intimate partner domestic violence, often follows a pattern of abuse and coercion. Third, the domestic violence definition only applies to adults, while forced marriage can take place at any age. Further, even though forced marriage shares some of the issues that 'conventional' domestic violence has (i.e. force, coercion, mental and physical violence, denial of freedoms, control over sexuality) (Hester et al. 2008), it can also lead to post-marriage intimate partner domestic violence (Siddiqui 2002; Home Office, Forced Marriage Unit and ACPO 2005). Other research in this area has highlighted how state practices around immigration control – including the two-year probation period on a spouse visa where the immigrant spouse has 'no recourse to public funds' (Burman and Chantler 2005; Wilson 2007) – are used by perpetrators of domestic violence and forced marriage to maintain their domination over victims. Recent studies have demonstrated that immigrant women on insecure visas are controlled in a number of ways, by their family, for example, keeping their passports, refusing to apply for permanent visas at the right time, using children to blackmail women into staying in violent relations. However, this control is legitimised by the state which refuses to allow women on insecure or temporary visas access to housing and other benefits, forcing them to stay in unhappy or forced marriages (Hague et al. 2006). As noted above, not only is entry forced in some cases, but women are coerced to stay on in marriages against their will because of financial and structural pressures. This has up to very recently been poorly understood by the mainstream violence against women movement in the UK.

The mainstream violence against women movement has more generally been somewhat reluctant to deal with particular forms of violence against women from minoritised communities. This can be attributed partly to a relativist framing of violence and abuse which argues for a contextual understanding and which has been interpreted as meaning that violence and abuse in minority communities are the responsibility of those communities rather than an issue for the violence against women movement at large. Coupled with a fear that intervening in violence against minoritised women is risky and might be perceived as 'culturally insensitive' and as imposing neocolonialist assumptions, the mainstream violence against women movement has generally steered clear of violence against minoritised women. The growth of minoritised women's refuges in the 1980s emerged in part as a result of the inability of many mainstream refuges to respond adequately to the needs of minoritised women (see Batsleer et al. 2002). This positioning of violence against women as cultural, of which forced marriage is a prime example, has been discussed above in our section on multiculturalism. Whilst this positioning may be shifting within the mainstream violence against women movement (though we would argue that evidence for this is yet unclear), another danger has emerged which merits further consideration.

Significantly, in relation to the forced marriage debate in the UK and in some European countries a worrying pattern is emerging concerning the manner in which the state is responding to feminist concerns on violence against women including issues such as forced marriage. Immigration policy is being widely used in the UK and other European Economic Area (EEA) countries in the name of protecting victims from forced marriage. This trend has been highlighted by a number of writers (e.g. Gedalof 2007; Dustin and Phillips 2008; and Chantler et al. 2009). In the UK, in November 2008 the government increased the age to 21 for sponsorship and spousal visas for spouses from outside the EEA. This was hailed as a progressive measure to prevent forced marriage, despite evidence which illustrates that there is widespread unease about the measure, both in the UK and in Denmark (Hester et al. 2008). In Denmark evidence suggests that increasing the age to 24 has had a disproportionate effect on minoritised communities and has increased racial tension (Phillips and Dustin 2004). The increase in age appears to have had no direct impact on forced marriages in Denmark, but some couples have migrated to other European countries such as Sweden in order to get married (Chantler et al. 2009). Similarly in the UK, concerns around discrimination, human rights, and challenges to the right to family reunification were raised by different ethnic communities (Hester et al. 2008).

Hence, as Razack (2004) and Gangoli and Chantler (2009) argue, it is imperative to be alert to the ways in which the state can and does co-opt feminist concerns and devises policies to respond to these in potentially racist ways via immigration policy.

As we have seen, conceptualising forced marriage in terms of difference can be limiting and potentially have racist implications. On the other hand, there are limitations in using the commonality approach (e.g. the extension of the definition of domestic violence, to include experiences of minoritised women, thus emphasising some commonalities), since neither the domestic violence, human rights or child protection approaches by themselves map onto women's experiences of forced marriage. Besides, existing definitions and understandings focus exclusively on the ability to consent to entry into marriage, and do not address women's ability to exit marriages. There is some value in understanding generalised heterosexual pressure to get married, but it is important to make a distinction between the different types of pressure experienced by gay women and men forced to marry and by heterosexual women and men being forced to marry. We will now address the issue of how forced marriage can be seen as a form of gender-based violence.

Forced marriage as gender-based violence
The UN defines violence against women as 'any act of gender-based violence that results in, or is likely to result in, physical, sexual or psychological harm or suffering to women, including threats of such acts, coercion or arbitrary deprivation of liberty, whether occurring in public or in private life'. This definition includes violence at the level of the family (such as domestic violence, sexual violence, 'traditional' forms of violence such as dowry-related violence and female genital mutilation); at the level of the community (rape, sexual harassment, trafficking) and at the level of the state (articles 1 and 2, UN Declaration on the Elimination of Violence against Women 1993).

Forced marriage can be seen as a form of gender-based violence for two reasons. First, existing data on forced marriage suggests that more women and girls experience forced marriage than do men and boys, with 85 per cent of cases reported to the UK's Forced Marriage Unit involving women and girls, and only 15 per cent involving men and boys (FMU website).[1] A recent study of the prevalence of forced marriage in ten local authorities in the UK revealed that 96 per cent of cases reported in these areas involved women and girls, and only 4 per cent involved men and boys (Kazimirski et al. 2009). Second, the impact of forced marriage is more serious on women and girls than on men, as they are more likely to experience sexual abuse, rape and post-marriage domestic violence as a consequence of forced marriage than are male victims of forced marriage (Hossain, n.d.; Outtarra et al. 1998; Hester et al. 2008).

The UN definition of violence against women could be a useful means to conceptualise forced marriage, as it addresses the gender-based nature of this violence. However, there are some potential limitations to this definition. Firstly, it makes a distinction between 'traditional' forms of violence, such as female genital mutilation and dowry-based violence and other forms of violence, but tradition is associated solely with practices of certain communities and nationalities, thus creating the usual binary and therefore hierarchy between 'traditional' and 'modern' cultures. Second, the definition, not unlike the domestic violence definition addressed above, is incident-based, and does not take into account the pattern of power and control that is inherent within forced marriage.

Forced marriage can also be considered as part of a gender-based violence continuum: Liz Kelly (1988b) first created the concept of continuum to expand the understanding of sexual violence. She cautioned that there was a difference between extending definitions to 'reflect the complexity of experiences and collapsing a number of forms of sexual violence into one category'. However, she argued that it was important to recognise that 'forms of sexual violence shade into one another at certain points' and that how women define their experiences of sexual violence 'varies, both between women and over time for any individual woman' (Kelly 1988a, 67). Kelly's idea of a continuum places everyday acts of violation within structural violence perpetrated against women (Kelly 1988b). The idea of continuum has also been accepted by the UN Secretary General's Report on Violence Against Women (2006, 36) which states that gender-based violence is 'a continuum of multiple, interrelated and sometimes recurring forms ... physical, sexual and psychological/emotional violence and economic abuse and exploitation, experienced in a range of settings, from private to public, and in today's globalised world, transcending national boundaries'.

This is resonant for experiences of forced marriage, which can include a continuum of violent and abusive behaviour, ranging from emotional pressure, coercion, threatening behaviour, abduction, battering, rape and sexual violence, at the point of entry into marriage, during marriage and when attempting to leave such relationships. Perpetrators as evident from Hester et al. 2008 can include family members (parents, siblings, other blood relatives, husbands and in-laws), wider community members (local community leaders, professionals, neighbours) and the state (immigration officers, the police).

Conclusion

We have seen that current explanations and conceptualisations of forced marriage are useful, but that each of the tropes has limitations. Understanding forced marriage as a human rights issue deflects attention from the rights of individual women and men; where individual human rights are concerned, the issue of consent is problematic. Conceptualising forced marriage as a multicultural issue can contribute to the stigmatisation of par-

ticular communities, while defining it as domestic violence can lead to only a partial understanding of the issue. Feminist conceptualisations of gender-based violence and the gendered continuum of violence are perhaps most useful to avoid such stereotyping of minoritised communities, particularly where these conceptualisations adopt an intersectional approach which attends to multiple dimensions of oppression and disadvantage, for example class, racism, heteronormativity.

However, as we have seen, definitions of forced marriage focus primarily on entry into marriage, and we argue that exit strategies (or lack of such strategies) may play an important role in experiences of forced marriage (Hester et al. 2008). Key research on strategies against forced marriage suggests that the state focus in the UK has been on exit strategies in forced marriage cases, that is, on encouraging young people to exit forced marriages at the cost of strategies focused on regulation or prevention of forced marriage. It is suggested that the 'right to exit' approach, while meeting an urgent and immediate need, is flawed not only because the emotional, financial and physical costs of exit can be too high for the individual concerned, but also because it offers a case-by-case approach that 'imposes the burden of resolving conflict on the individual' and does not address the underlying causes and power relations that lead to forced marriage (Phillips and Dustin 2004, 545). Phillips and Dustin argue that an overemphasis on exit strategies can be counterproductive. However, our research indicates that current policy, for example immigration restrictions on entry, focuses more on regulating entry than on enabling exit, especially for first-generation immigration women who may be trapped into the marriage. Further, current forced marriage definitions focus exclusively on the point of entry into a marriage. The Home Office defines forced marriage as occurring: 'Where one or both parties are coerced into a marriage against their will and under duress' (Home Office 2006). This definition is based on consent or duress at the point of entry into the marriage. While this is a useful definition, Hester et al. (2008) point out that survivor experiences of forced marriage may not easily map on to this neat understanding. This also poses questions of exit options (particularly where consent has not been given or is questionable) and the pressure (emotional, physical, financial, cultural, immigration status and so on) that is put upon women and men to stay in a forced marriage. Pressure here includes a prioritisation of preserving the marital relationship rather than protecting women, and a stigmatisation of divorce.

Exit out of such relationships also needs to be considered, including the systems (state practices and their intersections with cultural practices) that keep women in forced marriages and thus may be deemed to increase risk. Whilst it is right that the focus should be on 'consent', and entry, what is clear is that consent is sometimes hard to establish. In addition, there may well be cases where despite refusal, a marriage will take place. These factors make it important to focus not only on 'entry into', but also 'exit out of' such relationships.

Focusing on the ability (or inability) to exit out of the relationship can also widen our understanding of forced marriage beyond particular communities. There is abundant research on how men employ a range of tactics, including using children, financial control, immigration status and emotional pressure, to force women to stay on in violent and abusive relationships (Chantler et al. 2003; Strube 1988; Stark 2007). Stark also reveals that the ideology of coercive control entraps women, and forces them to stay on in violent relationships. Stark's conceptualisation of coercive control (2007) offers a comprehensive understanding of domestic violence, suggesting that domestic violence is based on a 'complex material-cultural nexus' that renders women powerless and men powerful, and able to exercise coercive control over women (Brush 2009). This includes the regulation of women's behaviour in line with normative understandings of femininity.

Further, the risk and reality of increased violence at the point of separation and post-separation forces women to return to their abusers. This is not restricted to women of a particular ethnic and/or religious community. We believe therefore that a holistic definition of forced marriage also needs to include force and coercion at the point of marriage (entry), during the marriage, and around exit.

Note

1   The Forced Marriage Unit is part of the Foreign and Commonwealth Office and offers nationwide support to victims of forced marriage and to professionals who work with such victims.

References

Ahluwalia, K. and Gupta, R. (1997) *Circle of Light*, London: Harper Collins.

Anitha, S. and Gill, A. (2009) 'Coercion, Consent and the Forced Marriage Debate in the UK', *Feminist Legal Studies*,17(2), 165–84

Barry, K. (1979) *Female Sexual Slavery*, Englewood Cliffs: Prentice-Hall.

Batsleer, J., Burman, E., Chantler, K., McIntosh, S.H., Pantling, K., Smailes, S. and Warner, S. (2002) *Domestic Violence and Minoritisation: Supporting Women to Independence*, Women's Studies Research Centre, Manchester Metropolitan University.

Brush, L. D. (2009) 'Guest Editor's Introduction', *Violence Against Women* 15(2), 1423–31.

Burman, E., and Chantler, K. (2005) 'Domestic Violence and Minoritisation: Legal and Policy Barriers Facing Minoritised Women Leaving Violent Relationships', *International Journal of Law and Psychiatry*, 28 (1), 59–74.

Carroll, L. (1988) 'Arranged Marriages: Law, Custom, and the Muslim Girl in the U.K', Women Living Under Muslim Law Dossier 20, 168.

Chantler, K., Burman, E. and Batsleer, J. (2003) 'South Asian Women: Systematic Inequalities in Services around Attempted Suicide and Self Harm', *European Journal of Social Work*, 6(1), 1369–457.

Chantler, K., Burman, E., Batsleer, J. and Bashir, C. (2001) *Attempted Suicide and Self-harm – South Asian Women*, Women's Studies Research Centre, Manchester Metropolitan University.

Chantler, K., Gangoli, G., and Hester, M. et al. (2009) 'Forced marriage in the UK: Religious, cultural, economic or state violence?' *Critical Social Policy*, 29(4), 587–612.

Chantler, K., and Gangoli, G. (forthcoming) 'Domestic Violence in Minority Communities: Cultural Norm or Cultural Anomaly?' In R. Thiara, M. Schroettle and S. Condon (eds.) *Violence against Women and Ethnicity: Commonalities and Differences across Europe – A Reader*.

Derné, S. (2005) 'The (limited) effect of cultural globalisation in India: implications for culture theory', *Poetics*, no. 33, 33–47.

Duluth (n.d.) www.theduluthmodel.org/documents/PhyVio.pdf, accessed on 10 August 2009.

Dustin, M. and Phillips, A. (2008) 'Whose agenda is it? Abuses of women and abuses of "culture" in Britain', *Ethnicities*, 8 (3), 405-24.

Forced Marriage Unit (2008) *The Right to Choose: Multi-Agency Statutory Guidance for Dealing with Forced Marriage*, London: Forced Marriage Unit.

Foreign and Commonwealth Office (2005) *Forced Marriage – a Wrong Not a Right*. London: Foreign and Commonwealth Office.

Foreign and Commonwealth Office, Home Office and NHS (2007) *Dealing with Cases of Forced Marriage. Guidance for Health Professionals*, London: Home Office.

Gangoli, G and Chantler, K. (2009) 'Protecting Victims of Forced Marriage: Is Age a Protective Factor?' *Feminist Legal Studies*, 17, 267–88

Gangoli, G., McCarry, M. and Razak, A. (2009) 'Child Marriage or Forced Marriage: South Asian Communities in North East England', *Children and Society*, 23(6), 418–29.

Gangoli, G., Razak, A. and McCarry, M. (2006) *Forced Marriages and Domestic Violence Among South Asian Communities in North East England*, Newcastle and Bristol: Northern Rock Foundation and University of Bristol.

Gedalof, I. (2007) 'Unhomely Homes: Women, Family and Belonging' in Hague, G. M. and Malos, E. M. (2005) *Domestic Violence: Action for Change*, 3rd edn, New Clarion Press.

Hague, G. M., Gangoli, G , Joseph, H. and Alphonse, M. (2006) *Domestic Violence, Marriage and Immigration: If you are immigrating into the UK to marry, what you might need to know*. School for Policy Studies, University of Bristol; Nirmala Niketan, University of Mumbai and British Academy.

Hester, M. (1992) *Lewd Women and Wicked Witches: a Study of the Dynamics of Male Domination*, London: Routledge.

Hester, M., Chantler, K., Gangoli, G., Devgon, J., Sharma, S. and Singleton, A. (2008) *Forced marriage: the risk factors and the effect of raising the minimum age for a sponsor, and of leave to enter the UK as a spouse or fiancé(e)*. Bristol, School for Policy Studies, University of Bristol and School of Nursing, Midwifery and Social Work, University of Manchester.

Home Office (2006) *Forced Marriage: The Risk Factors and the Effect of Raising the Minimum Age for a Sponsor, and of Leave to Enter The UK as a Spouse* (SRG/05/037). London: Home Office.

Home Office (n.d.) 'Crime and Victims' website, http://www.homeoffice.gov.uk/crime-victims/reducing-crime/domestic-violence, accessed 14 March 2008.

Home Office, Forced Marriage Unit and ACPO (2005) 'Dealing with cases of forced marriage. Guidance for police officers', London: ACPO.

Hossain, S. (n.d.). 'Abduction for Forced Marriage – Rights and Remedies in Bangladesh and Pakistan'. www.soas.ac.uk/honourcrimes/FMarticleHossain.pdf

Interights, Ain O Salish Kendra (ASK) and Shirkat Gah (2000) 'Submission to Home Office Working Group – Information Gathering Exercise on Forced Marriages'. http://www.soas.ac.uk/honourcrimes/FMsubmission.htm, accessed on 4 January 2010.

Kazimirski, A., Keogh, P., Kumari, V., Smith, R., Gowland, S., Purdon, S. and Khanum, N. (2009) *Forced Marriage: Prevalence and Service Response*, National Centre for Social Research. Research Report for DCSF – RR128.

Kelly, L. (1988a) 'What's in a name? Defining Child Sexual Abuse', *Feminist Review*, 28, 65–73.

Kelly, L. (1988b) *Surviving Sexual Violence*, Polity Press, Oxford.

Mackinnon, C. (1987) *Feminism Unmodified: Discourses on Life and Law*, Cambridge, MA: Harvard University Press.

Otoo-Oyertey, N. and Pobi, S. (2003) 'Early Marriage and Poverty: Exploring Links and Key Policy Issues', *Gender and Development* 11(2), 42–51.

Outtarra, M., Sen, P. and Thompson, M. (1998) 'Forced marriage, forced sex: the perils of childhood for girls', *Gender and Development*, 6(3), 27–33.

Patel, P. (2008) 'Faith in the State? Asian women's struggles for human rights in the UK', *Feminist Legal Studies*, 16, 9–36

Phillips, A. and Dustin, M. (2004). 'UK initiatives on Forced Marriage: Regulation, Dialogue and Exit', *Political Studies*, 52, 531–51.

Razack, S. (2004) 'Imperilled Muslim Women, Dangerous Muslim Men and Civilised Europeans: Legal and Social Responses to Forced Marriages', *Feminist Legal Studies*, 12 (2), 129 –74.

Rich, A. (1980) 'Compulsory Heterosexuality and Lesbian Existence', *Journal of Women's History*, 15(3) (2003), 11–48.

Rose, N. (1990) *Governing the Soul: the Shaping of the Private Self*, London: Routledge.

Samad, Y. and Eade, J. (2002) *Community Perceptions of Forced Marriage*, London: Foreign and Commonwealth Office.

Sanghera, J. (2007) *Shame*, London: Hodder and Stoughton.

Sanghera, J. (2009) *Daughters of Shame*, London: Hodder and Stoughton.

Scharf, M. and Mattler, S. (2005) *Forced Marriage: Exploring the Viability of the Special Court for Sierra Leone's New Crime Against Humanity*. Case Research Paper Series in Legal Studies, Working Paper 05-35, http://ssrn.com/ abstract=824291, accessed 4 January 2010.

Shan, S. (1991) *In My Own Name*, Women's Press, London.

Siddiqui, H. (2002) 'Forced Marriages: An Abuse of Women's Human Rights', *Rights of Women Bulletin*, Spring 2002, 2–4.

Singer, Sir Peter (2001) 'When is an arranged marriage a forced marriage?' *International Family Law Journal*, 2001, IFL 30.

Stark, E. (2007) *Coercive Control: The Entrapment of Women in Personal Life*, Oxford University Press.

Stobard, E. (2002) *Guidelines to the Police in Dealing with Cases of Forced Marriages*, Association of Chief Police Officers, Foreign and Commonwealth Office and Home Office.

Strube, M. (1988) 'The Decision to Leave an Abusive Relationship: Empirical Evidence and Theoretical Issues', *Psychological Bulletin*, 104, 2, 236–50.

Talwar Oldenburg, V. (2002) *Dowry Murder: The imperial origins of a cultural crime*, Oxford University Press, New Delhi.

Trawick, M. (1992) *Notes on Love in a Tamil Marriage*, Berkeley, University of California.

Uddin, B. and Ahmed, L. (2000). *A Choice by Right: the Report of the Working Group on Forced Marriage*, Home Office, London.

UN (1993) Declaration on the Elimination of Violence against Women. Available online at http://www.un.org/documents/ga/res/48/a48r104.htm, accessed 14 October 2009.

UN Secretary General Report on Violence Against Women (2006). Available at http://daccess-dds-ny.un.org/doc/UNDOC/GEN/N06/419/74/PDF/ N0641974.pdf?OpenElement, accessed 25 January 2011.

Wadley, S. (1980) 'Hindu Women's Family and Household Rites in a North Indian

Village', in N. Falk and R. Goss. (eds.) *Unspoken Worlds: Women's Religious Roles*, Harper and Row: San Francisco and London: 95–106.

Wilson, A. (2007) 'Forced Marriage Debate and the British State', *Race and Class*, 49(1), 25–38.

2

Reconceptualising consent and coercion within an intersectional understanding of forced marriage

Sundari Anitha and Aisha K. Gill*

This chapter aims to trace the definitional evolution of forced marriage through an examination of the legal and policy discourses on forced marriage in the UK. Despite the expansion of the ambit of what is understood to constitute coercion in marriage, the binary conceptualisation of coercion and consent fails to capture women's experiences and practitioners' concerns. This chapter explores how a deeper understanding of the types of coercion associated with forced marriage might be achieved by taking into account women's location within a matrix of intersecting inequalities: socio-economic constraints, cultural practices within their communities, racism and the normative status of heterosexuality in wider society, and the gendered nature of legal discourses and state policies (especially immigration policies). The final section discusses a number of measures and policy recommendations for addressing the needs of survivors of specific forms of violence from a holistic, intersectional perspective that situates forced marriage on the continuum of violence against women.

Locating forced marriage within debates on violence against women

Since 1990, there have been substantial changes in social policy and criminal justice system responses to domestic violence in the UK. Key agencies such as the Crown Prosecution Service have reviewed and overhauled their policies on domestic violence and moved towards a more proactive approach to evidence gathering for prosecution. Specialist domestic violence courts have been established; these may be rolled out across the UK. There has been significant growth in specialist services to provide outreach assistance, advocacy, and

* Both authors contributed equally to this chapter.

victim and family support (e.g. supervised contact with children). There has also been a review of legislation, *Safety and Justice* (Home Office 2003), consultations with survivors, and legislative developments, the most important of these being the Domestic Violence Crime and Victims Act, which expanded victims' rights to protection. However, research indicates that practitioners at the grassroots level, especially those working to implement new policies, have been fairly resistant to change (Hall and Whyte 2003), not least because not all changes have been positive: increasing focus on criminal justice responses to violence against women, and on high-risk cases (e.g. Multi Agency Risk Assessment Conferences), has had a detrimental effect on education and awareness-raising work. For instance, some criminologists have been sceptical about the 'what works' approach that characterises current crime reduction policies (Braithwaite 2003; Crawford 1997; Garland 2001; Hillyard et al. 2004). Though feminist scholars and activists have supported evidence-based practices and community action (like Crime Disorder Reduction Partnerships; see, for example, Taylor-Browne 2001), they have also expressed similar concerns about the low priority accorded to long-term preventative work, which is never easy to quantify.

Of further concern is the fact that policy trends in one area have tended to undermine reforms elsewhere (Radford et al. 2000); current crime reduction policy has focused on criminalisation at the expense of support services (Young 1999). For instance, while the police and other agencies urge women to leave abusers, family courts often lock them into relationships post-separation by making unsafe contact orders for children (Saunders and Barron 2003). Moreover, victims' access to long-term financial support and accommodation is limited and limiting (Morrow, Hankivsky and Varcoe 2004), not least because the expansion of sanctuary schemes, which give abused women the option to continue to live in their own homes and thereby save the state the costs associated with rehousing. Women's organisations have expressed concerns that the expansion of these schemes might come at the cost of funding for refuge services (Scottish Women's Aid 2010).

Though awareness and reporting of gender-based violence have increased, some professionals and academics claim that little has changed since the 1980s as fewer rape or domestic violence cases are now prosecuted (Coy et al. 2009; Lees 1997; Snider 1998). Regional and local variations in the responses to incidents have led to the coining of the term 'domestic violence lottery' (Regan 2001). However, while the term 'lottery' invokes a sense of outrage at differential treatment, it does not speak to the power structures at play in relation to access to services: after all, in a lottery everyone is equally likely to win or lose. Both access to services and the quality of support provided by public agencies are influenced by issues of difference and social exclusion, especially in relation to race, sexuality, age and income level (Burman et al. 2004): these variations are not a matter of chance, as the word 'lottery' implies. Factors that can ameliorate these problems for particular individuals include feminist activism and the rather more contingent interventions by individuals in local branches of national agencies and local government (Hague et al. 1996). Despite progress, many victims of domestic violence continue to receive inadequate care and support (Radford and Gill 2006).

Despite the increased interest in violence against women since the late 1970s, women from minority religious and ethnic groups in Western European countries have not been identified by policy makers as being in need of particular protection (Phillips and Dustin 2004). Consequently, they have been rendered nearly invisible, and the specificity of their needs has been almost entirely ignored. One exception was the provision of specialist domestic violence services, including refuges, aimed at women from specific communities. These services were developed in the late 1970s and early 1980s in response to campaigning by black and minority ethnic and refugee women who were not well-served by mainstream services which had little understanding of their specific needs. However, specific forms of violence against black and minority ethnic and refugee women continued to be invisibilised in policy discourses. Recently, however, the debate on forced marriage has brought to light particular forms of violence faced by women from minority ethnic communities; this has encouraged governments across Western Europe to address this problem directly.

Despite the stated efforts of the last Labour government to be 'sensitive' in its dealings with minority communities, in striving to ameliorate the problem of forced marriage the government framed the issue in cultural terms rather than viewing it as a specific manifestation of the wider problem of gendered and patriarchal violence (see Chapter 5). Indeed, the UK government's policy on forced marriage is epistemologically predicated on a desire to modernise minority communities that is, in turn, based on a concept of cultural *othering*: in other words, current policy initiatives attribute the cause of forced marriage to culture, region, and/or religion, all of which are considered to lie outside the realm of governmental responsibility (Gill and Mitra-Kahn 2010). At the time of writing, the policy of the Conservative-Liberal Democrat coalition government on violence against women, and on forced marriage in particular, has not been clearly articulated.

The oversimplified view of forced marriage as belonging to an *othered* culture serves two distinct purposes. First, constructing the issue as a culturally sanctioned crime divorces forced marriage from a clear violence against women agenda. Second, viewing forced marriage as a culturally sanctioned act positions the host nation as a liberal and neutral force – a socially superior society within which legal remedies to the problem of forced marriage can be constructed – with the corollary that the *othered* society is essentialised as atavistic and illiberal (Razack 2004). The legal remedies to forced marriage available to women in the UK have less to do with the human rights of minority women, and more to do with the policing of minority communities and the patrolling of the nation's borders. These remedies are premised on the idea that black and minority ethnic women do not have the ability to change patriarchal practices in their communities from *within*. Thus, it follows that responses to forced marriage cannot be found within minority communities and, instead, must be imposed from without (Gill and Mitra-Kahn 2010).

Forced marriage and the law in the UK

There is a long history of legal engagement with the problem of forced marriage in the UK. However, the issue has only become the focus of media attention and policy debate as a result of the publicity surrounding three high-profile cases in the late 1990s (Hall 1999; Watt 1999). Following these cases, a Home Office report on forced marriage was published in 2000. This report (Uddin and Ahmed 2000) distinguished between arranged marriage, a practice which operates in numerous countries worldwide and in certain minority communities in the UK, and which is facilitated by families but requires the consent of both partners, and forced marriage, which was defined as a marriage conducted without consent by either partner (Uddin and Ahmed 2000, 10).

In the UK, available statistics indicate that forced marriage is a problem that primarily affects women originating from the Indian subcontinent (FCO and Home Office 2005, 15), though it also affects women originating from Iran, Afghanistan, Turkey, Armenia, Somalia, Eritrea and Sudan, and from Irish traveller communities (Hester et al. 2008). Estimates of the incidence of forced marriage made by specialist domestic violence services range from 450 (Newham Asian Women's Project 2007) to 1,000 (Southall

Black Sisters 2001) cases a year. Recent media reports have spoken of the '500 missing girls' who are thought to have been removed from schools in the UK and forced into marriage in the Indian subcontinent; by adding to this their estimates of older victims of forced marriage, some reports speculate that there may be up to 4,000 cases of forced marriage a year (Taylor 2008). Reliable figures are hard to obtain in part because of the difficulty of distinguishing between coercion and consent: research on black and minority ethnic communities in the UK indicates that, while most people perceive a difference between arranged and forced marriages, they also recognise some overlap (Gangoli et al. 2006). As with all other forms of violence against women, the extent of forced marriage is occluded by underreporting.

Before it is possible to understand the modern legal approach to forced marriage, it is necessary to know something about its history, not least because current legislation is based on presuppositions that have gone unchallenged for decades. Before the mid 1980s, coercion or duress was interpreted narrowly by the courts and taken to mean either physical force or the threat of physical force: 'an immediate threat to life, limb or liberty' (Phillips and Dustin 2004). In the case of *Hussein (Otherwise Blitz) v Hussein* (1938), for example, the petitioner asked that her marriage to the respondent be annulled on the grounds that she had only contracted the marriage because he had repeatedly threatened to kill her if she did not. In granting a *decree nisi*, the court upheld that the plaintiff's free will had been undermined by the respondent's conduct and that she had been coerced into the marriage. This case is representative: the most common claims of duress that have come before courts have involved duress imposed either by one of the parties to the marriage or by the family of one of the parties (*McLarnon v McLarnon* 1968; *Harper v Harper* 1981; *KR* 1999).

The case of *Hirani v Hirani* (1983) marked a new phase in the understanding of coercion. The applicant was a 19-year-old Hindu woman whose parents had arranged a marriage to prevent her from associating with a Muslim man. Having separated from her husband after only six weeks of marriage, she petitioned for a *decree nisi* on the grounds of duress exercised by her parents, upon whom she was financially dependent and who had threatened to turn her out of the home if she did not go through with the marriage. Although her petition was initially rejected, in allowing her the right to appeal and eventually granting her the *decree nisi*, the court held that 'The crucial question ... is whether the threats, pressure, or whatever it is, is such as to destroy the reality of consent and overbears the will of the individual.' Phillips and Dustin (2004, 538) have pointed out that this judgment marks a definite shift in legal rhetoric from a restrictive definition of duress centred upon threats of physical violence to one in which the key issue was 'whether the mind of the applicant (the victim) has in fact been overborne, howsoever that was caused'. In subsequent cases (e.g. *Mahmood v Mahmood* 1993; *Mahmud v Mahmud* 1994; *Sohrab v Khan* 2002) the courts examined the impact of emotional pressure, which they understood as taking a variety of forms (e.g. being made to feel responsible for bringing about a loved one's death, and threats of suicide on the part of the coercer).

In 2005, it was in response to the increasing media profile of forced marriage from the late 1990s that new legislation proposed to treat forced marriage as a specific criminal offence. Following criticism of the proposed legislation from several non-governmental organisations on the basis that (a) it was divorced from practice and would, thus, prove ineffective (Gill 2005; Mookherjee and Reddy 2005), (b) it would reinforce racist stereotypes (Imkaan 2006), and (c) it would fragment laws pertaining to violence against women, a civil bill was then proposed which was eventually incorporated *within* the Family Law Act. The Forced Marriage (Civil Protection) Act received Royal Assent on 26 July 2007 as a new part (Part 4A) of the Family Law Act, 1996, thus locating forced marriage within the broader context of violence against women. The meaning of 'force' (in the sense of forcing someone to do something) is defined in section 63A (6) of this act as 'to coerce by threats or other psychological means'. Thus, under the new law, forced marriage has been rendered an actionable and specific civil wrong, with specific remedies (chiefly forced marriage protection orders) designed to protect those threatened with, or subjected to, this wrong (for a detailed discussion of this Act, see Chapter 6 in this collection).

Understanding consent and coercion in forced marriage: from binaries to continuum

The Home Office report on forced marriage emphasised the distinction between arranged and forced marriage to allay concerns among minority communities that the initiative might cast suspicion on the former (Uddin and Ahmed 2000).[1] The courts have also been anxious to distinguish between the two types of marriage, though often with troubling consequences. In two cases in which the applicant's petition for nullity was granted on the grounds of emotional duress, the courts somewhat paradoxically reasserted the legitimacy of parental pressure: for instance, in *Mahmood v Mahmood* (1993), the judge commented:

> I accept entirely that parental consent is perfectly legitimate and proper ... I also accept that the consent which has to be given to marriage need not be enthusiastic consent, but even reluctant consent will suffice provided that the consent is genuine.

Similarly, in *Mahmud v Mahmud* (1994), the judge stressed that, if 'under pressure – and perhaps very considerable pressure – a party does indeed change his or her mind and consents to a marriage, with however ill a grace and however resentfully, then the marriage is in my opinion valid'. The problem here is a pressing one: how can 'reluctant' or 'resentful' consent resulting from 'very considerable pressure' not amount to coercion?

Feminists have long recognised the variety of pressures on women to marry, including issues related to poverty, pregnancy and sexuality, as well as social norms and expectations underpinned by patriarchal structures and institutions. Indeed, research on the marriage practices of black and minority ethnic women in the UK indicates that the sanctions that uphold the dominant moral codes of minority communities influence how individuals in these communities exercise agency. In research that has examined the marriage choices and decision-making processes of young South Asian women in the UK, this statement was one of many that pointed to the range of pressures that are perceived by women: 'If a girl says no, it's considered a bad thing,' and 'if you didn't [i.e. go along with the marriage], there would be hell to pay from your parents and all your relatives' (Bhopal 1999, 121; see also Gangoli et al. 2006, 10; and Wilson 2006, 18–19, 91–3). In such a situation, the court may be able to assess the strength and the reasonableness of the woman's convictions on the basis of the family's history: for example, if the woman's sister had been disowned for refusing to consent to an arranged marriage, she would have a valid reason to believe that withholding consent would lead to sanctions. However, in the absence of explicit threats, the coercive potential of social expectations which are familiar to many women has seldom been recognised in prevailing understandings of forced marriage.

In *Singh v Singh* (1971), the petitioner was a 17-year-old Sikh girl ('P') who had consented to an arranged marriage. According to Sikh custom, following a civil ceremony the parties separated while a religious ceremony in a Sikh temple was arranged. However, P refused to attend the religious ceremony or have anything further to do with her husband. She petitioned unsuccessfully for the marriage to be nullified on the grounds of, *inter alia*, duress induced by parental coercion; she claimed that she had gone through with the first ceremony out of respect for her parents and religion, despite deciding that she did not wish to do so when she first met her prospective husband at the registry office before the ceremony. In dismissing her appeal, the Court held that in order to establish that there had been duress that vitiated consent to the marriage a petitioner would have to show that his/her will was overborne by genuine fear induced by threats of immediate danger to life, limb or liberty.

P's application was dismissed because of the absence of any explicit threat. Though explicit emotional duress has since been recognised by courts in the UK, the power of societal norms continues to be disregarded. However, respect for parents and religion is not a spontaneous feeling that arises within the subject. It is a gendered, socially and culturally constructed mode of behaviour (Manion 2003), which in particular communities is enforced through a range of related concepts: in this case, honour (*izzat*)[2] and shame (*sharam*) (Gill 2004; Wilson 2006). Women's agency is always exercised in the context of a number of coercive forces, including constructs of femininity and specific forms of socialisation (e.g. being taught to value success in relationships). Not all black and minority ethnic women in the UK confront the same norms or confront them in the same way. However, research indicates that in some South Asian communities women are considered the bearers of family honour. In this context, the gendered concept of shame may well cause a woman to feel that she has no choice but to consent to a marriage to avoid stigmatising her family and, thus, to preserve her own sense of self and self-worth (Gangoli et al. 2006, 11).

The grey areas between coercion and consent have been alluded to in another recent case where forced marriage was feared in the case of an adult woman (SK) who went 'missing' after being taken to Bangladesh. Justice Singer (*SK* 2004) issued a summons to SK's family to produce her at the British High Commission and applied injunctive relief, restraining her family from threatening, intimidating, harassing or using violence against her, or proceeding with the supposed wedding. Singer argued:

> there is a spectrum of FM [forced marriage], from physical force or fear of injury or death in their most literal form, through to the undue imposition of emotional pressure which is at the other end of the FM range, and that a grey area then separates unacceptable FM from marriages arranged traditionally which are in no way to be condemned, but rather supported as a conventional concept in many societies. Social expectations can of themselves impose

emotional pressure, and the grey area to which I have referred is where one may slip into the other: arranged may become forced but forced is always different from arranged.

Despite the extension of the definitional ambit of coercion to include such hazily defined grey areas, and despite the allusion to social expectations, the notion of free will remains central to the legal discourse on forced marriage in the UK. This preoccupation with free will ignores the fact that consent is constructed in the context of power imbalances and gendered norms and, crucially, often in the absence of explicit threats. This conceptualisation of the legal subject as an autonomous agent who is able to choose and act freely elides the experiences of gendered, raced beings in favour of a subject predicated on the assumption that the experiences of white men are normative.

Feminist legal scholars have long noted that the atomistic, unencumbered subject deemed to be in full command of self, personhood, labour and property bears little resemblance to women's experiences as socially situated and heterogeneous subjects constrained by gendered norms (Richardson 2004; Walker 1999). The construction of personhood among women can be said to be constituted with reference to complex relations of dependency shaped by political and social hierarchies (Mackenzie and Stoljar 2000; Meyers 1989). Within communities where arranged marriage is practised, determining whom a woman can and cannot marry in fact serves to delineate the boundaries between communities and castes (Wilson 2006), a conflation of women's bodies with the boundaries of the nation and community that is not unique to (im)migrant cultures (Yuval-Davis 1997). Refuges for South Asian women in the UK have long dealt with the ostracism that many women face as a consequence of disclosing domestic abuse and choosing to leave an abusive relationship. Being exiled from social networks can involve more than the emotional loss of significant others: it may mean the loss of one's own identity, what Reitman (2005) terms the 'sociopsychological costs of exit', the loss of a sense of belonging that defines the self (Weinstock 2005). In this context, a refusal to consent to a marriage that will result in a potential loss of family, and thus community, is surely perceived as inherently coercive by many women. As has been argued by feminists in other contexts, the presumption of choice and consent exercised by a formal, neutral, legal subject (Hunter and Cowan 2007; Naffine 2003) does not incorporate the experiences of women. Furthermore, for many women of South Asian origin, as indeed for any woman of colour, the option of exit from their family and (often) thereby, their community is to 'escape' into a racist society, one potentially hostile to (im)migrants, particularly since the 11 September 2001 attacks on the World Trade Center and other targets.

Coercive control is exercised in ways that are far more subtle than those provided for in current definitions of forced marriage, and research indicates that inequalities and specificities inherent in women's racialised, gendered and classed location constitutes specific acts of coercion in marriage. It is within a range of both articulated and unarticulated constraints and opportunities that particular groups of black and minority ethnic women exercise their agency, to varying degrees, in determining (1) whether or not to marry, (2) their choice of marriage partner, and (3) the timing of their marriage. Focusing on the extent of the coercive pressure (whether physical or emotional) that has been actively brought to bear on a victim of forced marriage may not reveal the total burden of coercion experienced by a woman (Feinberg 1986). This concept of the total burden incorporates all of the experiences and the contextual location of the individual to assess how pervasive, frightening and/or intense the pressure is. Feinberg's (1986) approach is useful precisely because, as already suggested, explicit threats do not exhaust the range of coercive techniques and structures experienced by black and minority ethnic women in the UK who face pressure to marry. To confine accounts of coercion to explicit threats – be they of physical force or explicitly articulated emotional pressure – ignores the ways in which a classed, gendered and racialised context creates coercion.

An intersectional approach to forced marriage

A new discourse on personal freedom and constraint is needed to capture the experiences of women, especially black and minority ethnic women, and to reflect on the diverse forces that influence women's choices in relation to marriage. The dominant media discourse on forced marriage, for example, superficially conflates arranged and forced marriage, and views them both through a culturalist lens, overwhelmingly portraying women as passive victims, rather than unpacking the gendered inequalities with which all women grapple, to varying degrees. Thus, in the media, some black and minority ethnic women are lauded as heroines for having resisted patriarchal structures within their communities (Sanghera 2007) and for managing to escape their control, while others are portrayed as passive victims awaiting rescue by the British state (Harding 2000). Similar perspectives also emerge in scholarship on agency (Frank 2006), where women's actions in oppressive contexts have been categorised as acquiescence to patriarchal authority, whereas agency is equated with women's overt resistance (Goddard 2000, 3; Morgan 1991; Wolf 1991), often demonstrated through the strategy of exit.

The need to move away from a binary conceptualisation of agency versus passivity is highlighted in research (Chetkovich 2004) that recognises the complexity of women's actions in oppressive contexts. Research evidence indicates the different ways in which black and minority ethnic women actively negotiate and make deliberate strategic choices about marriage in order to manoeuvre within the grey areas that exist between (relative) coercion and consent (Bradby 1999; Gangoli et al. 2006; Samad and Eade 2002). The multiple constraints within which women exercise their agency originate both within families and communities as well as from external factors like racism and essentialist attitudes towards their communities. Bredal's (2005) research draws attention to the complex motivations behind perceptions of marriage choice among young black and minority ethnic and refugee women in Norway who articulated their desire to uphold certain traditional norms by actively pursuing arranged marriages out of a *positive* need to assert their sense of belonging within a community under siege post-9/11.

This intersectional nature of the constraints and opportunities faced by victims/survivors of forced marriage has implications for the state's responses to forced marriage, especially the right to exit. As discussed above, the intersectional approach (Crenshaw 1991) suggests that black and minority ethnic women experience racial, gendered, sexual and class oppression, and that these multiple forms of oppression do not merely occur simultaneously but, instead, are interrelated and mutually reinforcing (Collins 2000). Intersectional theorists reject derivative analyses that posit a single, key oppression that all other areas of oppression derive from. Intersectionality also differs from the additive model of oppression, which assumes that black and minority ethnic women are subject to racial and gendered 'double jeopardy' (Brah and Phoenix 2004; Mirza 1997). Thus, although debate about what intersectionality actually means has been rife (Brah and Phoenix 2004; Browne and Misra 2003; Yuval-Davis 2006), there has been relative agreement on its principal tenets. First, the constituent categories of intersectionality are socially defined and the meanings of these categories are historically contingent. Second, specific locations in this matrix of intersecting axes of oppression represent unique experiences that are more significant than the sum of their parts: this reflects the multiplicative nature of intersecting oppressions (Crenshaw 1991). Third, intersecting forms of discrimination create both oppression and opportunity (Collins 2000). Fourth, because hierarchies of power are cross-cutting, it is likely that a person will be simultaneously advantaged by certain identities and disadvantaged by others, and the two are linked (Zinn and Dill 1996). Fifth, and finally, these hierarchies intersect at all levels of social life, both through social structure and through social interaction. Intersectional approaches also recognise that categories of oppression can often be broken down further: for instance, some women are situated in positions of power relative to other women (e.g. mothers and mothers-in-law tend to have power over daughters and daughters-in-law).

In the UK, numerous influences, including state policies (particularly immigration policies), country of origin, and individual diasporic experiences intersect to shape the nature of coercion in matters of marriage. There is a growing body of research which indicates the gendered processes related to the diasporic experience: in some cases, parents impose an unwanted marriage to stem the influence of Western culture over their daughters or to end their daughters' associations with 'unsuitable partners' (Gangoli et al. 2006, 13–14; Samad and Eade 2002, 67). Successive legislation has restricted immigration routes into the UK so that marriage remains one of the few means of settlement. Research indicates that in the diasporic context, the issue of consanguineous marriage may be reasserted as a traditional cultural practice to facilitate the migration of kin out of a sense of obligation and the need to maintain links with the original communities (Shaw 2001).

Women's agency is also shaped by the nature of service responses and the availability of resources to meet their needs. The current emphasis on the cultural uniqueness of particular forms of domestic violence (e.g. forced marriage and so-called 'honour crimes') informs, and is informed by, racist and essentialist stereotypes that feed into anti-immigration agendas (Dustin and Phillips 2008) that are dressed up as steps to combat forced marriage. It is within this context that research indicates that women from black and other minority ethnic communities are less likely than other women to access statutory services for help in relation to domestic violence for a variety of reasons, including fear of racism and the desire to avoid reinforcing stereotypes about their communities (Batsleer et al. 2002; also see Rai and Thiara 1997). Despite this evidence, following the recent policy shift towards community cohesion, domestic violence services that cater to the needs of black and minority ethnic women face closures; this situation threatens the only routes via which many black and minority ethnic women are willing and/or able to seek support in resisting coercion and violence within their families.

Intersectionality can shed light on the ways in which women's class, education and employment status, sexuality, generational differences in outlook, differences in migration routes into the UK, region of origin, position within community networks in the UK, perception and experiences of racism, and their access to appropriate support and services all intersect to create the constraints and opportunities within which women exercise agency. These constraints do not go unchallenged, most visibly by those women who choose to exit abusive situations and relationships. However, the same women may continue to define themselves with reference to gendered norms in contradictory and conflicting ways, while simultaneously challenging these norms through their actions as they seek to rebuild their lives following exit from (fear of) coercive marriages.

Another area in which intersectional approaches could have a significant impact is the criminal justice system, especially in relation to obtaining testimony from victims. A range of complex factors – personal, social, cultural and institutional – influence a woman's decision to remain silent or to speak out about abuse: intersectionality offers a method for analysing the complexities behind these silences and utterances. However, understanding the factors (and their interaction) that lead to disclosure or silence is only the starting point. Sokoloff and Dupont argue that 'intersections colour the meaning and nature of domestic violence, how it is experienced by the self and responded to by others, how personal and social consequences are represented and how and whether escape and safety can be obtained' (Sokoloff and Dupont 2005, 43). Thus, intersectionality has much to offer in relation to exploring women's experiences of forced marriage and their different needs in response to it so that policy and service delivery can be better targeted to meet those needs.

Conclusion

This chapter identifies three key issues that should be taken into account in working to better understand forced marriage and other forms of violence against women and to improve and refine efforts to address this problem:

The need to conceptualise coercion and consent within a continuum
Awareness of the socio-historical, political and cultural context of women's lives, and their location at the intersection of several vectors of inequality, is crucial to understanding the relationship between consent and coercion in

58

matters of marriage. Current definitions of arranged and forced marriage are based on a flawed binary distinction between consent and coercion. Instead, women's experiences in matters of marriage should be conceptualised as forming a continuum. Though consent and coercion are clearly distinct and at opposing ends of this continuum, they are connected through degrees of social expectations, control, persuasion, pressure, threat, and force, which operate in the context of gender inequalities and carry the potential for exploitation. Women exercise agency in complex and often contradictory ways as they assess the options that are open to them, weigh the costs and benefits of possible actions, and seek to balance competing needs with the expectations and constraints that weigh upon them.

Recognising that gendered power imbalances create the conditions in which women's consent is constrained in minority *and* majority communities involves moving away from a foregrounding of culture in discourses on forced marriage and other specific forms of violence against women. However, this is not to deny the importance of explicating the specific forms that coercion assumes in particular contexts: attempts to formulate measures to prevent forced marriage are meaningless if these attempts do not address the contexts in which forced marriage occurs. At the same time, the connections and commonalities in women's experiences of violence should not be minimised or ignored. Identifying these commonalities is vital in demonstrating how groups (and the practitioners who work to support them) can share information and best practice, and work towards social change and the achieving of social justice. A better understanding of violence against women as it affects all women, and/or particular subgroups of women, is important in terms of giving impetus to efforts to develop existing legislation, policies and services, and to create new initiatives, particularly preventive ones.

The dangers of cultural explanations of forced marriage and the possibilities of an intersectional approach identifying similarities and differences between various forms of violence against women

Despite the attempt to signal the acceptance of minority cultural practices by the adopting of a misleading binary distinction between arranged marriage and forced marriage, media and policy discourses continue to frame the problem of forced marriage in cultural terms, rather than viewing it as a specific manifestation of a wider problem of violence against women. Little attention is given to the many ways in which all women are located within a matrix of structural and socio-cultural inequalities and, thus, face social expectations, pressures and constraints in matters of marriage. The coercion involved in forced marriage is characterised as a feature of particular communities, which are represented as 'patriarchal and inherently uncivilised' (Razack 2004, 129). Women within these communities are represented as particularly oppressed and lacking in agency in relation to liberated Western women, who are seen 'as educated, as modern, as having control over their own bodies and sexualities, and the freedom to make their own decisions' (Mohanty 1988, 65). These media and policy discourses also invoke specific cultural or religious traits (often interchangeably) to explain violence against women in minority communities, whereas culture is not similarly invoked to explain the forms of violence that affect women from mainstream backgrounds: transnational feminist scholars have highlighted this problem in other contexts (Abu-Odeh 1997; Narayan 1997, 84–5 and 1998; Volpp 2000).

The consequences of adopting this colonial stance towards black and minority ethnic communities are far-reaching. For the purposes of this discussion, the most important is that this approach conceives of tradition as something static and ahistorical, thereby effacing the ideologies and politics that define certain practices as traditional. It also ignores the ways in which the categorical construction of 'women from minority communities' homogenises individuals so that they become stereotyped as 'Third World women being victimised by Traditional Patriarchal Cultural Practices' (Narayan 1997, 57). However, decrying what some commentators have called 'abuses of culture' (Dustin and Phillips 2008) does not mean that we should ignore the specific socio-political contexts that underpin the practice of forced marriage. As Purna Sen argues, just as it is flawed to posit a cultural specificity that fails to address the links between different types of violence against women, 'to deny specificity if it exists is also problematic' (Sen 2005, 50).

When forced marriage is viewed as part of the continuum of violence against women and conceptualised through an intersectional analysis, it is clear that 'culture' shapes the phenomenon and the responses of victims, but that isolating 'culture' as an explanatory factor does not offer an adequate explanation. Intersectional analyses focus on the ways in which different forms of oppression interact, with not merely additive but multiplicative effects; this allows for a better understanding of how culture itself is variable, and shaped by issues of racism, class and the diasporic context.

The need to look beyond criminal justice interventions and the right to exit

When the cultures of minority communities are perceived as being to blame for specific forms of violence against women concentrated within black and minority ethnic communities (i.e. forced marriage and 'honour'-based crimes), the primacy of the right to exit in state responses seems natural and the political agenda driving the exclusive stress on this response is occluded. The UK government's response to forced marriage has focused on criminal justice interventions aimed at securing women's exit from already contracted or threatened forced marriage, and, more recently has taken the form of injunctions aimed at preventing forced marriage (the Forced Marriage [Civil Protection] Act 2007). However, existing legislation only recognises a restricted range of forms of coercion: many of the constraints that women (especially black and minority ethnic women) face in matters of marriage are not recognised under existing laws. Black and minority ethnic women are further marginalised by this legal discourse because of the assumption that exercising agency means exercising their right to exit. However, in particular communities, refusing to marry, or pursuing exit from the marital relationship, may entail abandoning family, friends, culture and community. Women who do not perceive this as a viable course of action may exercise their agency in complex and contradictory ways that fall short of exit. Inability to exit, therefore, should not be equated with acquiescence to patriarchal values and traditions.

Women's groups have long argued that not all women want to leave abusive marriages and/or families; an even smaller number want to initiate criminal or civil proceedings against family members, especially in cases of forced marriage (see Chapter 7 by Gupta and Sapnara). However, this does not mean that these women do not wish to act in order to prevent further violence. Services, legislation and policy must change in order to support women who choose not to exit or pursue criminal sanctions against the family. A diverse range of measures to help victims of violence against women are needed. These include specialist outreach services where women can meet and share their experiences with other survivors and receive appropriate support and advice, as well as education and awareness raising in schools and the community, and the continued provision of refuge spaces.

Notes

1 This section of the chapter draws on Anitha and Gill (2009), 'Coercion, Consent and the Forced Marriage Debate in the UK', *Feminist Legal Studies*, vol. 17, no. 2.

2 *Izzat* has multiple connotations and overlapping meanings, including connotations of respect, esteem, dignity, reputation and virtue, all of which are equated with the regulation of women's sexuality and the avoidance of social deviation. Inherent in this code of honour is the need to strive constantly to maintain honour and avoid shame. However, even among communities that subscribe to this code, the specific acts that are deemed to increase or erode *izzat* are subject to constant contestation and vary among black and minority ethnic communities in both the diasporic context and South Asia.

Cases cited

Harper v Harper [1981] CLY 730
Hirani v Hirani [1983] 4 FLR 232
Hussein (Otherwise Blitz) v Hussein [1938]
KR [1999] 4 All ER 954
Mahmood v Mahmood [1993] SLT 589
Mahmud v Mahmud [1994] SLT 599
McLarnon v McLarnon [1968] 112 SJ 419
Singh v Singh [1971] 2 All ER 828
Sohrab v Khan [2002] SCLR 663
SK, Re [2004] EWHC 3202

References

Abu-Odeh, L. (1997) 'Comparatively Speaking: The "Honour" of the "East" and the "Passion" of the "West"', *Utah Law Review*, vol. 2.

Batsleer, J., Burman, E., Chantler, K., Shirley McIntosh, H., Pantling, K., Smailes, S. and Warner, S. (2002). *Domestic Violence and Minoritisation – Supporting Women to Independence*, Manchester Metropolitan University, Media Services, Manchester.

Bhopal, K. (1999) 'South Asian Women and Arranged Marriages in East London', in Barot, R., Bradley, H. and Fenton, S. (eds.), *Ethnicity, Gender, and Social Change*, Macmillan, Basingstoke.

Bradby, H. (1999) 'Negotiating Marriage: Young Punjabi Women's Assessment of Their Individual and Family Interests', in Barot, R., Bradley, H. and Fenton, S. (eds.), *Ethnicity, Gender, and Social Change*, Macmillan, Basingstoke.

Brah, A. and Phoenix, A. (2004) 'Ain't I a Woman? Revisiting Intersectionality',

Journal of International Women's Studies, vol. 5, no. 3, May.

Braithwaite, J. (2003) 'What's Wrong with the Sociology of Punishment?' *Theoretical Criminology*, vol. 7, no. 1, 5–28.

Bredal, A. (2005) 'Arranged Marriages as a Multicultural Battle Field', in Mette Andersson, M., Lithman, Y. and Sernhede, O. (eds.), *Youth, Otherness, and the Plural City: Modes of Belonging and Social Life*, Daidalos, Gothenburg.

Browne, I. and Misra, J. (2003) 'The Intersection of Gender and Race in Labor Markets', *Annual Review of Sociology*, vol. 29, August.

Burman, E., Smailes, S. and Chantler, K. (2004) '"Culture" as a Barrier to Domestic Violence Services for Minoritised Women', *Critical Social Policy*, vol. 24, no. 3, August.

Chetkovich, C. (2004) 'Women's Agency in a Context of Oppression: Assessing Strategies for Personal Action and Public Policy', *Hypatia,* vol. 19, no. 4, Fall.

Collins, P. (2000) *Black Feminist Thought: Knowledge, Consciousness, and the Politics of Empowerment*, Routledge, New York.

Coy, M., Kelly, L. and Foord, J. (2009) *Map of Gaps 2: The Postcode Lottery of Violence against Women Support Services in Britain*, End Violence Against Women and Equality and Human Rights Commission, London.

Crawford, A. (1997) *The Local Governance of Crime: Appeals to Community and Partnerships*, Clarendon, Oxford.

Crenshaw, K. (1991) 'Mapping the Margins: Intersectionality, Identity Politics, and Violence against Women of Colour', *Stanford Law Review,* vol. 43, no. 6.

Dustin, M. and Phillips, A. (2008) 'Whose Agenda Is It? Abuses of Women and Abuses of "Culture" in Britain', *Ethnicities,* vol. 8, no. 3, September.

Feinberg, J. (1986) *Harm to Self,* Oxford University Press, New York.

FCO and Home Office (2005) *Forced Marriage: A Wrong not a Right,* Foreign and Commonwealth Office, London.

Frank, K. (2006) 'Agency', *Anthropological Theory,* vol. 6, no. 3, September.

Gangoli, G., Razak, A. and McCarry, M. J. (2006) *Forced Marriage and Domestic Violence Among South Asian Communities in North East England*, University of Bristol.

Garland, D. (2001) *The Culture of Control: Crime and Social Order in Contemporary Society*, Oxford University Press.

Gill, A. (2004) 'Voicing the Silent Fear: South Asian Women's Experiences of Domestic Violence', *Howard Journal of Criminal Justice,* vol. 43, no. 5, December.

Gill, A. (2005) 'Governing Violence: Gender, Community and State Interventions', *Community Safety Journal*, vol. 4, no. 2, April.

Gill, A. and Mitra-Kahn, T. (2010) 'Modernising the "Other": Assessing the Ideological Underpinnings of the Policy Discourse on Forced Marriage in the UK', *Journal of Policy and Politics.*

Goddard, V. (ed.) (2000) *Gender, Agency and Change: Anthropological Perspectives,*

Routledge, New York.

Hague, G., Malos, E. and Deer, W. (1996) *Multi-agency Work and Domestic Violence*, Policy Press, Bristol.

Hall, S. (1999) 'Life for "Honour" Killing of Pregnant Teenager by Mother and Brother', *Guardian*, May 26. http://www.guardian.co.uk/uk_news/story/0,3604, 299095,00.html (accessed 4 November 2008)

Hall, T. and Whyte, D. (2003) 'On the Margins of Provision: Community Safety, Partnerships and the Policing of Domestic Violence on Merseyside', *Policy and Politics*, vol. 31, no. 1.

Harding, L. (2000) 'Student Saved from Arranged Marriage', *Guardian*, 14 March.

Hester, M., Chantler, K. and Gangoli, G. (2008) 'Forced Marriage: The Risk Factors and the Effect of Raising the Minimum Age for a Sponsor, and of Leave to Enter the UK as a Spouse or Fiancé(e)', University of Bristol, Bristol.

Hillyard, P., Sim , J., Tombs, S. and Whyte, D. (2004) 'Leaving a "Stain upon the Silence": Contemporary Criminology and the Politics of Dissent', *British Journal of Criminology* , vol. 44 , no. 3, May.

Home Office (2003) *Safety and Justice: the Government's Proposals on Domestic Violence*, Home Office, London. http://www.archive2.official-documents.co.uk/ document/cm58/5847/5847.pdf (accessed 16 June 2010)

Hunter, R. and Cowan, S. (eds.) (2007) *Choice and Consent: Feminist Engagements with Law and Subjectivity*, Routledge-Cavendish, London.

Imkaan (2006) *Response to Home Office Consultation Document – 'Forced Marriage: A Wrong not a Right'*, Imkaan, London.

Lees, S. (1997) *Ruling Passions: Sexual Violence, Reputation and the Law*, Open University Press, Buckingham.

Mackenzie, C. and Stoljar, N (eds.) (2000) *Relational Autonomy: Feminist Perspectives on Autonomy, Agency, and the Social Self*, Oxford University Press, New York.

Manion, J. C. (2003) 'Girls Blush, Sometimes: Gender, Moral Agency, and the Problem of Shame', *Hypatia*, vol. 18, no. 3, Autumn.

Meyers, D. T. (1989) *Self, Society, and Personal Choice*, Columbia University Press, New York.

Mirza, H.S. (1997) *Black British Feminism: A Reader*, Routledge, London.

Mohanty, C. (1988) 'Under Western Eyes: Feminist Scholarship and Colonial Discourses', *Feminist Review*, vol. 30, Autumn.

Mookherjee, M. and Reddy, R. (2005) *Response to the Home Office Consultation Document – 'Forced Marriage: A Wrong not a Right'*, University of Kent, Kent. http://www.kent.ac.uk/clgs/documents/pdfs/clgsforcedmarriageresponse.pdf (accessed 21 June 2010).

Morgan, K. (1991) 'Women and the Knife: Cosmetic Surgery and the Colonization of Women's Bodies', *Hypatia*, vol. 6, no. 3, Fall.

Morrow, M., Hankivsky, O. and Varcoe, C. (2004) 'Women and Violence: The Effects of Dismantling the Welfare State', *Critical Social Policy,* vol. 24, no. 3, August.

Naffine, N. (2003) 'Who Are Law's Persons? From Cheshire Cats to Responsible Subjects', *Modern Law Review,* vol. 66, no. 3, May.

Narayan, U. (1997) *Dislocating Cultures: Identities, Traditions, and Third-World Feminism,* Routledge, New York.

Newham Asian Women's Project (2007) *Forced Marriage Civil Protection Bill – Response to the Consultation on Amendments to Family Law Act,* Newham Asian Women's Project, London.

Phillips, A. and Dustin, M. (2004) 'UK Initiatives on Forced Marriage: Regulation, Dialogue and Exit', *Political Studies,* vol. 52, no. 3, October.

Radford, J. Friedberg, M. and Harne, L. (eds.) (2000) *Women, Violence and Strategies for Action,* Open University Press, Buckingham.

Radford, L. and Gill, A. (2006) 'Losing the Plot? Researching Community Safety Partnership Work against Domestic Violence', *Howard Journal of Criminal Justice,* vol. 45, no. 4, September.

Rai, D. K. and Thiara, R. K. (1997) *Redefining Spaces: The Needs of Black Women and Children Using Refuge Services in England: Their Feelings, Needs and Priority Areas for Development in Refuges,* Women's Aid Federation of England, Bristol.

Razack, S. (2004) 'Imperilled Muslim Women, Dangerous Muslim Men and Civilised Europeans: Legal and Social Responses to Forced Marriages', *Feminist Legal Studies,* vol. 12, no. 2, October.

Regan, L. (2001) 'Children and Domestic Violence'. Paper presented at the Children and Domestic Violence Conference, National Police Training/Southampton University, City Conference Centre, 31 October.

Reitman, O. (2005) 'On Exit', in Spinner-Halev, J. and Eisenberg, A. (eds.), *Minorities Within Minorities: Equality, Rights and Diversity,* Cambridge University Press, Cambridge.

Richardson, J. (2004) *Selves, Persons and Individuals,* Ashgate, Aldershot.

Samad, Y. and Eade, J. (2002) *Community Perceptions of Forced Marriage,* Foreign and Commonwealth Office, London.

Sanghera, J. (2007) *Shame,* Hodder & Stoughton, London.

Saunders, H. and Barron, J. (2003) *Failure to Protect: Domestic Violence and the Experiences of Abused Women and Children in the Family Courts,* Women's Aid Federation of England, Bristol.

Scottish Women's Aid (2010) *Sanctuary Schemes,* Scottish Women's Aid, http://www.scottishwomensaid.org.uk/assets/files/publications/practitioners_brie fings/SWA_Sanctuary_Schemes_Briefing.pdf (accessed 27 January 2011).

Sen, P. (2005) '"Crimes of Honour", Value and Meaning', in Welchman, L. and Hossain, S. (eds.), *'Honour': Crimes, Paradigms and Violence Against Women,* Zed Books, London.

Shaw, A. (2001) 'Kinship, Cultural Preference and Immigration: Consanguineous

Marriage Among British Pakistanis', *Journal of Royal Anthropological Institute*, vol. 7, no. 2, June.

Snider, L. (1998) 'Towards Safer Societies: Punishment, Masculinities and Violence against Women', *British Journal of Criminology*, vol. 38, no. 1, 1–39.

Sokoloff, N. and Dupont, I. (2005) 'Domestic Violence at the Intersections of Race, Class, and Gender: Challenges and Contributions to Understanding Violence Against Marginalized Women in Diverse Communities', *Violence Against Women*, vol. 11, no. 1, January.

Southall Black Sisters (2001) *Forced Marriage: An Abuse of Human Rights One Year After 'A Choice by Right'*, Southall Black Sisters, London.

Taylor-Browne, J. (ed). (2001) *What Works in Reducing Domestic Violence?*, Whiting and Birch, London.

Taylor, M. (2008) 'Victims of Forced Marriages Could Total 4,000, Says Study', *Guardian*, 11 March.

Uddin, P. and Ahmed, N. (2000) *A Choice by Right: The Report of the Working Group on Forced Marriage*, Home Office Communications Directorate, London.

Volpp, L. (2000) 'Blaming Culture for Bad Behaviour', *Yale Journal of Law and Humanities*, vol. 12, no. 1, Winter.

Walker, M. U. (1999) 'Getting Out of Line: Alternatives to Life as a Career', in Walker, M. U. (ed.), *Mother Time: Women, Ageing and Ethics*, Rowman and Littlefield, Lanham, MD.

Watt, N. (1999) 'Terror of Couple Fleeing a Forced Marriage', *Guardian*, 27 May.

Weinstock, D. M. (2005) 'Beyond Exit Rights: Reframing the Debate', in Spinner-Halev, J. and Eisenberg, A. (eds.), *Minorities Within Minorities: Equality, Rights and Diversity*, Cambridge University Press.

Wilson, A. (2006) *Dreams, Questions, Struggles: South Asian Women in Britain*, Pluto Press, London.

Wolf, N. (1991) *The Beauty Myth: How Images of Beauty Are Used Against Women*, Doubleday, New York.

Young, J. (1999) *The Exclusive Society*, Sage, London.

Yuval-Davis, N. (1997) *Gender and Nation*, Sage, London.

Yuval-Davis, N. (2006) 'Intersectionality and Feminist Politics', *European Journal of Women's Studies*, vol. 13, no. 3, August.

Zinn, M., and Dill, B. (1996) 'Theorizing Difference from Multiracial Feminism', *Feminist Studies*, vol. 22, no. 2, Summer.

3

Forced marriage: the European Convention on Human Rights and the Human Rights Act 1998

Shazia Choudhry

This chapter explores the contribution of human rights discourse to the work of feminist activists, jurists and researchers working on violence against women and forced marriage. While the concept of human rights has been most enthusiastically adopted by women's movements in developing countries, it has also become more prominent in the developed world, especially since the United Nations (UN) and Council of Europe adopted policies on violence against women and forced marriage that are rooted in human rights discourses. The chapter argues that whilst human rights is an uncommon language for many academics and activists within the field it is, nonetheless, an approach which has the potential to provide concrete means of redress for victims of forced marriage at both regional and international legal levels. The chapter will use the European Convention on Human Rights (ECHR) and the UK's Human Rights Act 1998 (HRA) as a focus for the discussion. The main point which will be emphasised in the discussion is that under the HRA public authorities are required to protect victims of violence. This means that the government, police, prosecution authorities and courts are required to take positive steps to protect victims of violence. Rights in the domestic violence context should therefore be seen not as restraining government activity, but rather as compelling it. In this discussion, the two most relevant articles of the HRA and the jurisprudence of the European Court of Human Rights relating to them will be analysed for their real potential to aid the victims of forced marriage and honour-based violence within the UK.

At the outset, it is important to acknowledge the general debate concerning whether the issue of forced marriage should be treated separately from domestic violence provision and legislation and what difference that would make to the availability of human rights instruments to the victims. A key argument against the integration of policies on forced marriage and honour-based violence into broader domestic violence policy has been that these issues ought to be considered separately in order to make sense of and deal with the issues in a targeted way (Home Affairs Committee 2007, 8).

However, the integration of such policies can in fact allow both issues to benefit from the resources and best practice developed in this area and help to prevent the development of 'differential policies which negatively impact on minority communities, such as racist immigration controls' (Siddiqui 2007, 23). Although treating the issue of forced marriage as separate will not, as we shall see, prevent the application of a human rights framework, an integrated approach will, nonetheless, enable forced marriage victims to access more easily a wider range of international and domestic human rights instruments which have a huge potential for achieving real outcomes in terms both of legal redress and of the provision of substantial governmental resources.

Current legal redress

Although there is no specific criminal offence in England and Wales of 'forcing someone to marry', criminal offences may nevertheless be committed. Perpetrators can therefore be prosecuted for offences including threatening behaviour, assault, kidnap, abduction, theft (of passport), rape, threats to kill, imprisonment and murder. There are also a number of civil and family orders that can be made to protect those threatened with, or already in, a forced marriage. For children, an application for a care or supervision order can be made under the Children Act 1989, and/or wardship proceedings may be issued in the High Court. Victims can also seek an order for protection from harassment, for non-molestation, and for the right to occupy the matrimonial home. Forced marriages will in general, however, remain valid under civil law until they are annulled or a divorce is granted by the court. Most forced marriages will be annulled on the grounds of a lack of consent due to duress and/or the failure to observe legal formalities concerning minimum age. In addition, strict legal requirements govern whether a marriage is valid under UK law, and the rules for recognising a marriage vary depending on which country the marriage took place in.

The use of human rights as a form of legal redress
The issue of forced marriage has also for some time been articulated as one involving human rights; this is evidenced by the numerous references made

to human rights in governmental guidance and policy (e.g. Forced Marriage Unit 2005, 1; Forced Marriage Unit 2009, 10). Indeed, such is the prevalence of the discourse in this area that a policy analysis of forced marriage legislation and policy in the UK can be found in chapters 6 and 7 of this book. Despite these important contributions, there is little or no explanation of what the use of a human rights discourse actually means for victims of forced marriage on a practical basis. Various relevant international human rights instruments are cited, usually as part of the background to policy initiatives, but the question of how, if at all, these provisions can be translated into real protection or duties for victims of forced marriage is rarely, if at all, articulated. Moreover, virtually no reference is made to the UK's domestic human rights legislation, the Human Rights Act, which arguably offers the most potential for the enforcement of duties which may be imposed on government and its agencies with respect to the victims of forced marriage. It is noteworthy that the only organisation that has mentioned human rights legislation is the Association of Chief Police Officers in its recently published 'Honour Based Violence Strategy'.[1] The rest of this chapter will attempt to fill this gap in governmental literature by outlining how the use of domestic human rights legislation may be capable of providing a further means of protection for victims of forced marriage.

The use and development of international human rights with respect to violence against women and forced marriage

Violence against women occurs on a domestic and global level. It has therefore become an issue of both national and international legal concern. The recognition of the issue at the international level was, however, brought about in large part by the intensive grassroots work and lobbying of the international women's movement and thus, as Chesney-Lind (2006) has argued, needs to be understood by reference to second-wave feminism. This work culminated at the World Conference on Human Rights in Vienna in 1993 where demands by feminist organisations that domestic violence be recognised as a violation of women's human rights directly contributed to the adoption of the Declaration on the Elimination of Violence against Women by the General Assembly later that year.[2] The declaration also urged states, in Article 4(c), to 'exercise due diligence to prevent, investigate and, in accordance with national legislation, punish acts of violence against women, whether those acts are perpetrated by the State or by private persons'.[3] The acceptance of the fact that violence against women was global, systematic, and rooted in power imbalances and structural inequalities between men and women was therefore integral to the international recognition of domestic violence as a human rights issue. Following Vienna, the Beijing Declaration and Platform for Action consolidated these gains by underlining that violence against women is both a violation of women's human rights and an impediment to the full enjoyment by women of all human rights.[4] The result is that a number of international[5] and regional[6] human rights instruments now exist which can be used to assert the rights of victims against their home countries on the basis that they articulate a state's duty to protect fundamental human rights that are commonly violated in domestic violence and forced marriage cases. Those rights include the right to life, the right to physical and mental integrity, the right to equal protection under the laws of the state, and the right to be free from discrimination and tortuous treatment. Thus, states must not only ensure that their criminal *and* civil laws adequately protect the victims of domestic violence but also that they do so on an equal footing with other victims of violence.

Specific provision for forced marriage
In his 2006 in-depth study of all forms of violence against women, the UN Secretary-General Kofi Annan stated that:

> [a] forced marriage is one that lacks the free and valid consent of at least one of the parties. In its most extreme form, forced marriage can involve threatening behaviour, abduction, imprisonment, physical violence, rape, and, in some cases, murder. (Annan 2006, para. 122)

This definition of forced marriage has facilitated the further recognition by the UN that forced marriages and other violent and coercive practices may 'justify gender-based violence as a form of protection or control of women' (Annan 2006, para. 45). This violence deprives women (and girls) of their equal enjoyment, exercise and knowledge of their human rights and fundamental freedoms, and keeps them in subordinate roles (CEDAW 1992, para. 11). In addition, forced marriage has been recognised as capable of being used as a method of recruitment for the purpose of trafficking in persons, and may be a result of trafficking in persons (Coomaraswamy 1997).

The articulation of violence against women as a human rights issue has, without a doubt, thus enabled the recognition of forced marriage as an issue which must also be taken seriously at the international level. As a result, numerous international legal instruments now specifically prohibit forced and early marriage. The main emphasis of these provisions builds upon the advances made with regard to state obligations in this area by concentrating on the need for the full and free consent of the parties to the marriage; this is reflected in the terms of the main international legal provisions in the area.[7]

In 2008, the United Nations Division for the Advancement of Women released a legislative model framework in an expert group report entitled 'Good practices in legislation on violence against women.' This model code includes provisions outlawing forced and early marriage. However, the criminalisation of this conduct is not universally accepted as the best way to eliminate the practice of forced marriage. In many jurisdictions, including Afghanistan, Austria, Ghana, Norway and Serbia, forced marriage is considered by the respective criminal codes as a crime in its own right. In other countries, including Algeria, Belarus, Canada, Colombia, Estonia, Finland, Germany, Guatemala, Israel, Italy, Lithuania, Mauritius, Moldova and the UK, which do not have a specific provision criminalising a forced marriage, an act of forced marriage may be subject to criminal proceedings under other related crimes including trafficking in human beings, sexual exploitation, abduction, prostitution and rape (Huda 2007, para. 20).

While such international measures are important for their ability to highlight the need for the development of national policies to combat and eradicate domestic violence, they also have their limitations. International declarations, in the main, carry political weight but they are not, on their own, legally binding instruments (that is, unless they are seen as embodying notions of customary human rights law, which has a legally binding effect upon states [Vesa 2004, 309]). As such, the implementation of such measures is highly dependent upon both political will and the commitment of significant resources. Neither are always available or, indeed, possible. Treaties that have been directly incorporated into UK national domestic law, such as the ECHR, are thus much more likely to be enforceable and therefore provide a form of real and practical redress to victims of forced marriage.

The European Convention on Human Rights and the Human Rights Act 1998

As noted in the previous section, the development of the ECHR, as a regional instrument, has proved itself to be much more effective than other such instruments in ensuring state compliance with the human rights norms it represents. These Convention rights are now, under the HRA, capable of direct enforcement in the UK. This can be done in two main ways. First, there is the 'vertical effect' of the Act which is demonstrated by Section 6 which states that public authorities can be held liable for the breach of Convention rights. An example within this context would be a claim made against the state on behalf of a victim of domestic violence who had been killed by the perpetrator on the basis that the state had failed to provide her with adequate protection with regard to its duties towards her under Article 2, the right to life. Second, there is the 'horizontal effect' of the Act which enables two private individuals to bring a claim against each other with respect to an alleged breach of any of the Convention rights. A classic example within the family sphere would be a claim brought by a non-resident father that his Article 8 rights to family life have been breached by the mother who has refused him contact with his child. The Convention contains a list of rights, the most relevant to forced marriage being Article 1 which requires all States Parties to secure the rights and freedoms delineated within the ECHR 'to everyone within their jurisdiction,' Article 3 which concerns the right to be free from torture and from inhuman or degrading treatment or punishment, and Article 8 which requires the right to private and family life to be respected.

Article 3 of the ECHR

Article 3 of the ECHR states: 'No one shall be subject to torture or to inhuman or degrading treatment or punishment.'

The phrase 'ill treatment' in Article 3 includes actual bodily harm or intense physical or mental suffering (*Ireland v. the United Kingdom* (1978) 2 EHRR 25). 'Degrading treatment' includes conduct which humiliates or debases an individual; shows a lack of respect for, or diminishes human dignity. It also includes conduct which arouses feelings of fear, anguish or inferiority capable of breaking an individual's moral and physical resistance (e.g. *Price v. the United Kingdom*, no. 33394/96, ECHR 2001-VII, paras. 24–30; *Valašinas v. Lithuania*, no. 44558/98, ECHR 2001-VIII, para. 117). In considering whether treatment is 'degrading' the Court will have regard both to whether its object was to humiliate and debase the victim and to the effect on the victim.

Article 3 not only prohibits the state from inflicting torture or inhuman or degrading treatment on its citizens, it also requires the state to protect one citizen from torture or inhuman or degrading treatment at the hands of another (*A v. UK* [1998] 3 FCR 597; *E v. UK* [2002] 3 FCR 700). A state will infringe an individual's right under Article 3 if it is aware that she or he is suffering the necessary degree of abuse at the hands of another and fails to take reasonable (*Z v. UK* [2001] 2 FCR 246) or adequate (*A v. UK*, para. 24) or effective (*Z v. UK*, para. 73) steps to protect that individual (*E v. UK*). There is a particular obligation on the state to protect the Article 3 rights of vulnerable people, such as children. The obligations imposed on the state include to ensure that there is an effective legal deterrent to protect victims from abuse; to ensure that there is proper legal investigation and prosecution of any infringement of the individual rights; and where necessary to intervene and remove a victim from a position in which she or he is suffering conduct which is prohibited by Article 3. Hence states have been found to infringe Article 3 when they have been aware that children are being abused but have not taken steps to protect them (*E v. UK*); where the law on sexual assault required proof that the victim had physically resisted the sexual assault (*MC v. Bulgaria*); and where the police failed to investigate properly or take steps to prosecute men alleged to have committed sexual assaults (*MC v. Bulgaria*).

The right under Article 3 is an absolute one. Unlike many of the other rights mentioned in the European Convention there are no circumstances in which it is permissible for the state to infringe this right. This makes it clear that the rights of another party cannot justify an infringement of someone's Article 3 rights. So, for example, it cannot be successfully argued that a family's right of privacy justifies non-intervention by the state if that non-intervention infringes one family member's Article 3 rights. Indeed, and perhaps this is more controversial, it is suggested that other rights of the victim cannot justify an infringement of Article 3. In other words, the state cannot justify its failure to protect a victim's Article 3 rights in a forced marriage case by referring to that person's right to respect for private life.

Is forced marriage inhuman and degrading treatment for the purposes of Article 3?

The effects of forced marriage will often be sufficiently intense to engage Article 3. Forced marriage that involves physical abuse is likely to fall within Article 3, unless its physical injuries are of a minor kind. Forced marriages which involve emotional abuse, intimidation or debasement can also fall within Article 3 as 'degrading treatment', particularly when these aspects of the practice are intended to humiliate and demean the victim (Edwards 1996). In addition, as discussed above, many victims of reported honour-based violence and forced marriage in the UK are under 18 years old. Young victims in particular may find themselves in an abusive and dangerous situation against their will with no power to seek help. Forced marriage can thus be a form of child abuse and domestic violence. A number of conclusions can thus be drawn regarding the application of Article 3 to the practice of forced marriage. First, it has been suggested that forced marriage represents a 'collection of practices, which are used to control behaviour within families to protect perceived cultural and religious beliefs'. It is also recognised as a crime predominantly (but not exclusively) committed against women within a context of male power and control (Crown Prosecution Service 2008, 8). Second, when forced marriage is viewed within the wider context of violence against women, as a number of feminist commentators have argued, it may be seen to be of a particularly degrading nature (Smith 1989; Freeman 1984). Under this analysis the lack of legal protection, at least historically, that women have been offered has, in effect, acted as a warrant for this abuse. Third, conduct which amounts to severe emotional abuse (and not physical violence alone) which leads to an overpowering of an individual's personality can form part of forced marriage practices and may also, in turn, amount to degradation. Finally, psychological research into victims of forced marriage reveals the clear and highly significant psychological impact that forced marriage can have on women, even where each individual incident may appear relatively minor when seen in isolation. Studies have shown that self-harm and suicide are significantly higher among South Asian women than among other groups and that contributory factors include lack of self-determination, excessive control, the weight of expectations of the role of women, and anxiety about their marriages (Hussain, Waheed and Hussain 2006).

The positive duty of the state under Article 3

Article 3 imposes primarily a negative obligation on states: to refrain from inflicting serious harm on persons within their jurisdiction. Most cases involving Article 3 have involved state agents or public authorities inflicting treatment on individuals.[8] However, the European Court of Human Rights has been developing a certain level of flexibility in addressing the application of Article 3 within the 'private context' (D. v. the United Kingdom ECHR 1997-III, para. 49). The Court has, for example, recognised that the state can be under positive obligations to protect one individual from having their rights under Article 3 infringed by another individual (*Tyrer v. United Kingdom* (1979-80) 2 EHRR1; *E and Others v. the United Kingdom* [2003] 36 E.H.R.R. 31).

A positive obligation on the state to provide protection against inhuman or degrading treatment from another individual has thus been found to arise in a number of cases. In *A. v. the United Kingdom* [1999] 27 E.H.R.R 611, a child applicant successfully complained that the government had failed to protect him from degrading treatment (caning) carried out towards him by his stepfather. The European Court of Human Rights reasoned that Article 3 does not only require states to protect individuals from treatment which breached Article 3 administered by private individuals; in addition, it added, 'Children and other vulnerable individuals, in particular, are entitled to state protection, in the form of effective deterrence, against such serious breaches of personal integrity.'[9] A violation of Article 3 had therefore occurred.

However, it was not until the decisions in *Z and Others v. the United Kingdom* [2001] 2 FLR 612 and *E v. UK* that the nature and extent of positive obligations under Article 3 arising within English civil law came before the European Court of Human Rights. Both cases concerned allegations that the respective local authorities had failed to take adequate protective measures in respect of the severe neglect and abuse which the applicants, as children, had suffered at the hands of their carers, contrary to Articles 3 and 8. These alleged breaches, it was argued, were due to the House of Lords having held in *X and Others v. Bedfordshire County Council* [1995] 3 All ER 352 that, as a matter of principle, local authorities could not be sued for negligence or for breach of statutory duty in respect of the discharge of their functions concerning the welfare of children. The applicants' action for damages for negligence and/or breach of statutory duty had, therefore, been struck out as revealing no cause of action.[10] In respect of Article 3 the European Court of Human Rights found that there had been a violation, as it was clear that the neglect and abuse suffered by the children reached the threshold of inhuman and degrading treatment.

In its judgments the Court reiterated the principle that states should provide effective protection in relation to children and vulnerable adults, particularly where the authorities had or ought to have had knowledge of abuse.[11] Of particular note is the Court's response to the UK government's argument that, notwithstanding any acknowledged shortcomings, it had not been shown that matters would have turned out any differently:

The test under Art.3 however does not require it to be shown that 'but for' the failing or omission of the public authority ill-treatment would not have happened. A failure to take reasonably available measures which could have had a real prospect of altering the outcome or mitigating the harm is sufficient to engage the responsibility of the State. (*E v. UK*, para. 99)

As a result, the Court was satisfied that the pattern of lack of investigation, communication and co-operation by the relevant authorities amounted to a breach of Article 3.

Although there have been no cases brought before the European Court of Human Rights on the specific issue of forced marriage, the question of whether domestic violence can fall within the definition of Article 3 treatment has now been settled. The question was directly addressed by the Court for the first time in its highly significant decision in *Opuz v. Turkey* [2010] 50 EHRR 28 in which the applicant, a victim of domestic violence, alleged that the injuries and anguish she had suffered as a result of the violence inflicted upon her by her husband had amounted to torture within the meaning of Article 3 of the European Convention. Furthermore, by consistently failing to take any action to protect her from his violence in response to her repeated requests for help, the state had made her feel debased, hopeless and vulnerable. The Court agreed, coming to this conclusion by a straightforward application of the principles it had developed in relation to Article 3 discussed above. Of particular relevance was the principle that children and other vulnerable individuals, in particular, are entitled to state protection, in the form of effective deterrence, against serious breaches of personal integrity. The Court thus considered, as the author had earlier predicted (Choudhry and Herring 2006a and 2006b), that the applicant and therefore other victims of domestic violence could fall within the group of 'vulnerable individuals' entitled to state protection that was referred to in *A. v. the United Kingdom*. Relevant factors in coming to this conclusion that were cited by the Court were: the violence suffered by the applicant in the past, the threats issued by her husband following his release from prison, and her fear of further violence. Significantly, the Court also took into account independent evidence that had been produced by a number of advocacy groups and by Amnesty International of the particular situation of domestic violence victims in Turkey (*Opuz v. Turkey*, paras. 91–106). Reference was thus made to the applicant's social background, 'namely the vulnerable situation of women in south-east Turkey' (*Opuz v. Turkey*, para. 160), as a further relevant factor. Importantly, the Court also acknowledged that domestic abuse which is non-physical can also come within Article 3:

> The Court observes also that the violence suffered by the applicant, in the form of physical injuries *and psychological pressure*, were sufficiently serious to amount to ill-treatment within the meaning of Article 3 of the Convention. (*Opuz v. Turkey*, para. 161; emphasis added)

The Court then turned to the question of whether the national authorities had taken all reasonable measures to prevent the recurrence of violent attacks against the applicant's physical integrity. After reviewing the response of the authorities in some detail, the Court considered that it had not. Although the authorities had responded each time a complaint had been made, the reliance upon the applicant's continued involvement for further action and the general inadequacy of the measures taken against her husband meant that the local authorities had failed to demonstrate the diligence required to prevent the recurrence of violent attacks against the applicant (*Opuz v. Turkey*, paras. 166–75). The Court thus concluded that there had been a violation of Article 3 of the Convention 'as a result of the State authorities' failure to take protective measures in the form of effective deterrence against serious breaches of the applicant's personal integrity by her husband' (*Opuz v. Turkey*, para. 176).

The potential significance of this decision for victims of forced marriage cannot be underestimated. First, it demonstrates the acceptance and application by the European Court of Human Rights of a number of international instruments and decisions in relation to domestic violence. Second, it demonstrates that a state's obligation under Article 3 cannot be satisfied simply by the passing of appropriate legislation. What is also required to be demonstrated is that the legislation is reasonably *effective*. The Court's decision thus underlines the need for states to implement fully and monitor carefully the effectiveness of domestic violence and therefore, forced marriage, policy and legislation. Finally, although uncontested in *Opuz v Turkey*, it is nevertheless clear that the Court's willingness to refer to the reports provided by NGOs and advocacy groups means that such evidence will be of considerable importance when it comes to any future assessment by the Court of a state's obligation in this regard.

In summary, the Court has established that particular regard will be given to children and vulnerable adults when considering the extent of the positive obligations that are to be imposed on member states towards them, notwithstanding that the 'treatment' at issue is being meted out by private individuals. Liability under Article 3 will thus be incurred if the following criteria are met:

- the treatment concerned comes within the definition established under Article 3;
- the state ought to have had or had knowledge that such treatment was occurring;
- the state failed to take reasonably available measures that could have mitigated the resulting harm (Rogers 2003).

It is clear, therefore, that although Article 3 is drafted in absolute terms, the duties imposed by it are not. The police, local authorities and courts are only under a duty to intervene in so far as is reasonable to protect a victim of forced marriage where the effects of the practice amount to torture, inhuman or degrading treatment. In practical terms, this could mean that a failure by the police to answer effectively a call for help from a victim of forced marriage or, having attended the scene, to provide effective protection from its further effects or, indeed, to fail to prosecute or otherwise offer protection could violate the victim's rights under Article 3.

Article 8

Article 8 of the ECHR provides that

1. Everyone has the right to respect for his private and family life, his home and his correspondence.
2. There shall be no interference by a public authority with the exercise of this right except such as is in accordance with the law and is necessary in a democratic society in the interests of national security, public safety or the economic well being of the country, for the prevention of disorder or crime, for the protection of heath or morals, or for the protection of the rights and freedoms of others.

The right to respect for 'family life'

The first point to note about this aspect of the right is that the existence or nonexistence of 'family life' for the purposes of Article 8 is essentially, a question of fact depending upon the real existence, in practice, of close personal ties (*K. and T. v. Finland* (2001) 31 EHRR 18, para. 150). Article 8 imposes positive obligations on the state. Most of the case law has concerned the positive obligations imposed on a state to protect the family life between a parent and child. It is well established in the case law of the European Court of Human Rights that the mutual enjoyment by parent and child of each other's company constitutes a fundamental element of family life, and domestic measures hindering such enjoyment can amount to an interference with the right protected by Article 8 of the Convention (e.g. *Johansen v. Norway* (1997) 23 EHRR 33, para. 52). Thus there may be, in addition, positive obligations inherent in effective 'respect' for private or family life (*X and Y v. Netherlands* (1985) 8 EHRR 235). These obligations may involve the adoption of measures designed to secure respect for family life in relations between private individuals, including both the provision of a regulatory framework of adjudication and enforcement to protect individual rights (*Glaser v. the United Kingdom* (2001) 33 EHRR 1, para. 63). As a result, the right of parents, in appropriate circumstances, to have measures taken to reunite them with their children has also been included within the positive obligations upon the state. Thus, where the existence of a family tie has been established, the state must, in principle, act in a manner calculated to enable that tie to be developed and take measures that will enable a parent and child to be reunited (see, e.g., *Eriksson v. Sweden* (1990) 12 EHRR 1, para. 71; *Gnahoré v. France* (2002) 34 EHRR 38, para. 51). However, the Court has also made it clear that the state's positive obligations concerning the reunification of a parent and a child on the breakdown of the parental relationship are not absolute (*Kosmopolou v. Greece*, Application no. 60457/00, 5 February 2004 at para. 45). Where contact with the parent might appear to interfere with those rights, it is for the national authorities to strike a fair balance between them (*Ignacollo-Zenide v. Romania*, Application no. 31679/96, ECHR 2000–I, para. 94). The key consideration is, therefore, whether the state has taken all such steps to facilitate contact as can reasonably be demanded in the particular circumstances of each case (*Hokkanen v. Finland* (1995) 19 EHRR 139, para 58).

However, in the context of the state's positive and negative obligations, regard must also be had to the fair balance which has to be struck between the competing interests of the individual and the community as a whole, including other concerned third parties. In both cases the state enjoys a certain margin of appreciation (*X, Y and Z v the United Kingdom* (1997) 24 EHRR 143, para. 41).

Thus, it can be seen that within the context of forced marriage the state may be required to intervene in order to protect the family lives of the child or young adult victim and his or her parents under both its Article 8 and Article 3 obligations.[12] This may then, in turn, create a positive obligation upon the state to intervene to protect their rights of family life. The envisaged intervention in this context would normally be to take action either in favour of the victim or against the perpetrators of the forced marriage. In some cases that could mean the removal of the victim and/or the institution of civil or criminal proceedings against the parents. However, here the potentially controversial consequence of the qualified nature of Article 8 becomes apparent. The balancing exercise may result in a clash of rights. Not only must the right to family life of each family member be balanced against that of the other but this right must also be balanced against the other rights and interests contained in Article 8 – the right to respect to private life and the right to respect for the home. The former right is of most relevance and will be discussed next.

The right to respect for private life

Within the right to respect for private life is the right to bodily integrity. But there is more to it than this. The right to private life includes the right to 'psychological integrity ... a right to personal development, and the right to establish and develop relationships with other human beings and the outside world' (*Pretty v. UK* (2002) 12 BHRC 149, para. 61). So not only does the article require protection of individuals from physical violence; it also protects them from conduct that attacks their emotional well-being to such an extent that their personal development is hindered. Nearly all incidents of forced marriage, for the reasons discussed above in relation to Article 3, will do that.

Like Article 3, Article 8 has been interpreted to mean not only that the state must not infringe someone's bodily or psychological integrity, but also that the state must ensure that one person's integrity is not interfered with at the hands of another. In other words, the right to respect for private life is not just a 'negative right' inhibiting state intrusion into citizen's private lives; it places 'positive obligations' on the state to intervene to protect individuals. However, unlike Article 3 this is a relative right. It is permissible for the state to fail to respect an individual's right to respect for private life if paragraph 2 is satisfied. If, therefore, the level of abuse is not sufficient to engage Article 3 and instead falls within Article 8 then it is necessary to balance the interests of other parties. It would therefore be possible to make an argument that the rights of the abuser, or perhaps even the victim, justify the state in not intervening in an Article 8 case. However, as has been argued elsewhere, the balance between the rights will still often come down in favour of intervention (Choudhry and Herring 2006a, 2006b and 2010).

Balancing Article 8 rights in civil cases and the process of qualification
When considering an application that an abusive partner be removed from a home, or have their contact with their child/children restricted, the Court will have to undertake a balancing exercise between the competing individual Article 8 rights of the parties. The respondent can, for example, make a claim concerning his/her own rights to respect for private and family life and the right to respect for the home. As Article 8 is a 'qualified' right, once the court has decided that Article 8(1) is 'engaged' by an alleged interference with the right it will then turn to a detailed consideration of whether the qualifications contained in Article 8(2) have been established. This will require an assessment of whether the interference was prescribed by the law, whether the interference was necessary in the interests of one of the listed, legitimate aims and, finally, whether the interference was necessary in a democratic society in pursuance of the legitimate aim.

Thus, any interference with a right must be shown to have been in response to a pressing social need to act for that purpose and to be a proportionate response to that purpose (*Silver v. United Kingdom* [1983] 5 EHRR 347, para. 97). In general, in determining the issue of proportionality whether the measures taken are 'necessary in a democratic society', the Court will consider whether, in the light of the case as a whole, the reasons adduced to justify them were relevant and sufficient for the purpose of paragraph 2 of Article 8 (*Olsson v. Sweden [No. 2]* [A/250] [1992] 17 EHRR 134, para. 68); in making this assessment, the Court will afford the national authorities a margin of appreciation, in recognition of the fact that they are better placed to make the primary judgment as to the needs of the parties involved and the appropriate balance to be struck between them. The extent of the margin of appreciation to be accorded to states in such circumstances will, however, vary in the light of the nature and seriousness of the interests at stake (*K. and T. v. Finland*, para. 166; *Kitzner v. Germany* [2002] 35 EHRR 25, para. 67). The margin also varies according to the context of the individual facts of a case (*Johansen v. Norway*, para. 64; *K v. Finland* (2003) 36 EHRR 18, para. 168).

Again, as there have not been any cases specifically concerning forced marriage and Article 8 we must draw out the potential of the Article from analogous case law. The European Court of Human Rights considered the issue of contact and domestic violence in *Bevacqua and another v. Bulgaria* Application no. 71127/01, 12 June 2008 in which, following the parents' separation and during extended custody proceedings in Bulgaria, the applicant mother complained that the authorities had failed to take the necessary measures to secure respect for their family life and failed to protect the first applicant (the child) against the violent behaviour of her former husband relying on Articles 3, 8, 13 and 14 of the Convention. After a detailed examination of the facts the Court held that:

> The cumulative effects of the District Court's failure to adopt interim custody measures without delay in a situation which affected adversely the applicants and, above all, the well-being of the second applicant and the lack of sufficient measures by the authorities during the same period in reaction to Mr N.'s behaviour amounted to a failure to assist the applicants contrary to the State's positive obligations under Article 8 of the Convention to secure respect for their private and family life. (*Bevacqua and another v. Bulgaria*, para. 84)

Although the case is of more significance for parents who seek to justify the withdrawal of contact of their child from the other violent parent, the case is nonetheless of some significance for the victims of forced marriage, particularly child victims. First, it is not always the case that both parents are involved and acquiesce to the forced marriage. This case is thus of some help to the parent who seeks help for herself and her child as it will provide a mechanism for defeating any claims by the other parent that his family life is being breached by a refusal of contact. Second, in relation to a child/young adult victim of forced marriage who is without any parental support in seeking help against a forced marriage, the case provides a strong justification for their removal from the family home for their own protection (under the auspices of child protection policy and legislation) and guards against any claims for unsupervised contact. The case is also noteworthy for its articulation of the child applicant's right to respect for family life independent to the other family members. Third, the reliance by the Court on a number of international instruments to emphasise the particular vulnerability of the victims of domestic violence and the need for active state involvement in their protection provides a further incentive to state agencies to ensure that the victims of forced marriage are given adequate protection. The terms of the Recommendation Rec (2002) 5 of the Committee of Ministers of the Council of Europe on the protection of women against violence[13] and the

United Nations General Assembly Declaration on the Elimination of Violence against Women Article 4(c)[14] were quoted in detail, as were comments by the Special Rapporteur on violence against women and the case law of a number of international bodies concerning the issue of domestic violence (*Bevacqua and another v. Bulgaria*, para. 53). Thus, although the Court reiterated that the sphere of the relations of individuals between themselves was in principle a matter that fell within the domestic authorities' margin of appreciation, it was also able to rely on the absence of compliance with the aforementioned provisions as a means of emphasising the failure to respect the Article 8 rights of the victims in this case notwithstanding the application of this margin (*Bevacqua and another v. Bulgaria*, paras. 82–3). Finally, and of most significance, was the articulation by the Court of the second applicant's (the child's) right to respect to family life and the ability to effectively exercise her or his right to regular contact with the mother. Of particular note was the clear recognition by the Court of the adverse affects upon the child of having to witness the violence between her or his parents (*Bevacqua and another v. Bulgaria*, para. 79).

Conclusions on the domestic enforcement of Convention rights – the HRA

As outlined above, the HRA enables the direct enforcement of European Convention rights within UK courts. This chapter has demonstrated that the specific potential of Articles 3 and 8 of the ECHR could be developed by domestic courts to further aid victims of forced marriage. There are three main ways in which claims could be brought under the HRA which would be advantageous to the victims of forced marriage. First, under the HRA, public authorities are required to protect victims of violence and therefore forced marriage (*Islam (AP)* v. *Secretary of State for the Home Department* [1999] 2 All ER 545). This means that the government, police, prosecution authorities and courts are required to take positive steps to protect victims. Rights in the forced marriage context should thus not be seen as restraining government activity, but rather as compelling it. Second, where the court must balance the property and privacy interests of the perpetrator and the right to protection of the victim, the HRA should be used to require the courts to place most weight on the interests of the victim. Third, the HRA requires particular attention to be paid to the interests of children and vulnerable adults. Growing evidence of the harmful impact of forced marriage upon children's and young adults' welfare can therefore be used to necessitate state intervention in order to protect them.

It is important to recognise at this point in the analysis, therefore, that applying a human rights framework *can* bring about concrete protection for the victims of domestic violence and forced marriage. In *Opuz v Turkey* the European Court of Human Rights accepted for the first time that victims of domestic violence could fall within the group of 'vulnerable individuals' entitled to state protection under Article 3. In *Bevacqua and another v. Bulgaria* we saw Article 8 being utilised to ensure that domestic legislatures manage the intersection between child contact and domestic violence in a manner which does not place both the child and adult victims of domestic violence at risk of further danger where this is clearly foreseeable. Thus, as UN Secretary-General Kofi Annan has argued, claims on the state in this respect can 'move from the realm of discretion and become legal entitlements' (Annan 2006, p. 18, para. 39). Addressing the issue as one of human rights is therefore capable of empowering women, 'positioning them not as passive recipients of discretionary benefits but as active rights holders' (Annan 2006, p.18, para. 40).

Unfortunately, certain problems remain at the domestic level. The oft-cited aim of the HRA to 'bring rights home' has not, as the author has noted elsewhere, materialised within the context of domestic violence (Choudhry and Herring 2010). What is particularly striking is the total lack of reference to human rights when discussing the issue by both the executive and the judiciary. For example, the 2005 National Action Plan on Domestic Violence published by the Home Office and the 2006 guidelines on sentencing in domestic violence cases (Sentencing Guidelines Council 2006) make no reference to human rights at all. Similarly, court decisions on domestic violence and forced marriage have paid little or no attention to how the HRA affects the issues raised.[15] In only one of the official documents produced by the Association of Chief Police Officers was the need for positive action towards victims of forced marriage, as a direct effect of the HRA, explicitly mentioned.[16] In addition, the continued adherence to certain domestic legal principles concerning the extremely limited liability of police authorities with regard to claims of negligence has made the enforcement of European Convention rights difficult to achieve. It is not surprising therefore that anecdotal evidence from those working within women's organisations demonstrates that there is very little knowledge of how to use the HRA and international instruments effectively (Pouwhare and Grabham 2008, 104–5).

In conclusion, although the HRA has the potential to be used as a powerful legal and political tool to combat domestic violence and forced marriage, a great deal of work towards understanding how individual victims of domestic violence can readily access, understand and use it to their immediate advantage remains to be achieved.

Notes

1　'Honour Based Violence Strategy' was created on 27 August 2008 and is available online to view at http://www.acpo.police.uk/.

2　United Nations General Assembly Resolution 48/104, 'Declaration on the Elimination of Violence against Women', UN Document no. A/RES/48/104, 20 December 1993. See also General Recommendation No. 19 (1992) of the Committee on the Elimination of Discrimination against Women.

3　Other declarations contain similar requirements as to due diligence: see General Recommendation No. 19 (1992) as above and Article 7(b) of the Inter-American Convention on the Prevention, Punishment and Eradication of Violence against Women (1994) (Convention of Belém do Para).

4　The Beijing Declaration and Platform for Action were adopted by 189 countries at the Fourth World Conference on Women in Beijing in 1995.

5　The International Bill of Human Rights, comprised of the Universal Declaration of Human Rights 1948, the International Covenant on Civil and Political Rights 1966, and the International Covenant on Economic, Social and Cultural Rights 1966, sets forth general human rights standards that victims of domestic violence may invoke against their state of citizenship if that state is a party to the above instruments. The same can be done under the Convention on the Elimination of All Forms of Discrimination against Women, 1979, together with its Optional Protocol of 2000, and under the Convention against Torture and Other Cruel, Inhuman, or Degrading Treatment or Punishment, 1984. See Byrnes and Bath (2008) for an overview of recent successes.

6　The ECHR 1950 and the American Convention on Human Rights 1969, together with the Inter-American Convention on the Prevention, Punishment and Eradication of Violence Against Women 1994 and the African Charter on Human and Peoples' Rights 1981, are the major regional human rights documents that may be invoked by victims of domestic violence.

7　Article 1(1) of the 1964 UN Convention on Consent to Marriage, Minimum Age for Marriage and Registration of Marriages; Article 23(3) of the International Covenant on Civil and Political Rights; Article 16 (2) of the Universal Declaration of Human Rights; and Article 16(1) of CEDAW. In addition, see para 274(e) of the 1995 Beijing Platform for Action.

8　Cases have ranged from prison and detention – see *Ireland v. the United Kingdom*

[1978] 2 EHRR 25 – to corporal punishment – see *Tyrer v United Kingdom* (1979-80) 2 EHRR 1, para. 31.

9   *A. v. the United Kingdom* (1999) 27 E.H.R.R 611, para. 22. Reference was also made to the United Nations Convention on the Rights of the Child, Articles 19 and 37.

10 This decision became the leading authority in the UK in this area; however, it was distinguished by the House of Lords in two significant judgments: *W and Others v. Essex County Council* [1998] 3 All ER 111 and *Barrett v. London Borough of Enfield* [1999] 3 WLR 79

11 See paragraph 88. *Z v. UK* applied. See also *Stubbings v. UK* 1996-IV, para. 64.

12 Where a child is herself or himself affected by the violence the case is likely to fall within Article 3.

13 Adopted on 30 April 2002, Recommendation 5 states that Member states should introduce, develop and/or improve where necessary national policies against violence based on maximum safety and protection of victims, support and assistance, adjustment of the criminal and civil law, the raising of public awareness, training for professionals confronted with violence against women and prevention.

14 Article 4(c) urges states to 'exercise due diligence to prevent, investigate and, in accordance with national legislation, punish acts of violence against women, whether those acts are perpetrated by the state or private persons'.

15 Court decisions have paid regard to the HRA only in relation to the committal proceedings that will concern Article 6 rights of the defendant. See *Mubarak v. Mubarak* [2001] 1 FCR 193 at 203 and 207.

16 In its 'Honour Based Violence Strategy' (see note 1).

Cases cited

A v. UK [1998] 3 FCR 597

A v. the United Kingdom (1999) 27 EHRR 611

Barrett v. London Borough of Enfield [1999] 3 WLR 79

Bevacqua and another v. Bulgaria Application no. 71127/01, 12 June 2008.

Clibbery v. Allan [2002] EWCA Civ 45, [2002] 1 FCR 385, [2002] 1 FLR 565

D v. the United Kingdom ECHR 1997-III

E v. UK [2002] 3 FCR 700

E and Others v. the United Kingdom (2003) 36 EHRR 31

Eriksson v. Sweden (1990) 12 EHRR 1

Glaser v. the United Kingdom (2001) 33 EHRR 1

Gnahoré v. France (2002) 34 EHRR 38

Hokkanen v. Finland (1995) 19 EHRR 139

Ignacollo-Zenide v. Romania Application no. 31679/96, ECHR 2000-I

Ireland v. the United Kingdom (1978) 2 EHRR 25
Islam (AP) v. *Secretary of State for the Home Department* [1999] 2 All ER 545
Johansen v. Norway (1997) 23 EHRR 33
K v. Finland (2003) 36 EHRR 18
K. and T. v. Finland (2001) 31 EHRR 18
Kitzner v. Germany (2002) 35 EHRR 25
Kosmopolou v. Greece Application no. 60457/00, 5 February 2004
MC v. Bulgaria (2005) 40 EHRR 20.
Mubarak v. Mubarak [2001] 1 FCR 193
Olsson v. Sweden (No. 2) (A/250) (1992) 17 EHRR 134
Opuz v. Turkey (2010) 50 EHRR 28
Pretty v. UK (2002) 12 BHRC 149
Price v. the United Kingdom, no. 33394/96, ECHR 2001-VII
Silver v. United Kingdom (1983) 5 EHRR 347
Stubbings v. UK 1996-IV
Tyrer v. United Kingdom (1979-80) 2 EHRR 1
Valašinas v. Lithuania no. 44558/98, ECHR 2001-VIII
W and Others v. Essex County Council [1998] 3 All ER 111
X and Others v. Bedfordshire County Council [1995] 3 All ER 352
X and Y v. Netherlands (1985) 8 EHRR 235
X, Y and Z v. the United Kingdom (1997) 24 EHRR 143
Z v. UK [2001] 2 FCR 246.
Z and Others v. the United Kingdom [2001] 2 FLR 612

References

African Charter on Human and Peoples' Rights 1981

American Convention on Human Rights 1969

Annan, K. (2006) 'In-depth study on All Forms of Violence against Women: Report of the Secretary-General', UN Document No. A/61/122/Add.1.

Beijing Platform for Action, 1995

Byrnes, A., and Bath, E. (2008) 'Violence against Women, the obligation of due diligence, and the Optional Protocol to the Convention on the Elimination of All Forms of Discrimination Against Women – recent developments', *Human Rights Law Review*, vol. 8, no. 3.

CEDAW (1992) 'General Recommendation No. 19: Violence against Women', UN Document no. A/47/38.

Chesney-Lind, M. (2006) 'Patriarchy, Crime and Justice: Feminist Criminology in an Era of Backlash', *Feminist Criminology*, vol. 1.

Choudhry, S., and Herring, J. (2006a) 'Domestic Violence and the Human Rights Act 1998: A New Means of Legal Intervention', *Public Law*, Winter.

Choudhry, S., and Herring, J. (2006b) 'Righting Domestic Violence', *International Journal of Law, Policy and the Family,* vol. 2, no. 20.

Choudhry, S., and Herring, J. (2010) 'Domestic Violence: The Extent of the Problem and the Recognition and Use of a Human Rights Discourse', Ch. 9 in *European Human Rights and Family Law,* Hart Publishing, Oxford.

Convention against Torture and Other Cruel, Inhuman, or Degrading Treatment or Punishment, 1984.

Convention on the Elimination of All Forms of Discrimination against Women, 1979.

Convention on the Elimination of All Forms of Discrimination against Women, Optional Protocol, 2000.

Coomaraswamy, R. (1997) 'Report of the Special Rapporteur on Violence against Women, Its Causes and Consequences', UN Commission on Human Rights, Document no. E/CN.4/1997/47.

Crown Prosecution Service (2008) *Violence against Women: Strategy and Action Plans,* Equality and Diversity Unit. Available from: www.cps.gov.uk/publications/equality/vaw/vaw_strategy.html

Edwards, S. (1996) *Sex, Gender and the Legal Process,* Blackstone, London.

European Convention for the Protection of Human Rights and Fundamental Freedoms, 1950.

Forced Marriage Unit (2005) 'Dealing with Cases of Forced Marriage', guidance for police officers, 2nd edn, FMU, London.

Forced Marriage Unit (2009) 'The Right to Choose – Multi-Agency Statutory Guidance for Dealing with Forced Marriage', HM Government, London.

Freeman, M. (1984) 'Legal Ideologies: Patriarchal Precedents and Domestic Violence', in M. Freeman (ed.) (1984), *The State, the Law and the Family: Critical Perspectives,* Sweet and Maxwell, London.

Home Affairs Committee (2007) *Forced Marriage (Civil Protection) Bill [HL] Committee Stage Report,* Research Paper 07/63, House of Commons Library.

Home Office (2005) 'Domestic Violence – A National Report'.

Huda, S. (2007) 'Report of the Special Rapporteur on the Human Rights Aspects of the Victims of Trafficking in Persons, Especially Women and Children', UN Human Rights Council, Document no. A/HRC/4/23.

Hussain, M., Waheed and Hussain, N. (2006) 'Self Harm in British South Asian Women: Psychosocial Correlates and Strategies for Prevention', *Annals of General Psychiatry,* vol. 5, no. 7.

Inter-American Convention on the Prevention, Punishment and Eradication of Violence Against Women 1994 (Convention of Belém do Para).

International Covenant on Civil and Political Rights 1966.

International Covenant on Economic, Social and Cultural Rights 1966.

Pouwhare, T., and Grabham, E. (2008) '"It's another way of making a really big fuss": Human Rights and Women Activism in the United Kingdom: an Interview with

Tania Pouwhare', *Feminist Legal Studies,* vol. 16, no. 1.

Recommendation No. 19 (1992) of the Committee on the Elimination of Discrimination against Women. Available from: www.un.org/womenwatch/ daw/cedaw/ recommendations/recomm.htm.

Rogers, J. (2003) 'Applying the Doctrine Of Positive Obligations in the European Convention on Human Rights to Domestic Substantive Criminal Law in Domestic Proceedings', *Criminal Law Review,* October.

Sentencing Guidelines Council (December 2006) 'Overarching Principles: Domestic Violence, Definitive Guideline', SGC, London.

Siddiqui, H. (2007) 'BME Women's Struggles against Forced Marriage and Honour Based Violence, *Safe,* vol. 22, p. 23.

Smith, L. (1989) *Domestic Violence: an Overview of the Literature,* Her Majesty's Stationery Office, London.

UN Convention on Consent to Marriage, Minimum Age for Marriage and Registration of Marriages, 1964.

United Nations Division for the Advancement of Women (2008) 'Good Practices in Legislation on Violence against Women. Available from: www.un.org/ womenwatch/daw/egm/vaw_legislation_2008/Report%20EGMGPLVAW %20 (final%2011.11.08).pdf. Accessed 1 February 2011.

United Nations General Assembly Resolution 48/104 'Declaration on the Elimination of Violence against Women', UN Document no. A/RES/48/104, 20 December 1993.

Universal Declaration of Human Rights 1948.

Vesa, A. (2004) 'International and Regional Standards for Protecting Victims of Domestic Violence', *American University Journal of Gender, Social Policy & Law,* vol. 12.

4

Border control to prevent forced marriages: choosing between protecting women and protecting the nation

Anja Bredal*

There is no doubt that radical-right populist parties in Europe have appropriated concerns about women's oppression into their anti-immigration agendas (Akkerman and Hagelund 2007; Razack 2008). At the same time, one may argue, as Akkerman and Hagelund (2007: 213) do, that 'the discourse on gender has helped to legitimate the shift away from multiculturalism among left parties'. Policy changes that are embraced by the right as tools to curb immigration are justified by the left as tools to protect young women from patriarchal power, these authors claim. In short, the issue of women's oppression has provided what Akkerman and Hagelund (2007: 214) call 'a space for the left and the right to act in common'. This chapter ventures to explore a case in point, namely the policies that posit immigration law as a tool to protect women from being forced into marriage.[1] My aim is to interrogate how forced marriage is discursively constructed through European immigration law and policy initiatives, using Denmark and Norway as empirical cases. These countries are among the pioneers in using immigration rules to tackle forced marriages, a tendency now seen throughout Europe. At the same time they represent some important differences in how such rules are designed and practised, in particular following a defeat of a proposed new age limit on spousal entry in Norway, preventing the government from following in Denmark's footsteps. This chapter is organised with a view to bring out such differences, as I intend to identify some highly problematic and some more promising ways to tackle forced marriage within immigration control.

In my analysis I am particularly interested in how initiatives on forced marriage are framed. Is the problem primarily about protecting women from

* My sincere thanks to the editors Aisha K. Gill and Sundari Anitha for their constructive comments and extreme patience.

abuse, or about promoting women's agency, or about securing the borders of the nation? More specifically I ask: What kinds of legislation and procedures have been introduced? How are these tools meant to work? What conceptions of coercion and women's agency are they based on? How is forced marriage defined in relation to arranged marriages and to various problems associated with family immigration?

After a brief statement about my own position I will describe in some detail the responses of Denmark and Norway to the problem of forced marriage, with a view to bring out certain basic conceptual underpinnings. The Norwegian presentation will be somewhat longer than the Danish as fairly recent debates on an age requirement are of special interest. I go on to discuss some similarities and differences between the countries, before I draw out some conclusions.

My own position

As I venture to analyse and criticise conceptions of forced marriages I owe the reader clarification of my own position. I see forced marriages as a kind of violence in close relations. Women are in the majority among known victims, but men are also affected. In this context a forced marriage is an arranged marriage that is forced upon one or both spouses against her or his will. [2] Arranged marriage is a way of organising the choice of marriage partners and entering into marriage that is associated with a collectivist social order. Both its underlying norms and the tradition of arranged marriage itself may be practised in a variety of ways and degrees, and an arranged marriage may be entered into voluntarily or involuntarily. As such, I see 'arranged marriage' as a generic term of which forced marriage is a subcategory. What we are discussing, therefore, is not the difference between forced and arranged marriages, but between volition and force within the practice of arranged marriage: in other words, degrees of coercion and volition. Quasi-consent can be enforced in a range of ways, of which psychological pressure is probably the most common. In my world, psychological coercion is as illegitimate as physical coercion, but it may be more difficult to detect – both by the person being forced and by the person forcing, as well as by the bystander. This may have important legal implications, for example in establishing evidence in a civil or criminal court case, but I believe that as a principle the privilege of defining what volition is should lie with the person concerned.[3] Of course, she may have problems defining coercion for herself, but then that is what support should focus on: empowering her to work out her own definition. In other words I see a basic difference between two ways of defining coercion, one based on the subjective perception of the individual(s) concerned and the other on what I will call external criteria. Although this distinction is not absolute in practice, I will insist that it is useful for both analytical and political purposes.

The Scandinavian case

In Denmark and Norway, the idea of using immigration laws to combat forced marriage had been introduced by the nineties. It was known that a large proportion of immigrants from non-Western countries, and their descendants, married a person from their country of origin. Furthermore most of these spouses applied for a residence permit under the rules of family reunification in Scandinavia.[4] As it was generally assumed that migration was a major driving force behind both the marriages as such, and the use of force to arrange them, it seemed natural to use immigration law to get at the coercion. While some claimed that the best way to tackle the issue would be to open the borders, this was never a political option. The tools of immigration control were. As their purpose is to guard the gate to which these marriages were a key, it seemed – for some – both rational and morally right to use immigration control to identify and assist vulnerable individuals, at the same time ensuring that immigration rules were not abused. The dynamic of this two-pronged concern – forced marriage as a violation of the human rights of individuals and as a violation of nation state borders – lies at the heart of this chapter.

Denmark

Following a period of increasing media focus on dramatic cases of forced marriage, Denmark was the first European state to turn to immigration law to tackle the problem. From 1998 the Danish Aliens Act stipulated that spousal reunification should be refused if the marriage was based on 'an agreement entered into by parties other than the spouses themselves'.[5] The rule only applied where one or both parties were under 25 years of age, and the purpose was 'to protect young people against undue pressure in connection with an arranged marriage'. It was designed to ensure that those handling applications from under-25s should make a special effort to ensure that the marriage was voluntary on a case-by-case basis.[6]

What did the Danish government mean by a marriage based on an agreement entered into by others than the parties themselves? This was not brought out clearly in the proposal for the law, a fact that was commented on in the consultation but never resolved. In connection with a research project in 1999, I asked the immigration authorities how the provision should be interpreted. While the answer explicitly indicates a narrow definition of forced marriage in relation to arranged marriages, it simultaneously establishes a constitutive link between the two:

> The provision will only be used in cases where the marriage is arranged by others than the spouses themselves. Should the immigration authorities assess that the spouses have truly wished to enter into marriage the provision will not be used. Thus, if the spouses themselves have chosen to marry the marriage is not based on an agreement entered into by others than the spouses. The fact that there is a condition of the parents approving the marriage afterwards does not make a difference. Neither will it be sufficient grounds for refusal if the parents have introduced the spouses, that the parents have encouraged the marriage, or that the parents have assisted in the practical aspects.[7]

In this logic it becomes virtually impossible to envisage that two persons could voluntarily choose to enter into 'a marriage arranged by others'. Either the marriage is arranged by others and thus not freely chosen or it is freely chosen and not arranged by others. By blurring the line between the question of who arranges the marriage and the question of consent, this quotation is typical of a discourse that bases the assessment of volition in arranged marriages on highly individualised notions of personhood. These notions would in fact seem arbitrary in most contexts since individual agency is always embedded in social relations and structures, but they are particularly problematic in relation to agency which is exercised within collectivist norms. However, my main point here is that a conflation of forced with arranged marriages was built into the law from the very start. Later, in 2003, the title of the Danish governmental 'Action Plan on Forced, Quasi-Forced and Arranged Marriages' confirmed in no uncertain terms that both voluntary and forced arranged marriages were under open attack in Denmark. The plan was published by the Ministry for Refugee, Immigration and Integration Affairs, which is still in charge of policies on forced marriages, including social support measures.

In 2002, a minimum age of 24 was made compulsory for all spousal entry from outside the European Union and the European Economic Area, that is, by so-called 'third country nationals' (TCNs), with forced marriage cited as the main reason. The rationale behind the rule was based on two interlinked assumptions. First, what I will call a 'maturity argument' reasoned that young people in concerned groups generally need more time, beyond the age of maturity, to develop the strength and capabilities needed to withstand pressure from their parents.[8] The second assumption was that delaying the *entry* of the spouse to Denmark would in effect delay the *marriage*. As it was not possible to raise the legal age of marriage for selected groups, due to basic principles in human rights law, preventing the spouse from entering the country was a second-best option. The idea was that parents would postpone marriage plans until the couple would be allowed to cohabit in Denmark. As such it was a matter of changing behaviour in a rather indirect way. However, the rule was more often presented as if it prohibited the marriage itself.

Furthermore two so-called rules of presumption were introduced. The first decides that a marriage should be treated as a forced marriage by definition when the spouses are close kin. The second provides that a marriage is seen as *potentially* forced if there is a history of marriage migration in the individual's close family (Danish Immigration Service 2010). In other words, these rules establish certain external criteria for establishing whether a marriage was forced or not, independent of the individual's perception. At the same time the burden of proof was reversed, as it became the duty of the spouses to prove that their marriage had been contracted according to their own free will. Furthermore, whereas the 1998 amendment required that it be *established* that the marriage was not voluntary, it later sufficed to establish *doubt* (Olsen et al. 2004).

When it comes to more detailed procedures for detecting forced marriages we find the following headline on the web page of the Immigration Service: 'How does the Immigration Service determine whether a marriage is forced?' Here, the Service lists several indicators in addition to the two presumption rules. It instructs that interviews should be conducted on suspicion, but it is clear that the information provided from the individual is only part of the inquiry.

Norway
Norway's first national plan against forced marriages was published in 1998 (Norwegian Ministry of Children and Family Affairs, 1998). The plan distinguishes between arranged marriages and forced marriages, framing

the latter as an abuse against young people in a context of family and cultural conflict. At the same time the Norwegian journalist and activist Hege Storhaug proposed a 24-year rule inspired by the first Danish age rule.[9] It was not until 2002, however, that politicians started taking up on the idea, as the murder of a young woman of Iraqi Kurdish descent, Fadime Sahindal, created an unprecedentedly fierce debate on abuse against young women in ethnic minority families. In contrast to Sweden, where the public debate focused on honour killings, forced marriage was at the centre of debate in Norway. Suggestions that the immigration law should be used were rife, but the support for an age limit like the Danish one was limited. Instead, the government introduced an 'age rule' concerning economic support. Since 2003 a Norwegian citizen has been required to prove that she/he can provide for the spouse where one of them is under the age of 23. As in the case of the Danish age limit, this was also introduced by way of a maturity argument.[10] It was reasoned that tightening the support requirement would motivate parents to increase their daughters' educational status. According to this logic, parents would realise that their daughters need a certain degree of education to be able to obtain jobs that would secure the prerequisite level of income. As a consequence, the assumption was, when girls were allowed to stay longer in the education system they would also marry later and hence have more time to develop the ability to resist.[11]

A year later, as part of a general review of Norway's immigration laws, a government-appointed committee proposed a 21-year age limit on the entry of spouses from outside the EU/EEA, based on maturity arguments (Norwegian Ministry of Local Government and Regional Development 2004). The proposal was modelled on the Danish 24-year rule, but the government insisted it was only motivated by a concern for victims of forced marriage, in contrast to Danish motives that included immigration reduction. Not surprisingly, the new Norwegian proposal caused heated public debate and a lengthy political process which included strong opposition from within the government coalition. The end result was that the 21-year proposal was not included when the government presented a new Immigration Act in 2007 (Norwegian Ministry of Labour and Inclusion 2007).[12] It remains to study the debate more closely, including what tipped the scales inside the coalition government. Here I shall concentrate on how forced marriage was conceptualised in the consultation process, as a women's rights or immigration issue.

Disentangling immigration and women's oppression

As mentioned, the age limit was presented as a means to protect young women. Opposition was based on two quite different sets of arguments. One group of opponents claimed that an age limit only for third-country nationals was discriminatory as well as disproportionate because it would force many people to be separated from their loved ones in order to help a small minority at risk of forced marriages. These actors never questioned the feasibility of the measure, and thus seemed to accept that it would in fact protect women at risk. In consequence, they appeared to give priority to those who were not at risk, an impression that was reinforced by the fact that they demonstrated little knowledge about forced marriages. The supporters of the measure then could rather easily present themselves as unyielding advocates for women's rights, accusing their opponents of belittling the problem.

However, when a second group of opponents introduced feminist arguments against a 21-year age limit, their position transcended this dynamic and drove a wedge into the established polarity. These actors were primarily concerned that the age limit would *not* necessarily prevent forced marriages, and that on the contrary it could have unintended negative effects for those at risk.[13] Most importantly, they questioned the whole logic of cause and effect that the proposal was based on. The crux of their argument was that a 21-year age limit would not necessarily delay marriages, seeing as the age restriction only pertained to the unification of the spouses, as explained above. On the contrary, these actors argued, a possible alternative scenario was that young women would still be forced to marry well before they reached 21 only to be held in Norway under strict control, or forced to live with their husbands abroad, until their husbands were allowed residency. Some women might even be shipped off to live with their spouse permanently, if he did not get a residence permit. References were made to information from the Danish women's shelters organisation LOKK that this was actually happening in Denmark. In other words, instead of improving protection, the most vulnerable girls and women would be worse off under the proposed legislation, as they would risk losing their home country, Norway.

This is obviously a simplified version of the arguments. My main point is that this reasoning posed a real threat to the proponents of a 21-year age limit because it confronted them with their own stated intentions. If protecting women is your first priority, this is not the way to do it, these actors said. More generally the feminist opponents challenged the construction of forced marriage as immigration-driven, in favour of a violence-against-women perspective. They insisted that forced marriage is foremost about controlling women's sexuality, and that closing the door to Norway for the foreign husbands does not change this motivation. In short, it became clear that the logic of the proposal was worked out from an immigration control perspective, not from what we know about the oppression of women. By sticking to their perspective, the feminist opposition challenged the conflation of the nation state's and women's interests.

Conflating forced marriage and marriage immigration

As several commentators – including those originally not notably interested in forced marriages as such – picked up on the risk arguments, in 2006 the government issued a second consultation document, entitled 'Protection against Forced Marriage – Measures to Prevent Young People from Being Sent to and Kept Back in Their Country of Origin in Order to Be Forced into Marriage' (Norwegian Ministry of Labour and Inclusion 2006).[14] As the title indicates, the explicit purpose was to accommodate the concern raised in the first round that a 21-year rule might have adverse effects for some victims, as explained above. Very briefly the government suggested the addition of some measures modelled on the Danish affiliation requirement.[15] Again the government minister responsible insisted that the aim was to combat forced marriages, not reduce immigration.[16] Still, in the document forced marriage is presented alongside so called 'fetching marriages', meaning marriages between a person of immigrant background and a spouse from his or her country of origin. Already established in public debate and the media by NGO actors working with victims of forced marriages, the term had considerable negative connotations, including coercion and abuse.[17] The document draws heavily on this discourse when it almost collapses the two 'types', as indicated by the subheading: 'Potential consequences of a forced and fetching marriage'. While the first part of the section deals with the individual trauma connected to abuse and rape that is typically associated with forced marriage, many of the other problems described would follow whether the marriage is voluntary or not, as spelt out in the following quote: 'In addition there will be a range of practical challenges and problems that a transnational forced marriage shares with arranged fetching marriages.' The next section on 'consequences for society' clearly shows that the government's concern reaches beyond involuntary marriages:

If many spouses are fetched from abroad, and especially if they are fetched against the person's will, this may affect integration. (...) With extensive use of transnational marriages (fetching marriages), both those contracted voluntarily and those involuntarily, an ever-increasing number of young persons in immigrant communities will not have taken part in a common platform in Norwegian society through Norwegian education. Values that are seen as basic in Norway, such as respect for the individual, gender equality and freedom, will thereby not necessarily be obvious to all. This type of marriage also makes the preservation of clan and caste systems within many immigrant communities in Norway possible.

We can see that the range of concerns is much broader than coercion against individuals, constructing marriage immigration from certain parts of the world as problematic *per se* – for Norwegian society. Continuity is established between the problem of forced marriages and other problems allegedly associated with transnational marriages among immigrants and their descendents, be they voluntary or not. Notably the shift in perspective from what is a problem for the individual (forced marriage) to what is a threat to the nation's integration goes almost unnoticed in the text. Furthermore, these problems associated with transnational marriages are focused to an extent that seems curiously out of proportion compared to the modest scope of a 21-year rule.[18] Thus, it can be argued that the most important political effect of the document is to discredit transnational arranged marriages among non-Western immigrants. In any case, the consultation ended, as mentioned, in 2007 in defeat for the 21-year rule, initiating a period when less attention was given to immigration measures against forced marriages. The government focused on its new action plan for 2008–11, where forced marriage is framed as violence in close relations (Norwegian Ministry of Children and Equality 2007). In an immigration control context, the focus has been on improving the individual assessment of applications. Hence, a compulsory interview was introduced as of August 2009. Sponsors under 25 years of age who marry abroad are requested to return to Norway to be interviewed by the immigration authorities, unless they already have been interviewed with a view to marriage before leaving Norway.[19]

Discussion

In this section I sum up some differences between the two countries when it comes to main aspects of the legal initiatives and other policies.

Different frames

Whereas forced marriage was framed as an immigration and integration issue right from the start in Danish policies, Norwegian policies have been more complex. Even if the immigration frame has always been prominent in the public debate, pioneer government policies placed forced marriages within a children and family affairs framework. During 2004–06 the proposed age limit caused a strong focus on immigration control measures, where the interests of women were conflated with those of the nation. The outcome of the process could be interpreted as a defeat of such conflations in favour of a violence-against-women framework. However, the picture is more complex, and as of 2010 forced marriage is now hovering between the policy fields of gendered violence and integration. In Denmark, while still framed as an immigration issue, forced marriage is also seen as a kind of domestic violence, but the political responsibility lies with the immigration and integration minister.

Different strategies

Both Norway and Denmark have used immigration law initiatives in their strategy to combat forced marriages. Two main types of measures can be distinguished according to their aim and the social logics involved – individual and general-preventive measures. The individual approach seeks to detect individual cases of already implemented forced marriages in concrete application processes. The general-preventive approach is based on legal restrictions on family immigration for certain groups – typically age limits for third-country nationals – that aim to prevent forced marriages from happening. While the former type attacks each marriage individually, the latter is designed to prevent the use of force by delaying spousal reunion for all marriages, including voluntary ones. The general-preventive measures are well established in Denmark but so far not equally prominent in Norway, despite the introduction of a new kind of age limit.[20]

Both countries have introduced individual measures. Thus, in Norway and Denmark the law explicitly states that forced marriages do not give grounds for spousal entry, and procedures are developed to help immigration officials reveal cases of forced marriages. However, there are some important differences in the way these procedures are framed and designed. Above all, Danish legislation defines some kinds of marriages as *a priori* forced whereas Norway has a stronger focus on individual assessment. Norway has chosen to make interviews compulsory, while Denmark's rules of presumption are clearly about identifying forced marriages regardless of – and even in contradiction to – the individuals own perception.

However, Norway too has provisions that give immigration authorities a power of refusal without the need for an evidential statement, that is, without the person testifying publicly that she has been coerced. This rule is based on the experience that forced marriage victims often fear reprisals or severe conflicts with their families and kin. They may confide in the immigration officer, asking that their spouse is denied entry without the true reason becoming known. The relatively new rule grants the power to refuse in accordance with the woman's wishes, protecting her without exposing her – as explained here in a quote from the official web pages of the Directorate of Immigration:

> Cases in which there is reason to believe the marriage has been contracted by force may lead to challenging considerations. The security of the person who has been married against his or her will is one of the challenges. Most of those who state that they have been subject to coercion, do not want, for instance, this information to be used in the wording of the decision since they fear sanctions from the family. Furthermore, it is up to the authorities to prove that the marriage has been contracted by force. (Norwegian Directorate of Immigration 2009a; English from the original)

As much as I think this carefully worded text bears witness to an intention to stay loyal to the individual woman's will, I think there is reason to be cautious about how these rules are and will be practised. I am concerned that they may develop into templates that lose touch with their original grounding in the subjectivity of the individual: her definition of the situation and her explicit though confidential wishes. These rules are a tool tailored to a situation where a person publically insists she had a voluntary marriage, but has confided that she was in fact coerced. There is however, nothing in the legal text that prevents the same provision from being used in completely opposite situations. What happens when a young woman consistently insists she was not forced to marry, but an immigration officer suspects that she was? What then, when procedures are in place to refuse on the grounds of an external assessment, where an individual testimony is not needed and in fact is programmatically treated as contrary to fact? In short, the question is whether mechanisms originally intended to protect victims could also be used to 'create' victims, through the refusing of entry for spouses in genuine arranged marriages.[21]

To elaborate why I raise this concern, I will return to some other recurring topics in the above presentation, namely the definition of forced marriage, the maturity argument, and the various conflations inherent in debates on forced marriage. Doing so I will identify two notions that underlie much of the thinking on forced marriage and immigration control – present to a varying extent in both Norwegian and Danish discourse – that I find particularly problematic. These are the constructions of what I propose to call suspect subjectivities and suspect marriages.

Suspect subjectivities

There has been much talk about the problem of defining, or knowing, what a forced marriage is. I think what is usually presented as 'a problem of knowing' should be rephrased as 'a problem of the knower'. When giving talks to and interviewing various professionals I have become increasingly intrigued by the lack of subjects in statements such as this, for instance, from a school nurse: 'It's so difficult to know what is forced and what is not.' Increasingly I tend to give a standard response: 'For whom is it difficult and with what implications?' This is because I think the problem of knowing is too often discussed as if asking the person concerned is not relevant at all. It is as if the answer one would get to the simple question 'Do you want this marriage to happen?' in any case would be faulty in some sense or the other. She would not dare to tell or admit, or she would not dare to let her testimony be used in evidence. In other words, the testimony 'Yes, I want this marriage' is generally seen as suspect and not to be trusted. Because a person who is forced would never dare say she was, a person who says she wasn't forced cannot be believed. And further down in these layers of distrust there is another more basic set of suspicions lurking: Would she actually be aware? If she thinks she wants this marriage, isn't that only because she subconsciously knows that she cannot say no? Or even more basic: strictly speaking, is she a qualified knower or chooser?

This brings me back to the maturity argument and the notions of subjectivity that it is based on. Without going into detail, I claim that this line of thought draws on a general assumption that young people in groups who practise arranged marriages are brought up differently from those who do not practise this custom, that they are raised in a cultural context where individual autonomy is not appreciated, or even actively resisted. Since they are deemed to lack the capacity to make individual, independent decisions for themselves, their agreement to enter into an arranged marriage is more often than not seen as a non-autonomous decision. Hence, their judgement cannot be trusted because they are not able to judge. Their capacity for autonomous, reflective and independent choice is deemed to develop later in life, and they should therefore be allowed to wait until they are more mature. As much as I agree that some parents – in what we may call authoritarian patriarchal families – actively prevent their children from developing a capacity for autonomy and individual choice, this is not valid as a general characteristic of whole groups. Furthermore, as already mentioned, to understand and assess agency within collectivist decision making we need more sophisticated and nuanced analytical tools than those that dominate political debates.

Fortunately, both scholars and activists have recently made valuable contributions toward this goal, often in a combined feminist and anti-racist/postcolonial framework. These are attempts at grasping the complexity of agency and volition within constraints, either for women in oppressive relations generally, or more specifically in the context of arranged marriages. One particularly promising attempt at deconstructing the polarised dichoto-my of 'almost all are voluntary' versus 'almost all are forced' is that of Anitha and Gill in their analysis of British court cases on the annulment of forced marriages (2009, 165):

> [C]onsent and coercion in relation to marriage can be better understood as two ends of a continuum, between which lie degrees of socio-cultural expectation, control, persuasion, pressure, threat and force. Women who face these constraints exercise their agency in complex and contradictory ways that are not always recognised by the existing exit-centred state initiatives designed to tackle this problem.

Anitha and Gill (2009) aptly demonstrate that insight into the grey areas between full coercion and full consent is invaluable to the struggle against forced marriage and in providing support and redress to victims (Anitha and Gill 2009; Bredal 2005). I fully support their attempts at understanding coercion in terms of degrees as well as both indirect and direct constraints. However, in the context of this chapter I think it is crucial to bear in mind that this insight has been developed in a certain context and therefore should come, I suggest, with some strings attached. The notion of 'grey areas' has been developed with an explicit aim of understanding and promoting the individual's own perception of her situation, for example in connection with a legal case for annulment, as in Anitha and Gill's (2009) material. As such, it is organised as an argument against parents or other actors, for example judges, who do not understand or are in denial of the full extent of the psychological and structural situation that impinges on the victim's consent. In short, it has been developed in opposition to the belittling of coercion in arranged marriages. When the same line of argument is cut out of this particular framework and imported into a context where transnational arranged marriages are already perceived as (almost) the same as forced marriage, 'grey area' arguments will be appropriated to confirm this conflation. In other words, the 'grey area' is perceived as only referring to different degrees of coercion, allowing no corresponding room for degrees of volition in an arranged marriage. Against this background I find it particularly useful that Anitha and Gill (2009, 178) explicitly point to the challenge of context and appropriation:

> This is a difficult argument to make in the current context, where populist explanations of forced marriage take place within essentialist discourses that stigmatise Muslim communities and feed into racist responses. The dominant media discourse on forced marriage comes to what on the surface may seem like a similar conflation of arranged and forced marriage.

As I understand them, Anitha and Gill (2009) are worried that their continuum approach on the surface resembles and may be cited in support of a conflation approach to the relation between arranged and forced marriages. Based on my own experience, I agree that there is cause for such worries and I would claim that this is particularly the case in connection with immigration cases. However, to my mind, Anitha and Gill's (2009) continuum is in fact the opposite of a conflation. Whereas a continuum denotes a gradual transition from one condition to a different condition, conflation occurs when two different things sharing some characteristics become confused to the extent of appearing to be the same. In our context, a conflation approach would say that all (lack of) agency within arranged marriage is 'grey' and therefore there is no distinction between forced and arranged marriage, while Anitha and Gill's (2009) continuum approach seeks to stretch out the fabric of agency to make sense of the varying degrees of coercion as well as volition in particular arranged marriages. I think this distinction between conflation and continuum may be useful when refining concepts and analyses of agency, along the lines that Anitha and Gill (2009) suggest. I also think that such analyses need to be contextually sensitive. As much as I support a complex analysis of consent and coercion in civil law suits or criminal cases, the conflation approach is so dominant in immigration policy debates that continuum arguments should be used with special care in such contexts. In other words, I totally support Anitha and Gill's (2009) arguments for abandoning a binary conception of consent and coercion in favour of a continuum, provided that it is used as intended – to understand and assess the complexity of a woman's agency in individual cases, and not to establish once and for all the lack of volition in arranged marriages as such.

Suspect marriages

In addition to constructing the subjectivities of particular groups of people as suspect, immigration debates and legislation construct the marriages of the same groups, usually identified in national, ethno-cultural or religious terms, as suspect marriages. While a marriage is generally regarded as genuine unless proven otherwise, in the discourse on transnational marriages of immigrants and their descendants the burden of evidence seems to become increasingly reversed. These marriages are to a large extent regarded as suspect and problematic, a logic which is spelled out in Danish presumption rules but which also has a strong presence in Norwegian policy and public discourse.

The construction of *suspect marriages* is the result of several related conflations. We have seen how policy documents and debates construct arranged marriages as almost the same as forced marriages. And a transnational marriage between an immigrant and a person from her country of origin is established as problematic in an array of ways, e.g. by the Norwegian term 'fetching marriages'. Consanguineous marriages are regarded as unnatural and therefore are assumed to be more or less forced. Furthermore, seeing transnational arranged marriages as generally immigration-driven gives pro forma connotations to both arranged and forced marriages. Through the adding and stirring of several ingredients a discursive brew is concocted which may be called transnational-arranged-fetching-sometimes-forced-and-definitely-problematic marriages, in short, 'suspect marriages'. This discursive dynamic works through so-called equivalence chains (Laclau and Mouffe 1985) where phenomena that are logically and empirically distinct, and may or may not be interrelated, are constructed as 'almost-the-same-as' or 'part-of-the-same'.

To expand on this point I will use the case of forced marriages in relation to pro forma marriages. Seen from the perspective of the immigration authorities the two may seem as two kinds of illegitimate marriages that should be revealed and rejected as they do not form the basis for family immigration. From the perspective of those involved, however, they are very different things. The implication of this shift of perspectives illustrates my point about disentangling the concern for national borders and the concern for vulnerable women.

A pro forma marriage is a phony marriage specifically contracted in order to circumvent immigration rules. It is defined by the fact that the motive is *not* to establish a partnership or family life, but to gain entry to a country on false pretences. As is stated on the web page of the Norwegian Directorate of Immigration, 'a marriage of convenience is a serious violation of the Immigration Act that may lead to criminal prosecution' against both parties (Norwegian Directorate of Immigration 2009b). As a legal marriage, however, it is valid and can only be dissolved by a legal divorce. In short the category of pro forma marriage is constructed in relation to immigration rules and it is basically an abuse against the nation state. Usually both marriage parties are the perpetrators. A forced marriage, on the other hand, is primarily an abuse against one or both the marriage parties, most often perpetrated by their parents or other relatives. A forced marriage may be annulled on the grounds that the consent to it was not free and therefore is invalid. Obviously, seeking residence on the basis of a forced (invalid) marriage would also be an abuse against the nation state, but this abuse is secondary to – and derived from – the abuse against the person. This is brought out in the text on forced marriages on the Norwegian web page: 'Coercing somebody into getting married against their own will is a violation of human rights as well as of Norwegian law [penal law, author's amendment]' (Norwegian Directorate of Immigration 2009a). A forced marriage may of course also be a pro forma marriage, but there is no doubt that most forced marriages are very much the opposite – they are contracted with a view to establish lasting family life and to make sure that the woman's sexuality is kept within legitimate confines.

Seen from this perspective it becomes clear that the two types merit very different strategies on the part of the immigration authorities. In the case of pro forma marriages both parties to the marriage are set on deceiving the immigration officer. Building trust and asking them directly is therefore an irrelevant strategy when trying to reveal the true nature of the marriage. This has led to authorities establishing lists of so-called 'elements that can indicate that the marriage is a marriage of convenience'. Such indicators have been criticised for being unreasonable and used in racist ways. My point here is a different one, however. Although the content and implementation of external criteria may be questioned, the logic of external assessment is reasonable in the case of pro forma marriages. Revealing a forced marriage is a different situation, and the immigration authorities can in fact work to establish confidence with the persons involved, with a view to reveal the individual volition and agency. Nevertheless I suspect that immigration authorities tend to see more similarities than differences between the two. It is my impression that the logic of pro forma procedures has rubbed off on forced marriage, strengthening the tendency toward external assessment. This conflation is particularly evident in Danish policies, but is also relevant – though less explicit – in Norway.

As a final point in the context of suspect marriages, I claim that measures against forced marriages are discussed and designed within a context of a multipurpose agenda. By this I mean that an immigration rule against forced marriage is often not simply that. Rather it is more a matter of killing several birds with one stone. This has important implications for assessing the accuracy and efficiency of a measure, since if the target is multidimensional and imprecise, there is a fair chance of hitting at least part of it. Thus, when the Danish government claims that the age limit has been a great success, it is often not clear what target the success is measured in relation to. The age limit has definitely reduced marriage immigration, but if some women who are still coerced into marriage are forced to live abroad with their husbands, is that a success in terms of fighting women's oppression? In short, forced marriage has functioned as an important leverage in tightening rules on family immigration that in reality are motivated by a much broader set of political goals than preventing coercion against women. While Denmark provides the most typical case in point, there is no doubt that the Norwegian government's policy on reducing 'fetching marriages' would seem much cruder without the connotations with forced marriages. Over time, however, as the marriages are firmly established as suspect, there is less need to use forced marriage to legitimate tighter rules. Consequently, laws that first were introduced as measures against forced marriages are now increasingly framed in immigration reduction and social cohesion terms throughout Europe.

Conclusion

From the preceding discussion it seems clear that the need to protect women from abuse all too often melds seamlessly with concerns to 'protect the nation', as if they were two overlapping and concurring projects. I see this as a deeply problematic conflation that is associated with other conflations in the field of marriage immigration, and I argue that they should be deconstructed and disentangled. Comparing Denmark and Norway, the former definitely has an explicit policy based on a string of such conflations, whereas the latter is more ambivalent. On an optimistic note, it looks as if the violence against women frame has gained ground in Norway these last few years, but it is far from unrealistic to predict a backlash into general-preventive immigration restrictions. In any case, feminists should be wary of agendas that do not see any conflict between protecting women and protecting the nation state. These are not only two separate concerns; they are on a collision course to the extent that loyalty to the one must be chosen over the other. Above all, feminists must know that immigration control offers no quick fix to women's oppression.

Policies and measures against forced marriage should not rely on dichotomous conceptions of volition and coercion. It is equally crucial to avoid the trap of belittling as that of exaggerating the degree of coercion in arranged marriages. Instead we need sophisticated tools to understand and engage with women's agency in these decision processes. Even if conceptuaising women's agency is a complex issue, doing so within an immigration control context should be guided by some rather simple principles. Assessment should be made on an individual basis, starting with and staying loyal to the perception and wishes of the woman. The Norwegian efforts to improve interview procedures seem promising in this respect, provided that the purpose is to increase opportunities for the woman to come forward. However, I am afraid that Denmark's increasing reliance on external criteria – whether based on explicit or on implicit presumptions – is more typical of the general tendency in Europe, and I warn that this is both discriminatory and counterproductive to fighting women's oppression, including forced marriages. Finally, I have launched the twin concepts of suspect subjectivities and suspect marriages to point out some deeply problematic notions inherent in immigration debates. I am convinced that initiatives to combat forced marriages have to break firmly with both ways of devaluing people's agency and life projects.

Notes

1   Obviously, men may also be forced to marry against their will, and coercion is exercised in a social context that involves both a gender and a generational hierarchy. However, since most known victims are women, and since the control of women's sexuality is so central to these cases, I will refer only to women throughout the chapter.

2   A search in Norwegian literature bases reveals that the term 'forced marriage' was

previously used to denote the case of an unmarried woman who became pregnant and was pressured to marry the father of the child.

3   In Norway forced marriage is criminalised through a special provision in the Penal Code, section 222 (see Bredal 2005).

4   For Norway, see Daugstad 2006; for Denmark, see Schmidt and Jacobsen 2004.

5   All quotations in this section are translated by the author from Danish.

6   Notably, at the time, no specific documentation or research was available on the nature or extent of the forced marriage problem, nor had any consequential analysis of the legal amendment been carried out. This data was gathered in a telephone conversation with Head of Division (Kontorsjef) Hans B. Thomsen of the Interior Ministry in connection with a research project for the Nordic Ministerial Council (Bredal 1999).

7   Letter from Udlændingestyrelsen, the predecessor of the Immigration Service, dated 27 January 1999. See Bredal 1999 for the original quotation in Danish.

8   See Gangoli and Chantler 2009 for an interesting discussion of this logic.

9   According to Storhaug she got the idea while doing research in the archives of Danish ministries for her book *Hellig tvang* (Sacred Coercion; 1998); correspondence by e-mail November 2009.

10 In Norwegian: 'en antakelse om at jo yngre partene er, dess vanskeligere er det å motstå press fra familien' (an assumption that the younger the parties are, the more difficult it is to resist pressure from the family) (Norwegian Ministry of Local Government and Regional Development 2003).

11 However, according to the Ministry's consultation document, it could also have the opposite effect, motivating the early withdrawal of girls from education to allow enough time to earn the requisite amount of money to facilitate her husband's entry. This was, however, rejected as an insufficiently weighty counter-argument, even though NGOs claim this is what has happened in several cases.

12 It is no coincidence that the new Act was presented at a press conference that also launched the new action plan against forced marriages, accompanied by an unprecedented allocation of 170 million Norwegian kroner over the period 2008–11. The government obviously needed to demonstrate that they would work strenuously to combat forced marriages in other ways and to redirect attention away from internal conflicts and political casualties associated with the debate on a 21-year age limit.

13 The author of this chapter belonged to this group.

14 All quotations have been translated into English by the author.

15 This rule stipulates that the couple should have a stronger affiliation with Denmark than with any other country. I will not go into detail on this complex rule here, only note that in Danish policy the affiliation requirement was never a measure geared at forced marriages, but rather a tool to reduce immigration on its own account. For more information on the rule, see Bredal 2005.

16 I here refer to the press conference where the document was launched.

17 Interestingly the term was picked up by Statistics Norway in a report on transnational marriages in the Norwegian population (Lie 2004), as a generic term for all transnational marriages, including white Norwegian men's marriages to women in other countries. The ambition was clearly to change and widen the usage of the term and point out that marriage immigration was not only 'caused' by immigrants. Unfortunately Statistics Norway's usage of the term remained an exception as the term was already so strongly associated with immigrants and their descendants' transnational marriages and with forced marriages. Rather, by giving it an academic legitimacy, Statistics Norway has inadvertently contributed to the institutionalisation of the word.

18 In 2005, according to the consultation document, 267 marriages were contracted by a Norwegian resident under the age of 21 with a foreign resident. A majority (191) were between a woman based in Norway and a man from abroad.

19 'Regulations concerning the entry of foreign nationals into the Kingdom of Norway and their presence in the realm', Section 25d.

20 So far a so-called four-year rule has been introduced requiring a person to have finished four years of education or work after secondary education before being allowed to sponsor a spouse. The rule does not pertain to nationals though, as yet. Furthermore, this rule has not primarily been framed as a measure against forced marriages.

21 I am not alone in this concern of course. This was raised in the consultation over a similar proposal in the UK, among others by Southall Black Sisters.

References

Akkerman, T., and Hagelund, A. (2007) 'Women and Children First! Anti-immigration Parties and Gender in Norway and the Netherlands', *Patterns of Prejudice*, 41.

Anitha, S., and Gill, A. (2009) 'Coercion, Consent and the Forced Marriage Debate in the UK", *Feminist Legal Studies*, vol. 17, no. 2, August.

Bredal, A. (1999) 'Arrangerte ekteskap og tvangsekteskap i Norden [Arranged marriages and forced marriages in the Nordic countries]', TemaNord 1999, 604, Nordic Ministerial Council, Copenhagen.

Bredal, A. (2005) 'Tackling Forced Marriages in the Nordic Countries: Between Women's Rights and Immigration Control', in Welchman, L. and Hossain, S. (eds.) *'Honour': Crimes, Paradigms and Violence against Women*, Zed Books, London.

Danish Immigration Service (2010) 'Forced Marriages', http://www.nyidanmark.dk/en-us/coming_to_dk/familyreunification/spouses/forced_marriages.htm (accessed 26 May 2010).

Daugstad, G. (2006) *Grenseløs kjærlighet? Familieinnvandring og ekteskapsmønstre i det flerkulturelle Norge* (Love without borders? Family immigration and marriage patterns in multicultural Norway), Statistics Norway Reports 2006/39.

Gangoli, G., and Chantler, K. (2009) 'Protecting Victims of Forced Marriage: Is Age a Protective Factor?' *Feminist Legal Studies,* vol. 17, no. 3, December.

Laclau, E. and Mouffe, C. (1985) *Hegemony and Socialist Strategy,* Verso, London.

Lie, B. (2004) *Ekteskapsmønstre i det flerkulturelle Norge* (Marriage patterns in multicultural Norway), Statistics Norway Reports 2004/1.

Norwegian Directorate of Immigration (2009a) 'Forced Marriages', 21 July, http://www.udi.no/Norwegian-Directorate-of-Immigration/Central-topics/Forced-marriage-/ (accessed 12 May 2010).

Norwegian Directorate of Immigration (2009b) 22 December 2009. http://www.udi.no/Norwegian-Directorate-of-Immigration/Central-topics/Family-immigration/Marriage-of-convenience/ (accessed 12 May 2010).

Norwegian Ministry of Children and Family Affairs (1998) Action plan against forced marriages.

Norwegian Ministry of Children and Equality (2007) 'Action Plan against Forced Marriages 2008–11', http://www.regjeringen.no/upload/BLD/Planer/ 2007/ Tvangsekteskap_engelsk2007.pdf (accessed May 2009).

Norwegian Ministry of Labour and Inclusion (2006) 'Beskyttelse mot tvangsekteskap – tiltak for å motvirke at unge personer sendes til og holdes tilbake i opprinnelseslandet for å tvangsgiftes' 12 October (Protection against forced marriage – measures to prevent young people being sent to, and detained in their countries of origin in order to be forced into marriage) http://www.regjeringen. no/nb/dep/ad/dok/hoeringer/hoeringsdok/2006/horing-beskyttelse-mot-tvangsekteskap-ti/1.html?id=271005 (accessed 12 May 2010).

Norwegian Ministry of Labour and Inclusion (2007) Ot.prp. nr. 75 (2006–2007) Om lov om utlendingers adgang til riket og deres opphold her (utlendingsloven) [About the Immigration Act], 29 June. http://www.regjeringen.no/pages/ 1990125/ PDFS/OTP200620070075000DDDPDFS.pdf (12 May 2010).

Norwegian Ministry of Local Government and Regional Development (2003) Rundskriv [circular] H 28/03, 17 October 2003, http://odin.dep.no/krd/norsk/regelverk/rundskriv/016081-250015/dok-bn.html (accessed 12 May 2010).

Norwegian Ministry of Local Government and Regional Development (2004) Ny utlendingslov [New Immigration Act], NOU 2004:20, http://www.regjeringen. no/Rpub/NOU/20042004/020/PDFS/NOU200420040020000DDDPDFS.p df (accessed 12 May 2010).

Olsen, B., Liisberg, M., and Kjærum M. (2004) Ægtefællesammenføring i Danmark [Family Reunification in Denmark], Institute for Human Rights, Udredning, no. 1.

Razack, S. (2008) *Casting Out: The Eviction of Muslims from Western Law and Politics*, University of Toronto Press.

Schmidt, G. and Jacobsen, V. (2004) *Pardannelsesmønstre blandt etniske minoriteter* (Marriage and Partner Choice among Ethnic Minorities in Denmark), Copenhagen, Socialforskningsinstituttet, Report 04:09.

Storhaug, H. (1998) *Hellig tvang: Unge norske muslimer om kjærlighet og ekteskap* [Sacred coercion: Young Norwegian Muslims on love and marriage], Oslo, Aschehoug.

5
The social construction of forced marriage and its 'victim' in media coverage and crime policy discourses

Sundari Anitha and Aisha K. Gill

The debate on forced marriage is intertwined with essentialist premises about South Asian women's passivity, and about the role of the West in protecting minority ethnic women from 'their' men. This discourse assumes an absolute cultural difference between mainstream Western society and South Asian communities; this, in turn, serves to demonise entire communities, particularly Muslims, and creates an environment within which racist policies can be enacted and normalised. This chapter interrogates and explores how news reporting of forced marriage, government initiatives aimed at tackling this problem, and policy debates on these initiatives, all obscure the gendered basis of this form of violence, with significant implications for advancing research and developing effective policies.

The media and policy debates we examine include those surrounding the implementation of the Forced Marriage (Civil Protection) Act (for an analysis of the Act, see Chapter 6), the raising of the minimum age at which foreign spouses can obtain visas, and the consultations preceding these changes. It is not our intention to conduct a detailed analysis of media reporting on forced marriage, nor do we seek to conduct a detailed review of policy or practice developments. Our aim in this chapter is to examine and thereby unpack the underlying, but seldom explicitly stated, assumptions that have served to problematise and frame forced marriage in particular ways over the past few years.

Problematisation and framing discourses

Foucault's concept of problematisation (1985, 10–11) directs attention to the terms in which a problem comes to be framed, and the implications of this framing for how certain practices are reflected upon and thought about in history. In a May 1984 interview with Paul Rabinow (Foucault 2000, 118), given shortly before his death, Foucault advanced this argument by explaining:

> This development of a given into a question, this transformation of a group of obstacles and difficulties into problems to which the diverse solutions will attempt to produce a response, this is what constitutes the point of problematization and the specific work of thought.

Borrowing from Foucault's concept of problematisation, we are interested in unpacking the construction of forced marriage in media and public policy discourses. This interest does not indicate the discovery of a new problem or suggest that attention has now been focused on something whose existence was hitherto entirely unrecognised. Instead, in employing the concept of problematisation, we are interested (1) in examining the underlying and often implicit terms and assumptions on the basis of which this perennial issue has been constructed as a problem and addressed by mainstream policy and media debates, and (2) in assessing the implications of the problematisation of forced marriage, both in terms of defining and understanding the problem, and developing potential solutions.

Analyses of media representations of social policy and crime have drawn attention to the process of framing, which consists of selection and salience thereby organising the world both for journalists who report it and for those who rely on their reports (Entman 1993; Reese 2001). Thus, framing determines how media content is typically shaped, and also how it is contextualised in terms of the points of reference and latent structures of meaning that underlie the construction of a particular media account: a construction that simultaneously reflects and influences public perception of the problem (McQuail 2005). The meanings of a particular account do not arise naturally but, rather, are constructed through the process of a dialectical relationship between the social, economic and institutional structures (Halliday 1978).

The factors that influence journalistic framing of narratives have been identified by Shoemaker and Reese (1996) as social norms and values, organisational pressures and constraints, pressure from interest groups, journalistic routines, and journalists' individual ideological and political beliefs. Benedict (1992) also identifies several social and practical factors that affect the framing of news stories about crimes against women, including conceptions of 'what sells', journalistic traditions, racism, sexism, class prejudice, the bias of sources, reporters' opinions, and hierarchy in the newsroom. She argues that these social factors affect the selection and reporting of every news story, transcending the point of view of the individual reporter.

It has been argued that print and TV media pay disproportionate attention to crime, and that this attention centres on criminal incidents and their victims, rather than analyses of patterns of crime or the possible causes of crime (Beckett and Sasson 2000; Reiner et al. 2003). It is difficult to assess the precise impact of the media representation of crime on people's attitudes towards crime because people may choose which newspaper to read on the basis of their existing views, not *vice versa*. However, it has been argued that though the press coverage of violence against women has increased dramatically since the 1980s, media representations of such crimes, and their victims, reflect dominant societal attitudes towards women and serve to perpetuate gender inequalities (Berns 2004; Meyers 1997; Taylor 2009). Media accounts of violence against women typically exclude the concept of male accountability and focus on the victim, who is 'celebrated for having the courage to leave the abusive relationship or, conversely, blamed for staying and letting the abuse continue' (Berns 2004, 3). Thus, victims are constructed as responsible for their own plight, and attention is diverted from the underlying causes that perpetuate the abuse of women by men (Berns 2004). Social constructionism allows for an examination of how problems are defined and how these definitions set limits on, and create opportunities that affect, the process of policy making and implementation aimed at addressing perceived social problems (Rochefort and Cobb 1994). The role of the media is crucial in this process, as the ways in which policy makers perceive the category of people affected by a particular social problem depend on how these people are represented in the media; these representations may stimulate or prevent action on the part of policy makers (Franklin 1999; Rochefort and Cobb 1994). There is a complex relationship between news media, news sources, the content of media coverage concerning social policy, and the impact of such coverage on audiences, public opinion and policy makers (Franklin 1999). However, while these contributory factors are manifold, the end result is that the dominant representation of the affected group strongly influences political willingness to make commitments to address the problem (Rochefort and Cobb 1994). When the affected group is perceived as comprising victims who deserve sympathy, or the perpetrators are seen as a group that deserves punishment, policy-makers are more likely to strive to find a solution to the issue at stake.

As active agents in the discourse on forced marriage, the media and 'experts' construct and propagate images of victims and devote space to narratives that provoke shock and moral outrage among their audience. Thus, the discourse on forced marriage in part constructs the phenomenon and defines its nature. Given the crucial role played by the media and policy debates in highlighting the problem of forced marriage as one that requires particular policy solutions, there is an urgent need to unpack the ways in which forced marriage is constructed, and its victims are represented.

On culturalist understandings of forced marriage

Since 1999, there has been an explosion of media interest in forced marriage and other forms of violence that are viewed as solely affecting minority ethnic women, such as so-called 'honour-based' killings, dowry violence and, more recently, so-called 'slave brides'.[1] Media reports (Slack 2008) and research commissioned by policy makers (Kazimirski et al. 2009; Khanum 2008) have made varying estimates of between 3,000 to 10,000 cases of forced marriage in the UK every year. Some recent media reports, citing police sources, have estimated that up to 17,000 women each year experience so-called 'honour-based' violence, a category within which forced marriage has been included (Independent 2008). These statistics are difficult to substantiate, but – crucially – the *perception* that this is a growing problem is created through sensationalist newspaper headlines, such as 'Tenfold rise in forced marriages in four years' (Daily Mail 2009). It is only recently that statistics on forced marriage and honour-based crimes have been collated by police forces and other services: previously, these crimes were recorded under the generic categories of domestic violence. Given this historical lack of documentation, it is likely that the recording of forced marriage and an increase in the number of women reporting such crimes to the authorities in consequence of recent publicity has been represented in the media as a growing problem.

This recent newsworthiness of forced marriage can be understood with reference to the structures of representation that influence how, where, and to what extent a story will be told in the news (Chermak 1995; Meyers 1997; Pritchard and Hughes 1997). In the past, the media was less inclined to report on forced marriage than on mainstream forms of domestic violence, just as they were more likely to report on sensational homicides rather than those arising from habitual forms of domestic violence. An analysis of the reporting of homicide in three British newspapers between 1993 and 1997 (Peelo et al. 2004, 261) compared 2,685 police-recorded homicides in this period with media reporting: just under 40 per cent of homicides were reported in at least one of the papers studied. Homicides motivated by monetary gain or sexual proprietariness – a 'jealousy or revenge motive' (Peelo et al. 2004, 272) – were most likely to be reported in all three newspapers, while homicides arising out of 'rage or quarrel' (Peelo et al. 2004, 269), including 'everyday' domestic violence, were least likely to be reported. Abdela (2008) notes the disproportionate headline coverage given to street stabbings of young people, while stories about women who have been killed by current or past intimates receive little coverage. Echoing academic research (Peelo et al. 2004), Ian Blair, then Metropolitan Police Commissioner, used the example of the extensive media coverage given to the murders in 2002 of two ten-year-old girls in Soham, England, by their school caretaker to argue that white, middle-class victims receive disproportionate media coverage while murders in minority communities appear 'not to interest the mainstream media' because of the 'institutional racism' of the media (Cozens 2006), a suggestion for which he received much flak in the media.

Given the historical lack of interest in both domestic violence and minority ethnic victims, how do we account for the recent burgeoning interest in specific forms of violence against minority ethnic women? Have the media and policy makers finally taken account of the years of campaigning by specialist women's organisations appealing for recognition of the forms of violence faced by minority ethnic women, for better protections under the law, and for improved access to specialist services? A preliminary examination of the attention paid to the problem of forced marriage in recent policy formulations and in media reporting may indicate that this indeed is the case. However, it is interesting to note that not all forms of violence inflicted on minority ethnic women draw the attention of the media. For example, the continued detention of women and girls who have faced the trauma of war, rape and dislocation before claiming asylum in the UK has attracted little media interest.

The forms of violence against minority ethnic women that have been foregrounded in these recent debates are not those that originate in or are perpetuated by state practices and policies, but those that are attributable to particular communities and individuals within these communities. The recent interest in violence against women (particularly forced marriage) in black and minority ethnic, refugee communities is connected to broader discourses about the boundaries of the nation, debates on immigration, citizenship and concepts of 'Britishness' (Enright 2009; Gedalof 2007; for a similar analysis of Dutch policy formulation, see Ghorashi 2010).

Consequently, whereas acts of violence against women from white majority communities are increasingly explained away as the result of individual pathology and, thus, are seen as separate from the socio-cultural context in which the acts occur (Berns 2004), in relation to violence against minority ethnic women the focus centres on the cultural context of the violence in such a way that the entire community is blamed (Narayan 1997; Razack 2004; Volpp 2000). We argue that both perspectives – individual pathology or culturalist explanations of gender-based violence – construct the problem and, thus, potential solutions in specific ways, thus eliding the intersections between economic, social, cultural and gendered inequalities.

Three diagnostic frames can be identified in the media reporting of forced marriage; these frames focus on the victims and the perpetrators in a manner distinct from the frames employed in relation to other forms of domestic violence.

First, as has been noted elsewhere, media accounts portray the victims of forced marriage as particularly lacking in agency: as already/always victim subjects of a deterministic culture (Narayan 1997; Razack 2004). This representation is reinforced through celebratory accounts about/by women who have survived forced marriage and reconfigured themselves and their struggles through the discourse of otherness, in narratives that harness orientalist tropes of absolute cultural difference between their patriarchal communities and the liberated West. Survivors of forced marriage speak out about their experiences of abuse at great risk to themselves, and for a variety of motivations – to recover their voice, to make visible what may have been rendered invisible, to raise awareness about the problem and campaign on it (Ali 2008; Sanghera 2007, 2009). While recognising their courage in taking that decision, we seek to question the assumptions on which their narratives have been accorded space within the mainstream media.

In a photograph accompanying a cover story on forced marriage in the *Observer* (Seal and Wiseman 2009), survivors of forced marriage were all dressed in black Western clothes – an imagery that seemed to emphasise the survivors' distance from their communities. In the article accompanying these images, Sanghera is quoted as saying, 'My father didn't leave his traditions behind at Heathrow' (Seal and Wiseman 2009), reiterating the commonplace view that migrants need to 'leave their culture behind' and assimilate to Western norms, which are unequivocally represented as privileging gender equality. Likewise, in a celebratory account of a woman who survived forced marriage and went on to marry her white boyfriend, the *Daily Mail* lauds her courage thus: 'Today, she prides herself on being a thoroughly modern Englishwoman – and with her fashionably streaked hair, elegantly painted nails and designer wardrobe of must-have designs, she looks every inch the part' (Cable 2006).

The second framing device centres on the accounts of perpetrators' motivations that are put forward in media reports which focuses on family conflict or 'culture clash'. In this frame, forced marriage is constructed as an inevitable feature of traditional Asian culture, rather than as a form of gendered violence. In the context of a Forced Marriage Protection Order sought by a 22-year-old woman, PC Pennal of Lancashire Police thought it fit to say, 'We've also offered the father support. We've explained and given him an understanding ... that when there's a clash between someone's culture and the law ... sometimes we have to make this sort of stand' (Collins 2009). This misplaced notion of cultural sensitivity, articulated as a defence of multiculturalism, has long been criticised by feminist groups for its assumption that gender-based violence is an essential feature of *the* 'South Asian culture' – seen as a single entity – and that sensitivity to this culture requires the state to be sympathetic to cultural explanations for perpetrators' motivations (Dustin and Phillips 2008). Such perspectives have also been blamed by grassroot organisations for implicitly foregrounding the role of male leaders as spokespersons for black and minority ethnic, refugee communities (Patel 2008; Wilson 2007): a problem, it has been argued, of 'too much multiculturalism' (Fekete 2008, 58). However, a truly multicultural perspective would be able to acknowledge the diversity and changeability of 'other' cultures, as is routinely done with reference to mainstream culture. Given that models of British multiculturalism have cast minority culture as static, deterministic and inherently patriarchal, it could be argued that this actually represents a case of too little multiculturalism, rather than a surfeit of it. The continuities between the earlier multiculturalist and recent community cohesion approaches are evident in that the same representations of migrant culture as deterministic also inform the current problematisation of forced marriage as an inevitable marker of static patriarchal cultures.

The third, related framing device revolves around issues of coercive control of women in certain (i.e. Muslim) communities whereby cultural difference is employed to explain individual acts of forced marriage and suggest potential solutions. In sentencing a woman to three years in prison for coercing her two daughters to marry their cousins in Pakistan, Judge Clement Goldstone QC stated that 'those who choose to live in this country and who, like you, are British subjects, must not abandon our laws in the practice of those beliefs and that culture' (Narain 2009). Thus, forced marriage is represented as a cultural practice that is antithetical to 'Britishness'; this ignores the many other 'normal' forms of gender-based violence that are not similarly problematised. Whereas 'normal' forms of domestic violence are represented through discourses focused on the individuals (whether the blame is attributed to the victim or, less commonly, to the perpetrator), the frame employed in relation to forced marriage focuses on cultural difference, and the blame here is attributed to the communities in which forced marriage occurs. For example, in publicity about a research study funded by the Home Office to document the regional picture on forced marriage in Luton, in one of three national pilot projects (Khanum 2008), the author criticised specific minority communities for perpetuating a 'wall of silence' around forced marriage (Taylor 2008). Black, minority ethnic and refugee women's groups have long been campaigning about forced marriage, but it would seem that they are not part of this 'community'. The key question pondered by journalists and commentators on newspaper websites when discussing the problem of forced marriage – 'Why do they [the families and communities involved] tolerate this violence'? – is a question that is seldom asked of mainstream white communities when it comes to routinised forms of domestic violence.

These framing devices have consequences for the construction of policy solutions: whereas mainstream forms of domestic violence are constructed as individualistic crimes and have led to a focus on individualistic exit-centred state responses, the framing of forced marriage suggests – indeed, it requires – additional solutions centred on specific communities and their culture. Despite attempts to bring a nuanced understanding of forced marriage as a specific form of gender-based violence to its guidelines for frontline practitioners (Stobart 2009), the Forced Marriage Unit's underlying framing of forced marriage is revealed in the headline used for flyers and posters publicising recent government initiatives to tackle forced marriage: 'Challenging the Culture'.

These differential representations of forced marriage also contribute to the perception that culturally specific forms of violence are more abhorrent than 'normal' domestic violence: they are 'endemic abuse of the worst kind' according to Wayne Ives, Head of the Forced Marriage Unit in 2008

(Beckford 2008). In the context of domestic homicides unmarked by tropes of alterity, the media often trivialises and normalises domestic violence through the use of gender-neutral terms such as 'family disputes' or 'difficult relationships': the language is unmarked by the power differentials that give rise to these acts of violence (Berns 2004; Taylor 2009). Transnational feminists have drawn attention to the ways in which women's rights have increasingly come to be marshalled in defence of neocolonial and imperialist projects that construct specific manifestations of violence against women (for example, trafficking of women for prostitution, forced marriage, so-called 'honour'-based killings, or female genital mutilation) as particular moral and social problems urgently requiring resolution (Dustin 2010; Fernandez 2009; Jaggar 2005; Roggeband 2010; Ticktin 2008). Singling out forced marriage as a particularly 'barbaric' and 'abhorrent' form of violence against women firmly locates it in an othered, unchanging, pre-modern world (Fernandez 2009); it also differentiates forced marriage from 'normal' forms of domestic violence, which are both minimised in popular media and simultaneously treated as unrepresentative of mainstream culture. These representations are not unique to crime policy in the UK. Writing about the formulation of the term 'harmful traditional practices' by the UN – a victory of sorts for campaigners who sought a recognition of the gendered harms that the UN had hitherto remained silent on – Winter et al. (2002, 72) criticise the assumption that the 'metropolitan centres of the West contain no "traditions" or "culture" harmful to women, and that the violence which does exist there is idiosyncratic and individualized rather than culturally condoned'.

Since the early 1980s, the representation of minority ethnic women in dominant media and policy discourses in the UK, and more broadly in Europe (Bredal, in Chapter 4; Dustin and Phillips 2008; Roggeband and Verloo 2007), has shifted: where previously these women were largely invisible, they are now hypervisible. This shift has not disrupted the emphasis on minority ethnic women's docility and enforced domesticity, which are viewed as the inevitable consequence of living within traditional cultures. Essentialist stereotypes about the otherness of women from such cultures have been used to explain the violence perpetrated against them without there being any reflection on the overlapping, simultaneous and reciprocal vectors of inequalities that affect them. Given the pervasiveness of these discourses, it is hardly surprising that the complex ways in which violence against women within minority communities is connected to forms of violence and inequalities outside minority communities (for example, minority ethnic women seeking asylum who are housed in detention centres may face violence from a range of sources) seldom garner media interest.

Forced marriage: from a cultural problem to the problematic culture

Media reporting and policy making have long identified forced marriage as an issue of minority ethnic British women being forced into transnational marriages with men seeking to enter Britain on spousal visas. This focus is not accidental, and does not necessarily reflect the nature of forced marriage in the UK. Following moves by other EU countries to employ broader border control measures in the name of tackling forced marriage (see Bredal in Chapter 4), in March 2007 Liam Byrne, the UK Immigration Minister, announced proposals to raise the age of entry for spouses from outside the European Economic Area to 21. It was anticipated that this would result in 3,000 fewer people entering Britain each year from outside Europe, though the proportion of these failed entries that would have involved forced marriages remained unknown (Ford 2007).

In September 2005, the Joint Foreign and Commonwealth Office and Home Office Forced Marriage Unit announced a consultation about the criminalisation of forced marriage. While these debates were taking place, Anne Cryer, MP for Keighley, presented a memorandum to the Home Affairs Select Committee on Immigration Control (Cryer 2006) outlining the problems she said she routinely dealt with in the course of her constituency work, in which she highlighted forced marriage and violence within marriages. In this document, she outlines what she describes as the problems arising from the current immigration system – namely, fraud, lack of enforcement, economic migration, and the social and economic consequences of migration (Cryer 2006, 3.1). It is this last problem to which she devotes the most attention.

After a brief reference to economic benefits of migration, she draws our attention to the 'question mark regarding immigration on the back of a marriage of convenience' (Cryer 2006, 3.5 [b]). However, the problem rapidly comes to be framed as one of the 'ghettoisation' of particular communities and the lack of integration between communities, rather than as a problem of gender-based violence. This lack of integration is squarely identified as stemming from the marriage practices of the 'other' community. She argues (Cryer 2006, 3.5 [f]):

Certainly in northern towns and cities there is a reliance on marriages arranged intercontinentally. Normally between first cousins, marriage takes place between a British born and bred sponsor and a bride or groom from the sub-continent. (...) The emphasis on marriage between a British sponsor and a bride or groom from the sub-continent effectively means that the creation of the second generation is impeded – possibly indefinitely.

Consanguineous marriage, forced marriage, lack of knowledge of English are all cited as the 'tragic problems (that) are facilitated by intercontinental marriages which, in turn, are facilitated by weak immigration control and spouse entry' (Cryer 2006, 3.5 [h]). Cryer argues that immigration control will solve these problems and more specifically advocates lifting the lower age limit for the spouse visa to 21 (2006, 6 [c]). The social and cultural contexts that sustain and encourage forced marriage, and initiatives to tackle these issues, are afforded no place in Cryer's discussion or in the solutions she offers. Forced marriage is mentioned again only in the conclusion of Cryer's memorandum:

We must continue to welcome, cherish and have respect for other traditions and cultures in our communities. However, when cultures and traditions impinge on the human rights of the most vulnerable in our community then it is our responsibility to stop those abuses. This could be achieved through tighter immigration controls[.]

The memorandum also refers to Cryer's appearance on the BBC's *Newsnight* programme, five years previously, during which she drew attention to the number of disabled babies born in her constituency to Pakistani parents; at the time, media reported her intervention as a call for marriage between cousins to be outlawed (BBC News 2005). The media furore over cousin marriages was reignited in February 2008 by the then Environment Minister, Phil Woolas (later promoted to Minister of State for Borders and Immigration). Woolas directed media attention to the risks of 'inbreeding' from 'Muslim arranged marriages', and warned prospective parents that 'it is likely that you will have a disabled child' (Chivers and agencies 2008). While the risk *is* indeed higher – commonly calculated as between 2 per cent additional risk and 4 per cent additional risk where there is a family history of consanguineous marriages (Paul and Spencer 2008; Shaw 2003) – it is by no means a likely outcome.

In a recent public lecture, Baroness Ruth Deech argued that 'There is no reason ... why there should not be a campaign to highlight the risks [of a consanguineous marriage] and the preventative measures every bit as vigorously as those centring on smoking, obesity and Aids' (Deech 2010, 6). Recent research suggests that the risks of genetic abnormality in children born from consanguineous marriages are no greater than those for women over forty (Paul and Spencer 2008), yet no one is suggesting that women over forty should be prevented from reproducing or be the target of a public campaign. Any suggestion that children born to mothers over forty have significant resource implications for the NHS, or that parents falling into this category should be targeted by preventative measures, would meet with justifiable criticism. Why have the responses to these not dissimilar issues been so different? We would argue that commentators are less concerned with the extent of the risks and more with the basis of the choices made by parents. Whereas the decision to marry a cousin is readily cast as a practice rooted in 'medieval culture' (Cryer, cited in BBC News 2008) – one that may have additional implications regarding immigration – the decision to reproduce later in life is represented in terms of women's hard-won right to choose when to have children. In her lecture, Deech (2010) notes that the practice of consanguineous marriage has long been associated with immigrants and the poor, and that it is viewed as being 'at odds with freedom of choice, romantic love and integration' (Deech 2010, 3–4). Presumably, this is what lies behind public disapproval of consanguineous marriage when it occurs in immigrant communities but not when it occurs in mainstream communities (Deech 2010, 5), as in the latter it does not entail immigration and reaffirms the ideal of romantic love.

Since the attacks on the World Trade Center and other targets on 11 September 2001, the problematisation of racial differences has increasingly come to be articulated through a rhetoric of exclusion predicated on the alleged cultural incompatibility of immigrant communities. The notion that there is a normative form of Britishness is utilised to argue that the onus lies with the immigrant community to adapt their cultural values and traditions in order to make them more like those of majority communities (Gedalof 2007). This alleged cultural incompatibility is attributed to the modes of cultural reproduction (i.e. the modes via which culture is reproduced and transmitted from one generation to the next) that are employed by immigrant communities, whereby transnational marriages come to be blamed for the persistence of immigrant culture. Forced marriage thus becomes the pretext for both the problematisation of arranged marriage and the migration of particular communities, as in Cryer's memorandum. Here, the problem of forced marriage becomes uncoupled from issues of coercion and through a focus on transnational arranged marriages, comes to be posited as a 'problem of continuous migration' (Migration Watch 2009), whereby migration itself and what are perceived to be the consequences of migration, rather than forced marriage or attitudes to migration come to be categorised as a problem. Bredal (in Chapter 4 of this volume) discusses a similar process in the context of policy formulations in Europe, whereby forced marriage is constructed as a phenomenon that is 'almost-the-same-as' arranged marriage, transcontinental marriage or marriage involving migration of what are constructed as problematic groups of migrants.

The discourses within which the debate on immigration is articulated were set in the White Paper *Secure Borders, Safe Haven* (Home Office 2001; for an analysis of this document, see Gedalof 2007) and have been reasserted in discussions on forced marriage. It is within these framing devices that the then Labour minister Blunkett's comments on arranged marriage, along with his suggestion that speaking native languages within family homes is socially divisive (Akbar 2002; Morris and Beard 2002), received extensive support from some sections of the media (BBC News 2002). Policy documents such as the Cantle Report (Cantle 2001), produced in the aftermath of the disturbances that took place in Oldham and other cities in 2001, singled out the use of native languages as a signifier of the clash of cultures that was constructed as the underlying explanation for the behaviour of young South Asian men (Blackledge 2004, 68). As both minority culture and foreign language use in the home are viewed as being perpetuated by arranged marriages, the policy papers focused on marriage patterns and the cultural lives of minority communities, rather than on the wider structures of disadvantage that may have better explained the disturbances (Blackledge, 2004; Yuval-Davis et al. 2005).

Forced marriage, arranged marriage and consanguineous marriage have come to be lumped together and collectively identified as markers of cultural difference (for a discussion of similar processes in the Netherlands, see Roggeband and Verloo 2007). Such markers reinforce the boundaries of the nation in what Berlant refers to as the 'privatisation of citizenship' (cited in Gedalof 2007, 91). It is within this context that the plight of two young newlyweds hit the headlines during the summer of 2009. Adam Wallis from Wales fell in love with and married nineteen-year-old Rochelle Roberts from Canada. However, she was unable to secure a spousal visa because the age of entry had been raised from eighteen to twenty-one. There was widespread media sympathy for the couple (Allen 2009; Jones 2009). Reports on their story emphasised that romantic love was the only motivation for their marriage, and underlined the injustice of the new law for the lovestruck couples caught in it. Internet blogs and comments on newspaper and political party websites utilised this media storm to argue that the 'real' problem that the change in the law was designed to tackle was the importation of immigrants by means of pre-modern customs (namely arranged marriage) to a country where modern notions of choice and unmediated romantic love inform marriage decisions. This debate indicates the extent to which the discourse on forced marriage works to normalise immigration rules targeted at particular communities: it is only when 'true' Westerners get caught up in them that we see hand-wringing about the consequences of such rules (Gupta 2009). Couples in arranged marriages who may have been separated from each other by UK immigration law have provoked no such media outrage, because such marriages and the subjectivities of women who contract such marriages are deemed suspect within dominant discourses of absolute unfettered choice in matters of marriage (see Bredal, Chapter 4). For example, none of the media coverage of couples separated by the increase in the minimum age for spousal visas implied that marriage with an overseas partner was inherently problematic; instead, they seemed to suggest that marriage to a foreigner is acceptable if the marriage is based on romantic love. Writing about Norwegian family reunification law, Myrdahl (2010) argues that romance-based marriage has become central to constructions of national subjects in a racial project that renders some groups of Norwegian citizens simultaneously invisible as national subjects and hypervisible as objects of national management – all with the ostensible purpose of combating forced marriage.

The concept of romantic love itself is identified here as a crucial marker of difference where forced marriage and arranged marriage (and the two are often used interchangeably) are everything that romantic love is not. Falling in love is paradoxically constructed as an irrational act, uncontrollable and unfettered, free from social mediation; indeed, it is seen as an expression of individual autonomy and agency. This form of agency is considered a key signifier of personhood, whereas social mediation, rational determinants, and family involvement in marriage are perceived as signs of lack of agency. Research in South Asia demonstrates the fluidity and diversity of routes into arranged marriage (de Munck 1998; Puri 1999), yet anything that deviates from the stereotype of arranged marriage is attributed to Westernisation (Puri

1999, 136). For the West, arranged marriage has come to stand for the exoticism of South Asian cultural practices and minority ethnic women's lack of autonomy, emotional contentment and sexual satisfaction in a binary logic that recalls familiar orientalist discourses on East and West (Khandelwal 2009, 585–6). This reification of South Asian cultural practices is not unique to Western writers: South Asians living in the West similarly reify and essentialise their own culture within the discourse of exaggerated cultural difference. A feature in the *Guardian*, for example, employed the same binary distinctions when analysing South Asian's use of an internet dating site (Manzoor 2009). While white people's use of these sites was lauded as an exercise of individual autonomy unmediated by social constructs, South Asians' use of the sites was derided: 'they are still imprisoned by the idea that finding an ideal partner is about creed and career rather than chemistry' (Manzoor 2009).

However, the idea that romantic love is the ideal basis for marriage is a historically- and contextually specific phenomenon, and is no more transgressive in the West than in South Asia (Khandelwal 2009, 603–5). Transnational feminists have argued that Westerners often overestimate their own agency and underestimate the agency of non-Western women (Mohanty 1988; Narayan 1997). Khandelwal (2009) offers a useful interrogation of the discourse of exaggerated difference between arranged marriage and romance-based marriage by examining the notions of compatibility that inform marriage decisions and argues that individuals are most likely to fall in love with others from a similar class, and and a similar social and cultural background. She argues that marriage facilitates cultural reproduction in both types of marriage: compatibility is constructed in terms of social attributes (family status/class, educational background, caste or community) in relation to arranged marriage, and in individualised terms (shared interests, personality, physical attraction and so forth) in relation to marriage 'for love' (Khandelwal 2009, 603–5).

Over the past decade, the hypervisibility of forced marriage in media and policy debates has come about through the construction of forced marriage as a signifier of cultural difference, rather than as one of the many forms of violence against women that exist within both majority and minority communities. This recasting of the problem of gender-based violence into that of migration and 'Britishness' has significant implications for policy. Prior to the raising of the age of entry for spouses, the Home Office commissioned independent research on the possible impact of this change. The study raised concerns about an increase in the age of sponsorship or entry (either to twenty-one or twenty-four) on the basis that (1) it could be perceived as discriminatory, (2) it might be detrimental to human rights, (3) it would not prevent forced marriage since this affects people of all ages, and (4) it would penalise those who genuinely wished to marry (Hester et al. 2006). These concerns were echoed by the House of Commons Home Affairs Committee, though its members also considered that the evidence about these possible consequences was inconclusive (House of Commons Home Affairs Committee 2008, 41–3). The Home Office chose to ignore these findings and went ahead with the changes. It was only following a Freedom of Information request by Colin Yeo, a barrister at Renaissance Chambers, that the Home Office released the full research report (Yeo 2009). The then Labour government's decision to ignore the recommendations of the research it commissioned, and also the advice of charities working on this issue, is closely connected to their framing of the problem of forced marriage. An understanding of cultural difference as a signifier of forced marriage suggests as a solution the eradication or minimisation of cultural heterogeneity through immigration control, and community cohesion strategies aimed at settled minority communities. In this context, even if there was no evidence that raising the age of spousal visa could prevent forced marriage, by making transnational arranged marriage more difficult and, thereby, impeding immigration, it was considered an effective solution (for an assessment of similar policy formulations in Europe, see Chapter 4).

Conclusion

The conflation of forced marriage, transnational marriage, consanguineous marriage and arranged marriage that is implied in media and policy discourses reinforces racist and essentialist responses that are often ineffective and may, indeed, add to the structural barriers faced by minority ethnic women when seeking support, redress and assistance in overcoming violence. It is of concern that within these culturalist discourses the non-coercive marriage practices of black and minority ethnic and refugee communities have also come to be constructed as problematic – whether as signifiers of women's passivity, as impediment to community cohesion, or as an immigration problem. Thus, the marriage practices of immigrant communities are often recast as measures of integration, particularly, but not exclusively, in the case of transnational arranged marriages.

This recent media outrage about and scrutiny of violence against minority ethnic women, and in this case forced marriage, does not necessarily achieve a better understanding of the particular forms of violence faced by minority ethnic women. Understanding of this specificity requires both a close study of the particular practices and a recognition of the variability of these practices based on diverse articulations of gender, class, race, heteronormity, the migratory history of minoritised groups, state policy and state practice. Better understanding also demands a recognition that these changes are not just the result of globalisation or modernisation in what are problematically defined as 'harmful traditional practices', but that change is an intrinsic feature of any 'traditional cultural practice', and that 'mainstream' forms of domestic violence are similarly culturalised. It also requires an understanding of the commonalities and connections between particular, variable and context-specific forms of gender-based violence.

Specialist services working with minority ethnic women have long attempted to draw attention to specific forms of violence against women and the importance of wider recognition of women's diverse needs in response to violence against women. These calls seem to have been heeded within media and policy debates on forced marriage in the UK. It may seem that recent attention to these forms of violence is a step forward when compared with the silence, imposed in the name of respecting the sensitivities of diverse communities, which previously surrounded the issue. However, the discourses that underlie policy debates and news reporting of forced marriage not only reveal and reproduce assumptions and biases that prevent this and other harmful practices from being addressed and challenged within a broader violence against women agenda (Coy, Kelly and Foord 2009), but also normalise racist responses to such violence. Consequently, minority ethnic women are increasingly expected to respond to violence by stepping outside their communities, into a presumably neutral space – mainstream communities, generic refuges and generic services. This chapter interrogates and unpacks the terms on which the recent debates around forced marriage have taken place precisely because of the potential of these seldom explicitly stated, but widely pervasive discourses to construct the problem and solutions in specific ways, and to foreclose other possible solutions.

Note

1   'Slave brides' (Bano 2010) refers to marriage migrants who, during the first two years of their stay in the UK, have no recourse to public funds and hence cannot access refuge spaces; they face potential deportation if they cannot prove that the marriage broke down because of the domestic violence – women in this situation therefore face severe constraints when in an abusive relationship. Yet again, this term utilised by the media shifts the focus away from the immigration and welfare policies of the state, and also away from the connections and commonalities between 'normal' forms of domestic violence and the domestic violence faced by women with insecure immigration status; it also serves to exoticise and 'other' this manifestation of gender-based violence.

References

Ali, S. (2008) *Belonging*, John Murray, London.

Abdela, A. (2008) 'Stop Looking the Other Way', *Guardian*, 25 November. http://www.guardian.co.uk/commentisfree/2008/nov/25/domestic-violence-gender (accessed 22 July 2010)

Akbar, A. (2002) 'Blunkett: British Asians Should Speak English at Home', *Independent*, 16 September. http://www.independent.co.uk/news/uk/politics/blunkett-british-asians-should-speak-english-at-home-642930.html (accessed 24 May 2010)

Allen, V. (2009) 'Newlyweds Face 18-month Separation After Falling Foul of Law Designed to Protect Asian Women from Forced Marriage', *Daily Mail*, 24 July. http://www.dailymail.co.uk/news/article- 1201886/Newlyweds-face-18-month-separation-falling-foul-law-designed-protect-Asian-women-forced-marriage.html (accessed 23 April)

Bano, R. (2010) 'South Asian "Slave Brides" Causing Concern in UK', *BBC News*, 14 March. http://news.bbc.co.uk/1/hi/uk/8566102.stm (accessed 15 March 2010).

BBC News (2002) 18 September. http://news.bbc.co.uk/1/hi/ talking_point/2248606.stm (accessed 24 May 2010).

BBC News (2005) 16 November. http://news.bbc.co.uk/1/hi/programmes/newsnight/4442646.stm (accessed 27 April 2010).

BBC News (2008) 10 February. http://news.bbc.co.uk/1/hi/uk/7237663.stm (accessed 22 July 2010).

Beckett, K. and Sasson, T. (2000) *The Politics of Injustice: Crime and Punishment in America,* Pine Forge Press, Thousand Oaks, CA.

Beckford, M. (2008) 'Forced Marriage Cases up by 80pc This Year as Investigators Find Parents Using "Bounty Hunters"', *Daily Telegraph*, 21 November. http://www.telegraph.co.uk/news/uknews/3496442/Forced-marriage-cases-up-by-80pc-this-year-as-investigators-find-parents-using-bounty-hunters.html (accessed 23 April 2010).

Benedict, H. (1992) *Virgin or Vamp: How the Press Covers Sex Crimes*, Oxford University Press, New York.

Berns, N. (2004) *Framing the Victim: Domestic Violence, Media and Social Problems*, Aldine de Gruyter, Hawthorne, NY.

Blackledge, A. (2004) 'Constructions Of Identity In Political Discourse In Multilingual Britain', in A. Pavlenko and A. Blackledge (eds.), *Negotiation Of Identities In Multilingual Contexts*, Multilingual Matters, Clevedon.

Cable, A. (2006) 'A Forced Marriage? I'd Rather Kill Myself', *Daily Mail*, 9 June. http://www.dailymail.co.uk/femail/article-389831/A-forced-marriage-Id-kill-myself.html (accessed 24 April 2010).

Cantle, T. (2001) *Community Cohesion: A Report of the Independent Review Team*, Home Office, London.

Chermak, S. (1995) *Victims in the News: Crime and the American News Media*, Westview Press, Boulder, CO.

Chivers, T. and Agencies. (2008) 'Minister Warns of Inbreeding Risk for Muslims', *Telegraph*, 10 February. http://www.telegraph.co.uk/news/ uknews/1578190/Minister-warns-of-inbreeding-risk-for-Muslims.html (accessed 23 April 2010).

Collins, L. (2009) 'Woman Uses New Forced Marriage Laws Against Father', *Independent*, 10 February. http://www.independent.co.uk/news/uk/home-news/woman-uses-new-forced-marriage-laws-against-father-1606038.html (accessed 23 April 2010).

Coy, M., Kelly, L. and Foord, J (2009) *Map of Gaps 2: The postcode lottery of Violence against Women support services in Britain*, End Violence Against Women and Equality and Human Rights Commission, London.

Cozens, C. (2006) 'Met Chief Accuses Media of Racism', *Guardian*, 26 January. http://www.guardian.co.uk/media/2006/jan/26/pressandpublishing.raceintheuk (accessed 14 July 2010).

Cryer, A. (2006) Select Committee on Home Affairs: Additional written evidence, Memorandum submitted by Ann Cryer MP. http://www.publications. parliament. uk/pa/cm200506/cmselect/cmhaff/775/775awe11.htm (accessed 27 April 2010).

Daily Mail (2009) 2 July. http://www.dailymail.co.uk/news/article-1196955/Ten-fold-rise-forced-marriages-just-years.html (accessed 23 April 2010).

de Munck, V. (1998) 'Lust, Love and Arranged Marriages in Sri Lanka', in V. de Munck (ed.), *Romantic Love and Sexual Practices: Perspectives from the Social Sciences*, Praeger, New York.

Deech, R. (2010) 'Family Relationships and the Law since the 1960s: Cousin Marriage', Public lecture, Gresham College, 23 March. http://www.gresham. ac.uk/uploads/Ruth%20Deech%20March%202010%20-%20Cousin%20Marriage.doc (accessed 23 April 2010)

Dustin, M. (2010) 'Female Genital Mutilation/Cutting in the UK: Challenging the Inconsistencies', *European Journal of Women's Studies*, vol. 17, no. 1, February.

Dustin, M. and Phillips, A. (2008) 'Whose Agenda is it?: Abuses of Women and Abuses of "Culture" in Britain', *Ethnicities*, vol. 8, no. 3, September.

Enright, M. (2009) 'Choice, Culture and the Politics of Belonging: The Emerging Law of Forced and Arranged Marriage', *Modern Law Review*, vol. 72, no. 3, May.

Entman, R. (1993) 'Framing: Toward Clarification of a Fractured Paradigm', *Journal of Communication*, vol. 43, no. 4, Winter.

Fekete, L. (2008) *Integration, Islamophobia and Civil Rights in Europe*, Institute for Race Relations, London.

Fernandez, S. (2009) 'The Crusade over the Bodies of Women', *Patterns of Prejudice*, vol. 43, no. 3, July.

Ford, R. (2007). 'Visa Rules Will Raise Marriage Age to 21', *The Times*, March 29. http://www.timesonline.co.uk/tol/news/uk/article1583310.ece (accessed 26 July 2010).

Foucault, M. (1985) *The Use of Pleasure: The History of Sexuality*, vol. 2, Penguin, London.

Foucault, M. (2000) 'Polemics, Politics and Problematizations: An Interview with Michel Foucault', in P. Rabinow (ed.), *Essential Works of Michel Foucault 1954-84*, vol. 1, *Ethics: Subjectivity and Truth)*, Penguin, London.

Franklin, B. (ed.) (1999) *Social Policy, the Media and Misrepresentation,* Routledge and Kegan Paul, London.

Gedalof, I. (2007) 'Unhomely Homes: Women, Family and Belonging in UK Discourses of Migration and Asylum', *Journal of Ethnic and Migration Studies*, vol. 33, no. 1, January.

Ghorashi, H. (2010) 'From Absolute Invisibility to Extreme Visibility: Emancipatory Trajectory of Migrant Women in the Netherlands', *Feminist Review*, vol. 94.

Gupta, R. (2009) 'White Weddings and Forced Marriage', *Guardian*, 19 August. http://www.guardian.co.uk/commentisfree/2009/aug/19/forced-marriage-legislation-immigration (accessed 15 June 2010).

Halliday, M. (1978) *Language as Social Semiotic*. Edward Arnold, London.

Roggeband, C. and Verloo, M. (2007) 'Dutch Women are Liberated, Migrant Women are a Problem: The Evolution of Policy Frames on Gender and Migration in the Netherlands, 1995–2005', *Social Policy & Administration*, vol. 41, no. 3, June.

Hester, M., Chantler, K., Gangoli, G., Ahmed, B., Burman, E., Sharma, S., Singleton, A., Westmarland, N. and McCarry, M. (2006) *Forced Marriage: The Risk Factors and the Effect of Raising the Minimum Age for a Sponsor, and of Leave to Enter the UK as a Spouse or Fiance(e)*, for Home Office. University of Bristol.

Home Office (2001) *Secure Borders, Safe Haven: Integration with Diversity in Modern Britain*. HMSO, London.

House of Commons Home Affairs Committee. (2008) *Domestic Violence, Forced*

Marriage, and 'Honour'-based Violence (Sixth Report of Session 2007–08). House of Commons, London.

Independent (2008) 10 Feb. 2008. http://www.independent.co.uk/news/uk/home-news/a-question-of-honour-police-say-17000-women-are-victims-every-year-780522.html (accessed 23 April 2010)

Jaggar, A. (2005) '"Saving Amina": Global Justice for Women and Intercultural Dialogue', *Ethics & International Affairs*, vol. 19, no. 3, November.

Jones, M. (2009) 'Enforced Marriage Law Forces Couples Apart', *BBC Newsnight*, 24 July. http://news.bbc.co.uk/1/hi/programmes/newsnight/8165684.stm (accessed 23 April 2010).

Kazimirski, A., Keogh, P., Kumari, V., Smith, R., Gowland, S., and Purdon, S. with Khanum, N. (2009) *Forced Marriage: Prevalence and Service Response*, Natcen, London.

Khandelwal, M. (2009) 'Arranging Love: Interrogating the Vantage Point in Cross-border Feminism', *Signs*, vol. 34, no. 3.

Khanum, N. (2008) *Forced Marriage, Family Cohesion and Community Engagement*, Equality in Diversity, Luton.

Manzoor, S. (2009) 'Forget Internet Dating, This Is Online Matchmaking', *The Guardian*, 24 August. http://www.guardian.co.uk/lifeandstyle/2009/aug/24/shaadia-marriage-dating-website (accessed 21 July 2010)

McQuail, D. (2005) *McQuail's Mass Communication Theory* (5th edn), Sage, London.

Meyers, M. (1997) *News Coverage of Violence Against Women: Engendering Blame*, Sage, Thousand Oaks, CA.

Migration Watch UK. (2009) *Immigration and Marriage: The Problem of Continuous Migration*, Migration Watch UK, Guildford.

Mohanty, C. (1988) 'Under Western Eyes: Feminist Scholarship and Colonial Discourses', *Feminist Review*, vol. 30.

Peelo, M., Francis, B., Soothill, K., Pearson, J. and Ackerley, E. (2004) 'Newspaper Reporting and the Public Construction of Homicide', *British Journal of Criminology*, vol. 44, no. 2, March.

Morris, N. and Beard, M. (2002) 'Blunkett: Guilty of Offensive Language or Just Delivering Some Home Truths?' *Independent*, 16 September. http://www.independent.co.uk/news/uk/politics/blunkett-guilty-of-offensive-language-or-just-delivering-some-home-truths-607349.html (accessed 24 May 2010).

Myrdahl, E. (2010) 'Legislating Love: Norwegian Family Reunification Law as a Racial Project', *Social & Cultural Geography*, vol. 11, no. 2, March.

Narain, J. (2009) 'Muslim Mother Who Forced her School-age Daughters to Marry their Cousins is Jailed for 3 Years', *Daily Mail*, 22 May. http://www.dailymail.co.uk/news/article-1185589/Muslim-mother-forced-school-age-daughters-marry-cousins-jailed-3-years.html (accessed 23 April 2010).

Narayan, U. (1997) *Dislocating cultures: Identities, traditions, and Third-World feminism,* Routledge, New York.

Patel, P. (2008) 'Faith in the State? Asian Women's Struggles for Human Rights in the UK', *Feminist Legal Studies,* vol. 16, no. 1, April.

Paul, D. and Spencer, H. (2008) '"It's Ok, We're Not Cousins by Blood": The Cousin Marriage Controversy in Historical Perspective', *PLoS Biology,* vol. 6, no. 12. http://www.plosbiology.org/article/info:doi/10.1371/journal.pbio.0060320 (accessed 12 April 2010).

Pritchard, D., and Hughes, K. (1997) 'Patterns of Deviance in Crime News', *Journal of Communication,* vol. 47, no. 3, Summer.

Puri, J. (1999) *Woman, Body, Desire in Post-colonial India: Narratives of Gender and Sexuality,* Routledge, New York.

Razack, S. (2004) 'Imperilled Muslim Women, Dangerous Muslim Men and Civilised Europeans: Legal and Social Responses to Forced Marriages', *Feminist Legal Studies* vol. 1, no. 2, October.

Reese, S. (2001) 'Prologue-Framing Public Life: A Bridging Model for Media Research', in Reese, S.D., Gandy Jr, H. and Grant, A. E. (eds.), *Framing Public Life,* Routledge, New York.

Reiner, R., Livingstone, S. and Allen, J. (2003) 'From Law and Order to Lynch Mobs: Crime News Since the Second World War', in P. Mason (ed.) *Criminal Visions: Media Representations of Crime and Justice,* Willan Publishing, Cullompton, UK.

Rochefort, D., and Cobb, R. (1994) *The Politics of Problem Definition,* University of Kansas Press, Lawrence.

Roggeband, C. (2010) 'The Victim-Agent Dilemma: How Migrant Women's Organizations in the Netherlands Deal with a Contradictory Policy Frame', *Signs,* vol. 35, no. 4.

Sanghera, J. (2007) *Shame,* Hodder & Stoughton, London.

Sanghera, J. (2009) *Daughters of Shame,* Hodder & Stoughton, London.

Seal, R., and Wiseman, E. (2009) 'Abducted. Abused. Raped. Survived', *Observer,* 11 January. http://www.guardian.co.uk/world/2009/jan/11/british-asian-forced-marriages (accessed 9 May 2010)

.Shaw, A. (2003) 'The Impact of Genetic Risk on UK Pakistani Families', Wellcome Trust, London. http://genome.wellcome.ac.uk/doc_wtd020975.html (accessed 15 July 2010)

Shoemaker, P. and Reese, S. (1996) *Mediating the Message: Theories of Influence on Mass Media Content.* Longman, New York.

Slack, J. (2008) 'More Than 3,000 Asian Children Vanishing from School and "Forced into Arranged Marriages"', *Daily Mail,* 11 March. http://www.dailymail.co.uk/news/article-530295/More-3-000-Asian-children-vanishing-school-forced-arranged-marriages.html (accessed 14 July).

Stobart, E. (2009) *Multi-agency Practice Guidelines: Handling Cases of Forced Marriage.* Forced Marriage Unit, London.

Taylor, M. (2008) 'Victims of Forced Marriages Could Total 4000, says study', *Guardian*, 11 March. http://www.guardian.co.uk/world/2008/mar/11/gender. communities (accessed 4 April).

Taylor, R. (2009) 'Slain and Slandered: A Content Analysis of the Portrayal of Femicide in Crime News', *Homicide Studies*, vol. 13, no. 1, February.

Ticktin, M. (2008) 'Sexual Violence as the Language of Border Control: Where French Feminist and Anti-immigrant Rhetoric Meet', *Signs*, vol. 33, no. 4, Summer.

Volpp, L. (2000) 'Blaming Culture for Bad Behaviour', *Yale Journal of Law and the Humanities*, vol. 12, no. 1, Winter.

Wilson, A. (2007) 'The Forced Marriage Debate and the British State', *Race and Class*, vol. 49, no. 1, July.

Winter, B., Thompson, D. and Jeffreys, S. (2002) 'The UN Approach to Harmful Traditional Practices', *International Feminist Journal of Politics*, vol. 4, no. 1, April.

Yeo, C. (2009) 'Raising the Spouse Visa Age', *Journal of Immigration Asylum and Nationality Law*, vol. 23, no. 4.

Yuval-Davis, N., Anthias, F., and Kofman, E. (2005) 'Secure Borders and Safe Haven and the Gendered Politics of Belonging: Beyond Social Cohesion', *Ethnic and Racial Studies* vol. 28, no. 3, May.

Part 2

Policy and practice

6
Forced marriage legislation in the UK: a critique

Aisha K. Gill and Sundari Anitha

Since the early 1980s, violence against women has become a matter of major public and academic interest. Investigative work has started to reveal the extent of the various forms of violence inflicted on women (ranging from domestic violence to sexual violence, and from female genital mutilation to forced marriages) (Coy, Kelly and Foord 2009). Since 2004, the UK government has established a number of initiatives to combat domestic violence; the Domestic Violence, Crime and Victim's Act 2004 is of particular importance as it was the first Act specifically created to protect both the victims of domestic violence and their families.

Until the 1980s, women from minority religious and ethnic groups were not identified by policy makers as a demographic group in need of particular protection in Western Europe. Consequently, the specificity of their needs was rendered nearly invisible and largely ignored. From the 1980s, campaigning and activism by black and minority ethnic women's organisations led to the establishment of specialist refuges. However, crime policy and legislation paid little regard to the specific forms of violence until recently, when policy and legal initiatives on particular forms of gendered violence – including forced marriage and so-called 'honour-based' crime – have burgeoned.

Dominant media and policy discourses on forced marriage in the UK have identified culture as the key causal factor (see Anitha and Gill in Chapter 5); this understanding, along with the conceptualisation of victims of forced marriage as passive women controlled by outmoded traditions, has shaped the state's response to the issue, resulting in a focus on protectionist remedies. Consequently, the UK government's evolving legal policy on forced marriage has revealed a fluctuating and, at times, ambiguous response to the problem that illuminates the deep-seated theoretical tensions at the heart of legislative attempts to deal with the issue. It is within this context that this chapter examines the background, provisions and implications of the Forced Marriage (Civil Protection) Act 2007. This chapter evaluates how effective forced marriage legislation has proved, thus far, in protecting black and minority ethnic women in the UK.

Definitions of forced marriage and legislative responses

Marriage shall be entered into only with the free and full consent of the intending spouses.

Universal Declaration of Human Rights, Article 16(21)

The Marriage Act 1949 and the Matrimonial Causes Act 1973 together constitute the law on marriage in England and Wales. Section 12c of the Matrimonial Causes Act 1973 states that a marriage shall be rendered void if 'either party to the marriage did not validly consent to it, whether in consequence of duress, mistake, unsoundness of mind, or otherwise'. Additionally, a marriage may be dissolved by a decree of divorce justified predominantly on the grounds of 'unreasonable behaviour', a provision that victims and survivors of forced marriage may also invoke. The practice (and even threat) of forced marriage, and the extreme mental and sometimes physical violence that often accompany it, violates not only UK law, but also key international and regional human rights standards (Liberty 2005). Article 12 of the European Convention on Human Rights declares that 'Men and women of marriageable age have the right to marry and to found a family, according to the national laws governing the exercise of that right.' National and international law demand that both spouses give free and full consent to a marriage, as mandated by the Convention's underlying principles of self-determination and human dignity (for more on the implications of human rights laws concerning forced marriage, see Choudhry in Chapter 3).[1]

Four high-profile cases of forced marriage have thrown a spotlight on the issue:

1 the murder of Rukhsana Naz by her family after she left her marriage and became pregnant by another man (Hall 1999);
2 the plight of Jack and Zena Briggs, who were forced into hiding to escape bounty hunters employed by Zena's family after she refused to marry a cousin in Pakistan (Watt 1999);
3 the successful return to England of a young Sikh girl after her parents abducted her and took her to India to be married (KR 1999); and

4 the case of 32-year-old NHS doctor Humayra Abedin, who was rescued from a forced marriage in December 2008 after being held captive by her parents since arriving in Bangladesh in August 2008 to visit them.[2]

A Home Office report on forced marriage was published in 2000 following the publicity surrounding the first three of these cases. As discussed in Chapter 2, this report distinguished between arranged marriage, prevalent in some minority communities in the UK and in countries across the world, and forced marriage: according to the report, arranged marriages are facilitated by family members with the consent of both partners, whereas forced marriage is a marriage where one or both parties fail to give consent, or only do so under duress (Uddin and Ahmed 2000, 10).

Since 1999, various policy initiatives have aimed to tackle this problem, leading to the development of a number of practical measures. However, policy responses need to be framed within an understanding of the diverse and interconnected influences on women's agency, and their experiences of coercion, if they are to address the problem of forced marriage effectively. The socio-cultural context plays a major role in determining not only the types of violence against women that are most common in different communities, but also shapes victims' experiences of violence against women and the measures that are most likely to be effective in addressing these abuses. It is in accordance with these concerns that the following sections examine the debates that gave rise to the Forced Marriage (Civil Protection) Act, outline the provisions of the Act, and lastly provide preliminary observations about the effectiveness of this initiative to date, with recommendations on how its implementation could be improved.

The criminalisation debate, the private member's bill and the merits of a civil remedy approach to forced marriage

Increasingly, the courts have taken an interest in accepting litigation in cases of specific forms of domestic violence, as in a recent case concerned with dowry ownership following the dissolution of a marriage. In 2000, Ms Verma, a bride from Bradford, successfully sued her husband's family for the return of a large dowry when the marriage ended after 70 days (Herbert 2000). In the case of forced marriage, case law indicates that the courts have acted on this issue for several decades now. For many decades after the 1938 case of *Hussein* (otherwise Blitz) *v Hussein*, the courts focused on questions of choice and whether the parties to the marriage had freely consented in the absence of duress defined as threats to life, limb, or liberty. However, after *Hirani v Hirani* (1983), the courts moved beyond a restrictive definition of duress as physical threats to accept that emotional pressure can also invalidate consent. In recent years, the English High Courts have also embraced the need to take steps to protect the interests of victims of forced marriage by declaring the nullity[3] of such marriages (rather than by instituting proceedings for divorce) without unnecessary delay or complexity of process. Emotionally, as well as legally, a declaration of nullity carries a very different meaning from divorce: a declaration of nullity recognises that the marriage was not legitimate, whereas divorce implies the reverse.

Although marriages contracted on the basis of coercion have long been illegal in the UK, in response to the publicity surrounding the high-profile cases discussed above, in September 2005 the Joint Foreign and Commonwealth Office and Home Office Forced Marriage Unit consulted on a proposal to create a specific criminal offence relating to forced marriage. They worked closely with leading academics and women's organisations (including Newham Asian Women's Project, Asha Projects, Ashiana, Rights of Women, Imkaan and Southall Black Sisters) to assess the viability of the proposed legislation (Gill 2006). However, many stakeholders regarded the proposed legislation as unlikely to be effective (Gill 2006).

One of the main arguments against the proposed legislation was that a criminal offence would not represent an effective deterrent, nor would it provide adequate protection for victims. Furthermore, by specifically addressing forced marriage, there would be a danger of fragmenting laws and policy measures aimed at tackling violence against women in its many guises. Those who argued against the measure contended that such legislation would add little to the existing body of law on murder, kidnapping and offences against the person (Imkaan 2007; Newham Asian Women's Project 2007). Opponents of the legislation also argued that, as it would be difficult to obtain sufficient evidence in individual cases to satisfy the criminal burden of proof required under the proposed law, the new law would have little to offer over existing legislation. Another concern was that this law would ultimately deter victims of forced marriage from seeking help from public authorities for fear that family members would be prosecuted as part of state-run legal proceedings over which they, as victims, would have very little control: any prosecution would be brought by the state in the *public* interest, rather than being initiated by the victim in his/her interest. Indeed, the literature demonstrates that women can perceive police intervention as counter-productive (Menjivar and Salcido 2002) in cases of violence against women, especially in minority communities.

Critics of the Bill stressed the need to create preventative and early-intervention mechanisms to combat forced marriage. As a result of this debate, in June 2006 the UK government decided not to introduce a forced marriage criminal statute. However, despite overwhelming support for this decision, a number of those consulted during this process, and some other relevant actors, continue to argue the case for criminalisation, believing that this will stop the practice or, at the very least, 'send a clear message' to potential perpetrators (Kite 2007).

In December 2006, Lord Lester of Herne Hill QC, in collaboration with Southall Black Sisters, proposed a Private Member's Bill that set out civil, rather than criminal, remedies under a stand-alone law to address forced marriage. The Bill attracted a wide range of supporters, including those who favoured criminalisation, in a coalition that Lord Lester referred to as the 'enlightened British Asians and other minorities' (Lester 2008). The proposed civil law promoted a more victim-centred approach than the criminal law proposal did as, under a civil bill, it is the victim who initiates legal action as opposed to the action being initiated by the state. The final draft of the Bill (January 2007) also allows for applications to be made not only by the victim (or potential victim) of a forced marriage but also by a friend or any other concerned person who has the permission of the court. This is a crucial, innovative feature as victims of forced marriage may not have access to a court.

Nevertheless, many women's organisations remained sceptical about the draft Bill because, in its original form, it failed to integrate the discourse of forced marriage into a wider discussion of violence against women, thereby reinforcing essentialist understandings of forced marriage as a cultural problem that, in turn, reinforce racist stereotypes (Imkaan 2007). These objections led to the January 2007 submission of an official critique of the draft Bill (sponsored by Imkaan, Newham Asian Women's Project, and the Equal Opportunities Commission). As the civil law relating to domestic violence in England and Wales is primarily contained in Part IV of the Family Law Act 1996, the critique highlighted the importance of establishing a civil response to forced marriage within this Act. The critique argued that, as the courts, police and family lawyers are already familiar with the workings of the Family Law Act in domestic abuse cases, incorporating forced marriage within the Family Law Act's remit would involve minimal disruption and costs: it would also help to ensure swift redress for victims. The proposal outlined in the critique was presented at a subsequent reading of the Bill in the House of Lords in January 2007.

The Forced Marriage (Civil Protection) Act 2007

On 26 July 2007, a restructured private member's bill received Royal Assent as the Forced Marriage (Civil Protection) Act within Part IV of the Family Law Act. Since 25 November 2008, family courts have been able to make Forced Marriage Protection Orders (FMPOs) to protect individuals from being forced into marriage. Thus, the Forced Marriage (Civil Protection) Act makes it possible for *potential* victims to make applications prior to a forced marriage taking place; this is critical, as previous legislation had ignored the importance of affording protections and remedies to prevent forced marriage in favour of dealing with cases after the fact. Those who fail to obey such orders may be found in contempt of court and sent to prison for up to two years.[4] The Forced Marriage (Civil Protection) Act expressly prohibits the practice, inducement, or aiding of forced marriage, which is defined as (a) forcing or attempting to force another person to enter into a marriage, or a purported marriage, without that other person's free and full consent, or (b) practising deception for the purpose of causing another person to enter into a marriage, or a purported marriage, without that other person's free and full consent. It provides powers to arrest and (when appropriate) to remand into custody those suspected of perpetrating the offence.

The civil remedies available under the Forced Marriage (Civil Protection) Act primarily focus on the protection of victims and the prevention of forced marriage, rather than on the punishment of perpetrators, though the Act does not preclude the possibility of a criminal prosecution: indeed, in certain instances, the public interest may require it. However, the Forced Marriage (Civil Protection) Act does not speak to the harm caused by the offence: it does not fully demonstrate why the criminal justice system should be interested in regulating or punishing forced marriage. Thus, while it offers the possibility of prosecutions in the public interest, it lays little ground for criminal cases to be brought. The focus on protection and prevention, rather than on prosecution, is the crucial distinction between the Forced Marriage (Civil Protection) Act and the criminal statute that was originally proposed.

The principal remedy under the Forced Marriage (Civil Protection) Act is the injunction: an order made by the court prohibiting certain acts that may lead to a forced marriage. Those in support of the Forced Marriage (Civil Protection) Act have argued that making injunctive relief available to (potential) victims is one of the most important and beneficial features of this measure as it enables them to attain swift and effective legal recourse before or after a forced marriage has taken place (Southall Black Sisters 2006). An added benefit that has been identified by victims and their advocates as particularly significant is that the victim often stands a greater chance of reconciling with his or her family (Newham Asian Women's Project 2007).

The limits of the current legal approaches to forced marriage

One of the drawbacks of the Forced Marriage (Civil Protection) Act is that it is geared towards a legalistic approach: the Act's focus on matters of law comes at the expense of recognising the subtleties of the socio-cultural practices and gendered experiences of coercion that underpin forced marriage. This problem needs to be understood in the context of the Labour government's focus on legal remedies in relation to the many different forms of violence against women: a focus that has resulted in a failure to adequately address the ways in which broader gender inequalities gives rise to, and legitimise, violence against women.

Through focusing on black and minority ethnic women, dominant media and policy discourses construct forced marriage as a cultural problem and a signifier of the difference (i.e., the lack of cohesion) between majority and minority ethnic communities in the UK. Not only does this elide the gendered nature of this harm (along with its connections to other forms of violence against women in both majority and minority communities), it has also enabled the Labour government to propose community cohesion as a solution to the problem of forced marriage. Recently, this translated into official condemnation of so-called 'single identity groups', and, despite a U-turn by the Labour government on the proposed withdrawal of funding from such groups (Wood 2009), the suspicion towards specialist services remains, and has strengthened in consequence of community cohesion agendas. Paradoxically, the construction of forced marriage as a cultural problem that denotes a lack of integration is part of a political framing that has come to threaten the existence of the very services capable of addressing the diverse forms of gendered violence occurring in the UK: specialist domestic violence services have been steadily eroded in the turn towards community cohesion, and their capacity for supporting victims from minority ethnic groups has been greatly reduced. As many of these organisations work under the assumption that violence against women is a gender-based, rather than a cultural issue, this has also served to undermine efforts to encourage more widespread engagement, especially on the part of the government, policy makers and frontline service providers, with this alternative understanding of the causes of forced marriage.

Public discourses on forced marriage contribute to the formulation and re-inscribing of specific British norms: the determination of a British 'we' necessarily entails judgements about those excluded from this identity. Public discussions about forced marriage provide British citizens with opportunities to contrast themselves with a non-British other living within Britain's national borders. The explicit subject of these discourses may be black and minority ethnic women and forced marriage, but the implicit frame of reference for normality in relation to issues concerning marriage derives from mainstream understandings of human rights, individual autonomy, bodily integrity, and women's equality. Accordingly, perceptions of forced marriage are concerned not only with 'them' (i.e. the backward minority other), but also with 'us' (i.e. progressive modern British individuals). As a result, British women are generally viewed as having autonomy, and their choices are seen as self-determined, while migrant/minority women are generally viewed as in need of protection. Thus, the politicisation of forced marriage as a cultural problem may contribute to political apathy towards other, more normalised forms of female oppression in the UK (see also Bredal in Chapter 4; Anitha and Gill, in Chapter 5).

The Labour government's narrow view of forced marriage as a cultural problem was revealed by its almost exclusive focus on policy initiatives to prevent the immigration of men suspected of being involved in forced marriages involving British women (Phillips and Dustin 2004; Hester et al. 2008). This is illustrated by the fact that the Community Liaison Unit, which was set up to tackle forced marriage, was initially based in the Foreign and Commonwealth Office (FCO), which previously had little experience in dealing with issues of gender-based/domestic violence. Although the Community Liaison Unit was relaunched in 2002 as a joint Home Office-FCO Forced Marriage Unit, it is still located in the FCO, rather than the Home Office, where cases of domestic violence are usually handled, reiterating the state's focus on immigration control rather than support for vulnerable women.

This situation is further compounded by the gender-neutral understanding of coercion employed in British law: the language of relevant legislation demonstrates that coercion is recognised as a possible factor in marriage for both men and women. While this is true, and statistics indicate that 15 per cent of callers to the FCO helpline are men (Foreign and Commonwealth Office 2010), this focus disregards both the fact that men and women tend to experience very different forms of duress as victims of forced marriage and the fact that men and women attempt to escape such oppressive situations in different ways. Not only do an overwhelming majority of reported cases of forced marriage in the UK involve women (FCO 2010), but, when men are victims of forced marriage, the implications of this 'victimhood' differ considerably.

Research on the experiences of marriage migrants from South Asia who survived domestic violence and insecure immigration status indicates that a significant number of women also experience abuse in relationships where it is the husband who has been pressurised into marriage, often in order to end his relationship with a woman his family perceived as unsuitable (Anitha, forthcoming). This research also documents that the consequences of such marriages were very different for the men, who often managed to continue their earlier relationships, benefited from the domestic labour and/or waged work undertaken by their wives, demanded sexual access to them, and, in many cases, also secured a dowry. For the women, the consequences of such marriages included neglect, abuse and eventual abandonment or exit from the abusive relationship, after which many of them faced deportation and/or destitution in consequence of the law on no recourse to public funds (Anitha, forthcoming).[5]

Although recent legislation recognises that victims of forced marriage are often deceived into the marriage, it is not clear whether the Forced Marriage (Civil Protection) Act will adequately address the deception practiced on consenting women in cases where it is the male spouse who has been coerced into marriage. If the law is invoked and such a marriage is nullified, the female spouse may face opprobrium for not 'making the marriage work' and/or threats of domestic violence, including, in extreme circumstances, the possibility of being murdered by her own family for returning home (i.e. to her country of origin) if she is unable to 'prove' domestic violence and, as a result, is deported under immigration law (Anitha, forthcoming). In such marriages, the legal option of exit via annulment that is available to male spouses may leave female marriage migrants with reduced options –

deportation to face abuse from their family for not making the marriage work (Anitha, forthcoming).

This disparity in experiences of forced marriage is caused by gender inequalities (including dowry costs) in consequence of which remaining in a marriage is particularly valued for women, as well as by the nature of British immigration policy; these inequalities are often structural and constitute violations of women's rights. Thus, a gender-neutral approach to the problem of forced marriage, especially one that focuses solely on the interests of the coerced party, is not necessarily conducive to achieving justice, which may involve a wider set of changes to both law and practice. Only a law that embraces an understanding of forced marriage that takes the gendered nature of this crime into account, and attempts to address the problem in a way that both recognises the impact of gender-based inequalities and prioritises safety and freedom from exploitation (including by providing practical and financial assistance), will properly and comprehensively address the issue.

The implementation of the Forced Marriage (Civil Protection) Act

At this early stage, it is difficult to assess effectively the impact of the Forced Marriage (Civil Protection) Act. However, it is possible to explore some preliminary trends through examining a policy paper (Prentice 2009) and other available information about the uptake of the statute prepared by the Ministry of Justice, though the absence of any other systematic review limits the scope and depth of this assessment. Table 6.1 details the number of applications made under the Forced Marriage (Civil Protection) Act and the total number of FMPOs in England and Wales during the period November 2008 to May 2010. Only one FMPO had been issued in Northern Ireland by June 2010.

Table 6.1 Applications made under the FM(CP)A, November 2008–May 2010

Total applications	Total orders	Applications where person to be protected is a child	Applicant in person with legal representation	Third -party applicants & others applications	Ex-parte applications	Power of arrest	No. of breaches
139	154	57	11	33	93	115	3

(Source: Ministry of Justice, personal communication, 2010)

Fifteen county courts have been designated to deal with applications for FMPOs, of which twelve are in areas that also have an accredited Specialist Domestic Violence Court (SDVC) system. Applications may also be heard at High Court level. The selection of the fifteen designated county courts was informed by the demographic characteristics of the catchment areas of the courts, with additional input from the Forced Marriage Unit (Prentice 2009, 15) about the likelihood of forced marriage cases arising within different jurisdictions. Detailed information about individual applications made and the FMPOs issued during this period has not been made public for fear of compromising confidentiality due to the small number of cases involved.

It is interesting to note that between November 2008 and October 2009, two thirds of the FMPOs were made in just three of the designated courts. Seven other courts made one to three orders. The remaining courts had issued no recorded FMPOs at the time the Ministry of Justice's review was published (Prentice 2009). It is not clear why the uptake of the Forced Marriage (Civil Protection) Act, and the use of FMPOs in particular, varied so widely across different regions during the first year of the statute's implementation. Possible contributory factors include lack of information about the Forced Marriage (Civil Protection) Act, the varying capacities of local agencies in terms of understanding and developing the requisite competencies to support victims and potential victims of forced marriage through the use of FMPOs (Kazimirski et al. 2009, 31–2), and fear of court involvement producing negative feeling on the part of already marginalised communities.

Just over one third of the applications made during the period in question related to children (i.e. persons aged seventeen or under). It has been argued that some local authorities have been slow to alter working methods, thereby hindering effective involvement in cases of potential forced marriage (Prentice 2009, 33): this reticence has been attributed to the lack of clarity regarding the boundaries between care proceedings under the Children's Act 1989, Court of Protection cases, and forced marriage cases (see also Gupta and Sapnara, in Chapter 7). It is possible that the jurisdictional differences in the uptake of the statute may, at least in part, be the result of different capabilities with regard to integrating child protection issues with assessments of the risk of forced marriage in individual cases. However, given that several orders were made outside the jurisdiction of the relevant courts (13 orders during the first year), it is also possible that cases from some of the under-represented areas were dealt with elsewhere.

A power of arrest was attached to most of the orders granted, enabling action to be taken to protect victims from a variety of coercive constraints and abuses. The low number of breaches of FMPOs could indicate the strength of the deterrent that the power of arrest represents. However, without additional information it is not possible to rule out other factors such as the reluctance to pursue one's family for a breach.

Interestingly, the number of FMPOs exceeded the number of applications: thus, in some cases, multiple FMPOs were made, presumably in order to ensure that the protections afforded to particularly vulnerable victims were suitably comprehensive. This hints at the proactive role of agencies in acting on behalf of (potential) victims of forced marriage. Indeed, one of the most significant findings of the Ministry of Justice review was that the third-party provision seems to have been well utilised. However, further information is not available about either the regional variation in the utilisation of the third-party provision or the nature of the agencies involved, though recent research has indicated that certain police forces have taken a lead in seeking FMPOs (Kazimirski et al. 2009; Prentice 2009). Third-party applications were conceived to enable action to be taken both to protect (potential) victims of forced marriage who are not in a position to act to secure protection and/or redress for themselves, and to minimise the risk of victims being ostracised by their families and the wider community for involving their families in court cases. However, concerns, which were originally raised during the consultation process on the Forced Marriage (Civil Protection) Act, that third-party applications may sometimes not be made in the best interests of (potential) victims remain unresolved, as no information about the circumstances of individual cases/FMPOs is currently available.

Kazimirski et al. (2009, 46) found that some statutory services routinely resorted to care orders or FMPOs – which they viewed as the sole indicator that they were 'taking a case seriously' – when encountering potential forced marriages, regardless of the circumstances of individual cases. Thus, instead of conducting a risk assessment in order to identify the needs of specific individuals, and then exploring which of the available support mechanisms might be most effectively employed in the case in question, many agencies were treating FMPOs as a first recourse, even when their own assessments suggested that statutory measures might seem 'heavy-handed' in relation to the level of risk (Kazimirski et al. 2009, 46). In the absence of measures or additional funds to strengthen non-statutory responses to forced marriage, the Forced Marriage (Civil Protection) Act may not represent an adequate or, in some cases, even appropriate tool for prevention or redress.

During parliamentary debates (HL Debates vol. 705, col. WA420, cited in Enright 2009: 344) it was suggested that the first year of the Forced Marriage (Civil Protection) Act would serve as a trial period, particularly with regard to the functioning of the provision for third party applications, following which the Labour government planned to run a two-part pilot scheme to monitor the 'open access' method for third party applications. The first part of the pilot was intended to focus on the work of a local authority: the second, on a domestic violence organisation. In early 2010, it was announced that another pilot project had been set up to assess their potential to act as Relevant Third Parties for the purposes of the Forced Marriage (Civil Protection) Act, and to explore the role of Independent Domestic Violence Advisers (IDVAs), including in relation to their involvement in SDVC systems (Reconstruct 2010, 6). A fourth project, involving consultations with the police to gauge support for the police acting as Relevant Third Parties (under the Forced Marriage [Civil Protection] Act) from 1 April 2010, was also planned (Reconstruct 2010, 6). However, following the change of government, it remains to be seen which, if any, of these schemes will be undertaken. Given the wider-than-anticipated use of FMPOs during the Forced Marriage (Civil Protection) Act's first year of implementation, there is an urgent need to examine the use of this statute, particularly with regard to the third-party provision, and its effectiveness from the perspective of the women (and men) whom it is intended to benefit.

Beyond the law: what can be done to address forced marriage in the UK?

The law is often perceived as an important means for transforming gender relations. It is an important instrumental and symbolic tool for changing entrenched attitudes and practices that contribute to the violation of women's rights, as well as a regulatory force for controlling people's behaviour. Feminist groups have sought recourse to the law to challenge socio-cultural and religious traditions that view women as subordinate and inferior to men; this is essential, as these values and traditions play a major role in rendering many gendered harms invisible. In terms of violence against women, the law has been invoked to control the behaviour of abusers, as well as to establish societal and cultural values that hold that violence against women, in all its forms, is unacceptable. That this turn to the law has required many a return visit, and has led to many unintended consequences, does not surprise legal scholars. As Romkens (2001) argues, in relation to using the law to effect social change, 'If we appeal to law, we sometimes call upon a Trojan horse: when we invite law in, law re-invites itself time and time again, but on its own terms and with its own agenda' (Romkens 2001, 290).

Laws cannot, in themselves, provide the progress towards social and cultural equality that is needed by feminists and other activists. The Labour government's preoccupation with legal solutions to the largely social problem of forced marriage was questioned by academics during a recent discussion in the black and minority ethnic sector (Home Affairs Select Committee Inquiry 2008). Many participants raised concerns that laws against forced marriage were being used to measure black and minority ethnic women's empowerment. They argued against this practice, noting that the mere passing of laws relating to forced marriage is not a satisfactory barometer for determining the actual occurrence of the offence. This is especially true when the fact that most countries have passed laws against this practice in response to international pressure, rather than as a result of a genuine commitment to women's rights, is taken into consideration (Park 2006).

The potential of the law to regulate and control the behaviour of individual perpetrators of gender-based violence is immense. However, research documents the fact that the workings of the law may also support gendered scripts of femininity that constitute the ideal victim and the 'real crime', even as laws are utilised to secure justice for individual women (Menon 2004; Carline 2005; Kapur 2005). Consequently, some feminist critical theorists have argued that the law is very much a two-edged sword for black and minority ethnic women: it can end up doing more harm than good (Gangoli 2007). According to these theorists, law is unlikely to deliver the outcomes that are needed because feminist objectives must be 'translated' into existing legal forms and concepts: these often do not take adequate account of the multiple and intersecting disadvantages that shape black and minority ethnic women's experiences. Moreover, once translated, these objectives may take on a life of their own because the next stage of trans-formation – from objective to law – is controlled, not by feminists, but by legal actors with their own agendas (Menon 2004).

One of the most important challenges facing those working to improve existing measures aimed at addressing forced marriage is the need to foster recognition that forced marriage is not gender-neutral and that it is fundamentally rooted in unequal power relationships between men and women. The case of Dr Abedin indicates that new, more complex narratives about violence against women need to be created in order to reflect the everyday experiences of victims, who cannot or will not always take the route of criminal prosecution in relation to gender-based violence, particularly when their parents are involved: when she was released into the care of the UK courts, Dr Abedin indicated that she did not wish for her parents to suffer any punishment for their actions towards her because she was their only child (Abedin 2008). The case highlights the fact that many woman's experiences do not fit neatly into legal categories; therefore, simplistically linking these categories with legal solutions is unlikely to give rise to effective mechanisms to address forced marriage (see also Hossain, in Chapter 10).

Efforts to encourage the creation and adoption of legal measures and policies that respond to the complexities of individual experiences of violence against women have repeatedly been undermined by what might be termed the 'implementation problem'. Rhode (1997, 16) has observed that 'once we pass a law or institute a policy, we often believe we've done our bit for women and move on to other issues'. Thus, in the words of Stanko, 'The most important part of any legislation is how decision makers put the provisions of the statutes into practice. Unfortunately, once legislation is passed, it is mistakenly credited with solving the problem' (1992, 165). Feminist law reform efforts have been particularly afflicted by these problems (Schneider 2000).

Judges in a number of recent forced marriage cases have identified another barrier to effective legal reform that applies particularly to civil remedies which, unlike criminal proceedings, are not undertaken by the state on behalf of the victim and therefore have to be paid for by the litigant. Recourse to civil law is expensive and, therefore, not available to all. Even when statutes such as the Forced Marriage (Civil Protection) Act are put into practice, recourse to the law for the purposes of seeking an annulment or injunction often depends on the availability of legal aid funds; this means that many female victims of forced marriage are not able to make use of the protections available under the Forced Marriage (Civil Protection) Act. Legal remedies should not be neglected but, for these to be effective, there is an urgent need for well-funded specialist organisations to help women navigate the legal system (Imkaan 2007).

A growing number of experts in the field of violence against women, including critics of the Labour government's approach to violence against women within black minority ethnic communities (Gangoli et al. 2006; Kelly 2006), look to social institutions (such as violence against women support groups, specialist refuges and outreach services) rather than the law to address the problem (Kelly 2006). The primary concern of these critics is the safety of abused women, rather than the prosecution of the offences committed against them: a priority that they hope will also be adopted by policy-makers. For this to happen, significant material resources would need be made available to aid women whether they choose to exit from abusive relationships or attempt to resolve their difficulties with their spouses and/or families. While appropriate sanctions are required to punish the perpetrators of gender-based violence, it is equally important that there be adequate support for victims. However, political and financial support has increasingly centred on law enforcement responses to forced marriage specifically and violence against women in general: this has resulted in a decrease in funding for specialist services. Giving the criminal justice system sole authority to define and manage this aspect of the politics of intimacy reflects short-term, crisis-orientated thinking, rather than an strong understanding of the problems underlying forced marriage and other forms of gender-based violence, particularly in black minority ethnic communities.

Conclusion

The binary understanding of consent and coercion in marriage that underlies the current criminal-justice-focused response to forced marriage cannot hope to embrace the range of constraints that women face in matters of marriage. Moreover, attempting to prevent forced marriages through injunctions and/or criminal proceedings must be understood as only part of the broader solution that is needed. Women's groups have long argued that not all women seek to leave abusive families and that an even smaller number want to initiate criminal (or even civil) proceedings against family members. Black feminists have articulated the need for a diverse range of responses to violence against women, including specialist outreach services, education and awareness-raising work in schools and in the community, welfare services and childcare facilities, and the provision of specialist refuge spaces. The recent legislative developments concerning forced marriage have not been accompanied by additional funding for these types of work. Anti-immigration rhetoric post-9/11 and post-7/7 has fostered essentialist policies and public discourses concerning violence against women, including forced marriage, within black minority ethnic communities: the consequent policy shift towards assimilation and community cohesion has led to a focus on misguided 'solutions' involving purely legal remedies, while the social remedies represented by specialist domestic violence services, many of which are facing mergers and closures, have been increasingly undervalued.

The authorities need to recognise that black minority ethnic women's experiences of violence, whether in the form of spousal abuse, forced marriage or 'honour'-based crimes, cannot be separated from other forms of violence against women (Gill 2009); neither can black minority ethnic women's experiences of coercion in matters of marriage be separated from their experiences within other structures of inequality. In working to address these so-called 'abuses of culture' (Dustin and Phillips 2008), it is vital to understand the specific socio-political contexts that underpin these practices. Simplistically positing that these forms of violence against women are culturally specific involves both a failure to recognise the links between different manifestations of violence against women, and a failure to recognise the racist and essentialist stereotypes that reinforce anti-immigrant policy responses to these problems (Anitha and Gill 2010; Bredal in Chapter 4; Dustin and Phillips 2008; Razack 2004; Wilson 2007).

Only by addressing these intersecting inequalities can an effective solution to the problem of violence against women be developed. In working to assist women facing the prospect of a forced marriage, there is an urgent need to abandon culturalist approaches in favour of conceptualising forced marriage as part of a wider problem of violence against women. In practical terms, this would require committing resources to preventative measures and financially securing specialist services. In exploring the promise and also the limits of both criminalisation of, and civil remedies for, forced marriage, it is important to recognise that these diverse types of responses need to be integrated, rather than applied in an either/or manner, if the state is to identify and punish forced marriage while simultaneously assisting victims (as opposed to further complicating their problems). Finding a long-term solution to forced marriage will require the state to implement measures that fully engage with issues of social justice and the socio-cultural values and practices that underlie and help to perpetuate all types of gender-based violence.

Notes

1 Cf. the UN Convention on Consent to Marriage, Minimum Age for Marriage and Registration of Marriages, Article 1; and the International Covenant on Civil and Political Rights ('No marriage shall be entered into without the free and full consent of the intending spouses'); and the Committee on the Elimination of Discrimination Against Women ('A woman's right to choose a spouse and enter freely into marriage is central to her life and her dignity and equality as a human being').

2 Although the Forced Marriage (Civil Protection) Act is not enforceable in Bangladesh, British lawyers (Anne Marie Hutchinson/Dawson Cornwell Solicitors) acting for Dr Abedin successfully worked with the authorities in Dhaka to ensure her release (in December 2008), despite the fact that she was not a UK citizen. Her family had duped her into returning to Bangladesh in August 2008 by claiming that her mother was seriously ill. They hid her passport and plane ticket, then held her captive for four months until she alerted her British Hindu boyfriend via email that she was in danger and was considering taking her own life. She had been subjected to physical violence and psychological abuse, and also denied contact with friends and lawyers. On her return to the UK (on 15 December 2008), her lawyers immediately appeared at the High Court in London to instigate nullity proceedings to void the marriage to which she had been subjected under coercion and duress in Dhaka (Blakely 2008).

3 See *NS v MI* [2006] EWHC 1646 (Fam) [2007] 1 FLR 444 (Nullity).

4 See forced marriage protection orders: http://www.hmcourtsservice.gov.uk/cms/14490.htm.

5 Women who come to the UK to join fiancés/husbands who are settled in the UK lose their right to remain in the UK, and therefore face deportation to their country of origin, if the relationship breaks down during the first two years; in the interim, they are barred from accessing public funds under the no recourse to public funds (NRPF) law. Under paragraph 289A of the Immigration Rules, known as the 'Domestic Violence Rule', if a woman is able to provide the requisite evidence that domestic violence was the cause of the marital breakdown, she can apply for indefinite leave to remain. However, while her application is being assessed, the NRPF clause stands. Therefore, benefits and public housing (such as refuges) are inaccessible to immigrant women unless they fall within a complex set of narrowly defined categories (Anitha 2010).

Cases cited

Hirani v Hirani [1983] 4 FLR 232

Hussein (Otherwise Blitz) v Hussein (1938)

KR [1999] 4 All ER 954. Available: http://webdb.lse.ac.uk/gender/Casefinallist.asp. Accessed 13 July 2008.

NS v MI [2006] EWHC 1646 (Fam) [2007] 1 FLR 444 (Nullity)

References

Abedin, H. (2008) 'Statement from Humayra Abedin', *Guardian*, 19 December http://www.guardian.co.uk/world/2008/dec/19/statement-nhs-doctor-abedin-forced-marriage (accessed 9 May 2009).

Anitha, S. (2010) 'No Recourse, No Support: State Policy and Practice Towards South Asian Women Facing Domestic Violence in England', *British Journal of Social Work*, vol. 40, no. 2, March.

Anitha, S. (forthcoming) 'Legislating Gender Inequalities: The Nature and Patterns of Domestic Violence Experienced by South Asian Women with Insecure Immigration Status in the UK', *Violence Against Women*.

Anitha, S. and A. Gill (2009) 'Coercion, Consent and the Forced Marriage Debate in the UK', *Feminist Legal Studies*, vol. 17, no. 2, June.

Blakely, R. (2008) '"Forced marriage" doctor, Humayra Abedin, freed by Bangladesh court', *The Times*, 15 December. http://www.timesonline.co.uk/ tol/news/uk/crime/article5340058.ece (accessed 30 April 2009).

Carline, A. (2005) 'Zoora Shah: An Unusual Woman', *Social and Legal Studies,* vol. 14, no. 2, June.

Coy, M., Kelly, L. and Foord, J. (2009) *Map of Gaps 2: The Postcode Lottery of Violence against Women Support Services in Britain,* End Violence Against Women and Equality and Human Rights Commission, London.

Dustin, M. and A. Phillips (2008) 'Whose Agenda Is It? Abuses of Women and Abuses of "Culture" in Britain', *Ethnicities,* vol. 8, no. 3, September.

Enright, M. (2009) 'Choice, Culture and the Politics of Belonging: The Emerging Law of Forced and Arranged Marriage', *Modern Law Review*, vol. 72, no. 3, May.

Foreign and Commonwealth Office (2010) *Victims of Forced Marriage,* Forced Marriage Unit, Home Office, London http://www.fco.gov.uk/en/travel-and-living-abroad/when-things-go-wrong/forced-marriage (accessed 8 June 2010).

Gangoli, G., Razack, A. and McCarry, M. (2006) *Forced Marriage and Domestic Violence Among South Asian Communities in North East England,* University of Bristol.

Gangoli, G. (2007) *Indian Feminisms: Campaigns Against Violence and Multiple Patriarchies,* Ashgate, Aldershot.

Hester, M., Chantler, K. and Gangoli, G. (2008) *Forced Marriage: The Risk Factors and the Effect of Raising the Minimum Age for a Sponsor, and of Leave to Enter the UK as a Spouse or Fiancé(e)*, University of Bristol, Bristol.

Gill, A. (2006) 'Patriarchal Violence in the Name of "Honour"', *International Journal of Criminal Justice Sciences*, vol. 1, no. 1, January.

Gill, A. (2009) '"Honour" Killings and the Quest for Justice in Black and Minority Ethnic Communities in the UK', *Criminal Justice Policy Review.* vol. 20, no. 4, January.

Hall, S. (1999) 'Life for "Honour" Killing of Pregnant Teenager by Mother and Brother', *Guardian*, 26 May. http://www.guardian.co.uk/uk_news/story/0,3604,299095,00.html (accessed 4 November 2008).

Herbert, I. (2000) 'Judge Tells Ex-husband's Family to Give Bride Back her Dowry of £40,000', *Independent*, 12 April.

Home Affairs Select Committee Inquiry (2008) *Domestic Violence, Forced Marriage and 'Honour'-based Violence*, House of Commons Select Committees Publications, London.

Imkaan (2007) *Forced Marriage Consultation Response to the Civil Protection Bill*, Imkaan, London.

Kapur, R. (2005) *Erotic Justice: Law and the New Politics of Post Colonialism*, Glass House Press, London.

Kazimirski, A., Keogh, P., Smith, R. and Gowland, S. (2009) *Forced Marriage: Prevalence and Service Response*, Natcen, London. http://www.education.gov.uk/research/data/uploadfiles/DCSF-RR128.pdf (accessed 20 June 2010).

Kelly, L. (2006) 'Why Violence Against Women is an Equalities Issue', keynote speech, Association of London Government, London, December.

Kite, M. (2007) 'Multi-culturalism Damages UK, says Cameron', *The Telegraph*, 28 January. http://www.telegraph.co.uk/news/uknews/1540790/Multi-culturalism-damages-UK-says-Cameron.html (accessed 11 November 2008).

Liberty (2005) *Liberty's Response to the Joint Home Office and Foreign Commonwealth Office Consultation on Forced Marriage*, Liberty, London.

Lester, A. (2008) 'Constitutional Safeguards for Human Rights', http://www.odysseustrust.org/lectures/285_Article_for_the_Legal_Democrat_on_Human_Rights_Act_FINAL.pdf (accessed 9 May 2009).

Menjivar, C. and Salcido, O. (2002) 'Immigrant Women and Domestic Violence: Common Experiences in Different Countries', *Gender and Society*, Vol. 6, No. 3, December.

Menon, N. (2004) *Recovering Subversion: Feminist Politics Beyond the Law*, University of Illinois Press, Chicago.

Newham Asian Women's Project (2007) *Forced Marriage Civil Protection Bill – Response to the Consultation on Amendments to Family Law Act*, Newham Asian Women's Project, London.

Park, A. (2006) '"Other Inhumane Acts": Forced Marriage, Girl Soldiers and the Special Court for Sierra Leone', *Social and Legal Studies*, vol. 15, no. 3, September.

Phillips, A. and Dustin, M. (2004) 'UK Initiatives on Forced Marriage: Regulation, Dialogue and Exit', *Political Studies*, vol. 52, no. 3, October.

Prentice, B. (2009) *One Year On: The Initial Impact of the Forced Marriage (Civil Protection) Act 2007 in Its First Year of Operation*, Ministry of Justice, London. http://www.justice.gov.uk/one-year-on-forced-marriage-act.pdf (accessed 13 January 2010).

Razack, S. (2004) 'Imperilled Muslim Women, Dangerous Muslim Men and Civilised Europeans: Legal and Social Responses to Forced Marriages', *Feminist Legal Studies*, vol. 12, no. 2, October.

Reconstruct (2010) 'Forced Marriage Act 2007: One Year On', Reconstruct, Uxbridge. http://www.hillingdon.gov.uk/media/pdf/f/7/forcedMarriageAct One Year OnJan10.pdf (accessed 20 June 2010).

Rhode, D. (1997) *Speaking of Sex: The Denial of Gender Inequality*, Harvard University Press, Cambridge, MA.

Romkens, R. (2001) 'Law as a Trojan Horse: Unintended Consequences of Rights-based Interventions to Support Battered Women', *Yale Journal of Law and Feminism*, vol. 13, 265–90.

Schneider, E. (2000) *Battered Women and Feminist Lawmaking*, Yale University Press, New Haven.

Southall Black Sisters (2006) *Forced Marriage Consultation Response to the Civil Protection Bill*, Southall Black Sisters, London.

Stanko, E. (1992) 'Domestic Violence', in G. Cordner and D. Hale (eds.), *What Works in Policing? Operations and Administration Examined*, Anderson Publishing, Cincinnati.

Uddin, P. and Ahmed, N. (2000) *A Choice by Right: The Report of the Working Group on Forced Marriage*, Home Office Communications Directorate, London.

Watt, N. (1999) 'Terror of Couple Fleeing a Forced Marriage', *Guardian*, 27 May.

Wilson, A. (2007) 'The Forced Marriage Debate and the British State', *Race and Class*, vol. 49, no. 1, July.

Wood, R. (2009) 'Government U-turn on "Single Identity Group" Funding', *Institute for Race Relations News*, 29 January. http://www.irr.org.uk/2009/january/bw000023.html (accessed 21 June 2010).

7
The law, the courts and their effectiveness

Teertha Gupta and Khatun Sapnara*

The enactment of the Forced Marriage (Civil Protection) Act 2007, which was added to Part IV of the Family Law Act 1996 (the existing legislation relating to domestic violence provisions in the family courts) was the culmination of a number of initiatives undertaken by the UK government. Key among these were the working group report *A Choice by Right*, which was published in 2000, and the December 2005 consultation on the possibility of criminalising forced marriage. The Forced Marriage (Civil Protection) Act came into effect on 25 November 2008 (for more on the consultations that preceded this statute and provisions of this Act, see Chapter 6).

In this chapter we examine the provisions of the Forced Marriage (Civil Protection) Act and other pre-existing legislation that has been utilised in cases of forced marriage, and make recommendations based on our experiences as practitioners. The first part of this chapter (on the Forced Marriage (Civil Protection) Act and the Family Law Act) outlines some of the ways in which the provisions of the Forced Marriage (Civil Protection) Act have helped to address victims' needs, while also noting the Act's short-comings and identifying alternative legal avenues of redress. We also examine the special provisions for children (i.e. persons aged 17 or under) who have experienced or who are at risk of experiencing forced marriage, discuss the adequacy of existing processes in relation to relevant case studies, identify areas of good practice, and provide recommendations for change. The second part discusses a hitherto less-explored aspect of forced marriage – nullity proceedings in forced marriage cases – to highlight their importance to

* We wish to thank the editors, Aisha K. Gill and Sundari Anitha, for their helpful comments and editorial suggestions during the preparation of this chapter.

victims, outlines the provisions in existing law on nullity, and assesses the effectiveness of these provisions in meeting the needs of survivors of forced marriage. The final section considers special measures that can be applied in cases of forced marriage and offers further guidelines for enhancing existing legal provisions.

The Forced Marriage (Civil Protection) Act and the Family Law Act

When the Forced Marriage (Civil Protection) Act came into force, it was envisaged that there would be between 5 and 50 applications a year under provisions designed to assist a 'person to be protected' (Ministry of Justice 2008, 36). In part, the Act was intended to have symbolic as much as practical force (i.e. a deterrent effect) in order to raise awareness. It was acknowledged that the nature of the communities that would be affected by the new legislation, with their close-knit ties and closed channels of communication, was such that the experiences of individual families involved in court processes pursuant to the Forced Marriage (Civil Protection) Act would be widely and rapidly disseminated amongst them.

However, a review of the Act after the first year of implementation revealed that it had been far more successful than envisaged, with family courts dealing with over 80 applications (Ministry of Justice 2009a). By the end of January 2010, the Ministry of Justice figures revealed, some 117 Forced Marriage Protection Orders had been made since November 2008 (Home Affairs Committee 2010, p. 54). As anticipated, applications were made by a range of litigants: victims (in person or through legal representatives), the police, local authorities, friends and families of victims, and voluntary sector organisations. During this period, Forced Marriage Protection Orders were made in almost every court designated to deal with applications under the Forced Marriage (Civil Protection) Act (a total of 15 across England and Wales, excluding the High Court). A number of applications were made by children (i.e. persons aged 17 or under) (Ministry of Justice 2009a, 19). The respondents to the applications, against whom orders were made, included brothers, sisters, mothers and fathers of victims.

The Forced Marriage (Civil Protection) Act was deliberately drafted to be applied very broadly in order to enable the courts to tailor orders to the circumstances of individual victims. Hence, the wording of the Forced Marriage (Civil Protection) Act excludes any express definition of forced marriage, but covers both the range of potential offences and the various ways in which people might be involved in planning and carrying out a forced marriage. The innovative provisions of the Forced Marriage (Civil Protection) Act have proved especially useful: these include the options for third parties to make applications on behalf of victims, for orders to be issued against third parties not named as respondents in the application (and, therefore, not formally party to the proceedings), and for measures to prevent extra-jurisdictional activities (i.e. taking the victim abroad for the purpose of carrying out a forced marriage).

Unlike the Family Law Act (1996), the Forced Marriage (Civil Protection) Act allows applications by third parties for non-molestation injunctions in domestic violence cases. This provision recognises that, in communities that practise forced marriage, there are situations in which an individual's actions are deemed to have brought a family, caste or entire community into disrepute; this allows perpetrators to recruit family members, friends and other members of the community to punish/control the individual concerned by coercing her (or, much more rarely, him) into a forced marriage in an effort to redeem the perceived shame. This recognition of the crucial role played by shame and honour is unique to the Forced Marriage (Civil Protection) Act (see Gill 2009).

The Act was intended to be a self-contained piece of legislation readily accessible to victims and persons acting on their behalf; therefore, the language is simple and the Act signposts all other available remedies. Designated county courts and the High Court have jurisdiction over cases pursuant to the Forced Marriage (Civil Protection) Act; it is a reflection of the seriousness with which the issue of forced marriage is regarded by government that proceedings pursuant to the Forced Marriage (Civil Protection) Act cannot be conducted in magistrates' courts (the lowest tier of family courts), even though courts at that level have an existing, wide-ranging jurisdiction in relation to family law that includes domestic violence.

Child protection

The law relating to the safeguarding of children is already well-developed. Cases of forced marriage involving children readily constitute 'significant harm' under the provisions of the Children Act 1989, so local authorities can intervene; indeed, under these provisions local authorities may seek an order to remove a child from the care of her parents and place her in foster care if they suspect that a forced marriage has been attempted or carried out. The

Forced Marriage (Civil Protection) Act enables local authorities to act with greater speed in securing protection for potential victims of forced marriage than previous legislation did. However, a child at risk of forced marriage is also frequently subject to other forms of harm, such as excessive chastisement or violence from parents, or failures on the part of parents to ensure adequate school attendance.

A significant challenge for both practitioners and the judiciary is to identify and protect potential victims, ideally through preventative action, in cases that are not identified as forced marriage but which nonetheless bear its characteristics. A large number of cases occur in the context of public law proceedings where a child may already be beyond parental control or where poor parenting is evident. Cases may also come to light in the private law arena when parents bring cases concerning conflicts about arrangements for the future welfare of a child, including when, where and to whom the child will be married. In such cases, issues of forced marriage may not be obvious; however, where recognised indicators of risk are present, these should be carefully considered by trained professionals. For instance, if a young girl says that her family is going to take her to Bangladesh and she fears that they may settle there and not return to the UK, then that can, to some extent, be regarded as a legitimate exercise of parental responsibility enshrined in law pursuant to Section 4 of the Children Act 1989 and not necessarily an issue in which the court should intervene. However, if, for example, hypothetically speaking the child says that she does not want to go, but that she is being told that she must because her grandmother is unwell, *and* if there is evidence that older siblings have previously been married whilst on 'holiday', then a professional alert to the features of forced marriage would likely identify the risk of a forced marriage and pursue the case further. However, this level of insight can only be achieved through experience in the long term, and training in the short to medium term of all professionals involved in the family justice system and in child protection. Early-stage information-sharing between the various professional disciplines is essential as a child may, for example, make such disclosures to a schoolteacher: it is vital that this information is passed on to the relevant authorities.

Public law proceedings pursuant to Section 31 of the Children Act 1989 (which asserts a statutory emphasis on working in partnership with families) and initiatives such as the Public Law Outline (a protocol requiring pre-action steps and evidence gathering) often mean that court applications/proceedings are delayed: thus, in such cases, the urgent nature of forced marriage is often ignored in practice. However, under the provisions of the Forced Marriage (Civil Protection) Act, there is nothing to prevent local authorities from obtaining the court's leave to make an emergency third-party application on behalf of the victim. Moreover, on 1 November 2009, it was announced that local authorities would be given 'relevant third party' status (pursuant to Section 63C [2] [b]), enabling applications to be made without the need to obtain leave of the court (Ministry of Justice 2009b). In practice, both applications for leave and applications for protection orders are heard at the same time; this prevents delays in securing urgent protection for victims. Thus, the Forced Marriage (Civil Protection) Act provides avenues for ensuring that the delays that are often contingent on applications made under other, relevant laws can be avoided. While the provisions of the Act enable timely applications to be made for Forced Marriage Protection Orders and other proceedings with regard to child protection, the complexities inherent in cases of forced marriage, in which the victim is usually expected to make claims against family members, can make legal recourse far from straightforward.

Victim credibility and legal support

Victims of forced marriage are, almost without exception, of limited means and, thus, are typically recipients of public funding for the purposes of litigation. This is not a particularly lucrative area of legal practice but, because of the priority given by the previous Labour government to domestic violence in general, public funding of forced marriage and domestic violence cases has been safeguarded at a time of considerable budgetary constraints on the public funding body (the Legal Services Commission) and publicly funded family law work in general. Such safeguards are essential in order to ensure that the Forced Marriage (Civil Protection) Act is effective.

Nevertheless, because of its low profile, domestic violence and forced marriage work is frequently undertaken by relatively junior solicitors and members of the bar. This often has significant implications for the effective representation of victims. For example, initial applications are made often on an emergency *ex parte* basis, so it is imperative that pleas setting out the factual histories that support applications are accurately and carefully drafted. Cases often hinge on particular understandings of victim credibility; these do not necessarily take into account the complexities of forced marriage and, without careful preparation by a qualified *and* experienced professional, a victim's subjective account of her experiences can collapse under cross-examination (for a discussion of the concept of victim credibility in different contexts, see Ellison and Munro 2010; Sweeney 2009; Balzani in Chapter 9). Perceptions of a victim's credibility can fundamentally affect the level of service she receives from the police, social services, lawyers and the courts. Victims are usually young and/or vulnerable adults. Moreover, sometimes forced marriage occurs in families that are otherwise law-abiding and that have demonstrated love and appropriate care for the victim during childhood. Thus, it is unsurprising that during the litigation process victims often present as being heavily conflicted and reluctant since they are torn between wanting protection for themselves and worrying about their parents' 'honour'; as such, they often attempt to limit confrontational measures. For example, when Dr Humayra Abedin, who was imprisoned and drugged by her parents in order to coerce her into a marriage, returned to the UK after a Bangladeshi court order was issued, she announced that she did not want to pursue any charges against her family, whom she still professed loved her; this decision was widely criticised in the tabloid press (Baig 2008; see Hossain in Chapter 10). Such contradictory impulses may manifest themselves in victims failing to give a full account of the family's abusive conduct and attempting to minimise family members' culpability; for example, a victim may argue that her parents are acting out of community and family pressures (see Chapter 10). If one considers the internal reservoir of courage and resilience that a victim must draw upon when taking her family to court, it is unsurprising that many victims are not stereotypically passive or weak despite the fact that they are all too frequently represented as such in media and policy discourses on forced marriage (Razack 2004).

Victims and potential victims often seek to balance complex and contradictory needs (Anitha and Gill 2009) by seeking protection from a forced marriage while also attempting to preserve relationships with their families and keep open channels of communication to aid the possibility of future reconciliation; in doing so, a victim may even undermine court orders and other protective frameworks (for example, by breaching the conditions of the arrangements put in place for contact with the family pursuant to a court order). Such exercises of an individual woman's agency may be seen to damage her credibility as these contradictory impulses are not always understood within the binary conception of victimhood and agency that characterises current understandings of forced marriage.

In its recent review of the Forced Marriage (Civil Protection) Act's effectiveness during its first year of implementation, the Ministry of Justice

(2009a) made positive assessments of the capacity and readiness of agencies to act in order to protect (potential) victims of forced marriage. Training and guidelines have been provided to facilitate the work of a number of agencies, particularly those that plan to make use of the third-party provision. For example, the Judicial Studies Board, which is responsible for the training of county court judges, has provided training for new and existing judges. However, the Judicial Studies Board's training of judges has been organised in such a way that it will take at least three years for all the relevant judges to receive appropriate training, though written material on the implementation of the Act is readily available to mitigate this problem. Existing guidelines for police, education, social services and healthcare agencies have been placed on a statutory footing. They have also been revised and condensed into one document: *Multi-agency Practice Guidelines: Handling Cases of Forced Marriage* (Stobart 2009).

The complexity of forced marriage cases means that those working in the field need a comprehensive awareness of both the nuances of the types of evidence that are routinely presented and the interface of forced marriage with other areas of law, such as public and international law. For instance, as noted above, forced marriage work is often carried out by relatively junior lawyers, who often lack the experience and expert knowledge needed to decide whether or not to invoke other family law provisions. Forced marriage cases sometimes operate on the cusp of private and public law proceedings, which means that proactive measures (such as making an interim care order for a child or even making the child a Ward of Court) are not always taken. However, without these measures, it is often impossible to afford (potential) victims adequate protection. Additionally, many professionals remain unaware of the existence of good practice guidelines, while others have received little or no in-depth training. This leads to situations in which cases are not handled properly and abuses go undetected. For instance, in one recent case Khatun Sapnara dealt with, the young victim was seen in her home on the day of her forced marriage, which took the form of a Muslim Nikkah ceremony and, thus, was not binding under English law. The victim was interviewed by police in her bedroom, while her new husband hid in the loft and family members hovered outside the door, which was only partially closed. Unsurprisingly, the victim failed to admit to any impropriety regarding the marriage; instead, she suggested that she was happy and had consented to it. The senior officer in the case, who had specific responsibility in the local police force for domestic violence and forced marriage, was unaware of the existence of guidelines which set out, *inter alia*, both the need for the alleged victim to be interviewed in a private, safe place and the importance of exploring the pressures in the family home that might inhibit free and full disclosure of complaints.

Forced marriage and nullity proceedings

The first part of this chapter focused on measures to prevent forced marriage rather than remedy forced marriages that have already taken place. In this section, we assess the importance of nullity proceedings, which are designed 'to restore the situation that would have existed if the act had not been committed' (Ferstman 2010). The grounds for divorcing a person and establishing that the marriage has broken down 'irretrievably' are set out in Section 1 of the Matrimonial Causes Act 1973: adultery, unreasonable behaviour, two years' separation, five years' separation, and desertion. However, the preferred route for many victims of forced marriage is not divorce, with its attendant social stigma (and *de facto* legitimising of the marriage) but rather the simpler route of seeking a declaration of nullity.

Nullity provisions

Whereas protective relief is available from Family Division judges in their role as Court of Protection judges, the route for obtaining a nullity is the Matrimonial Causes Act (MCA) 1973. Under the MCA, a marriage can be rendered void, if it is not automatically deemed void from the start (*ab initio*), because it is invalid for a variety of straightforward reasons: for example, if the spouses are siblings, are already married, or are under sixteen and have married without their parents' consent.[1] However, the most simple and straightforward route for nullifying a forced marriage is by having it declared as null on the grounds of duress, pursuant to 12(c) of the MCA,[2] on the grounds:

> a) that either party to the marriage did not validly consent to it, whether in consequence of duress, mistake, unsoundness of mind or otherwise; that at the time of the marriage either party, though capable of giving valid consent, was suffering (whether continuously or intermittently) from mental disorder within the meaning of the Mental Health Act 1983 of such a kind or to such an extent as to be unfitted for marriage;

A full analysis of the procedure for obtaining nullity on the grounds of duress has been provided by Mr Justice Munby in *NS v MI* (Nullity) (2006) EWHC

1646 (Fam) [2007] 1 FLR 444 and also in an article in March 2006's edition of *International Family Law* [2006] IFL 20. [3] Nullity proceedings can be commenced quickly using the emergency procedure in the High Court (Family Division):[4] this also allows the victim's address to be kept secret,[5] and enables injunctive relief to be obtained for the duration of the proceedings or beyond, if necessary. During the proceedings and at the final hearing, the court is more likely to be sensitive to cultural differences and alive to the need for heightened security if the victim's fears are set out clearly to the judge.[6]

The burden of proof in nullity proceedings

In nullity proceedings, the victim bears the burden of proof. Usually, this involves the victim acting as a witness by giving oral evidence and being cross-examined by the respondent's counsel. It cannot be overstated how difficult victims find this process. Moreover, victims of forced marriage are often obliged to prove a negative: that they did not consent to the marriage. This is not easy when evidence (such as a bride crying at her wedding) can be interpreted in ways that do not imply lack of consent or consent given under duress (many brides are overwhelmed by the occasion and cry at their weddings out of joy). Furthermore, it can be difficult to find witnesses willing to speak in support of the petitioner because of community sanctions against disclosure of any type of domestic violence or abuse (Gill 2004).

However, in some cases (though these are relatively rare), victims are openly angry, humiliated by having been made to go through with a marriage that they did not consent to. These individuals, such as the petitioner in *SH v NB (MARRIAGE: CONSENT)* [2009], positively look forward to the nullity process and the prospect of setting the record straight. In one case where the victim was represented by Teertha Gupta, she requested that screens be used in the courtroom not because she felt intimidated by the respondent, but because she felt that she would not be able to control her anger if she were to see him.

One misconception that is common to many victims is worth exploring. Many victims believe that a religious wedding in England automatically equates to a civil ceremony; this is not so, although many religious institutions conduct the signing of the civil register aspect of a marriage at the end of the religious ceremony. Thus, many victims mistakenly believe that they require a nullity when, in fact, in law no recognisable marriage has taken place.

The standard of proof necessary for the successful prosecution of nullity proceedings in forced marriage cases involves the normal, civil balance of probabilities: evidence of duress must be as clear and cogent as possible, as Mr Justice Munby pointed out in *NS v MI* (*supra* para. 33 and 36). This judgment reiterated that the ambit of coercion went beyond the exercise of physical force to include

> Importunity or threats, such as the testator has not the courage to resist, moral command asserted and yielded to for the sake of peace and quiet, or of escaping from distress of mind or social discomfort, these, if carried to a degree in which the free play of the testator's judgment, discretion or wishes, is overborne, will constitute undue influence, though no force is either used or threatened.

This judgment also sought to distinguish between pressure and coercion, by no means an easy distinction to make: 'In a word, a testator may be led but not driven; and his will must be the offspring of his own volition, and not the record of someone else's.' However, this judgment also recognised the difficulties associated with nullity proceedings:

> the court must be careful to ensure, particularly perhaps where a nullity suit is undefended, that a proper case is being put forward and not one contrived to enable a spouse to escape from a perfectly lawful and proper marriage which has turned out to be irksome.

This public policy approach underpins the law regarding nullity applications in cases of forced marriage. Even if the respondent does not attend the final hearing and does not formally oppose the application, oral evidence from the petitioner is still required (albeit in truncated form) so that the judge may question the victim to satisfy himself or herself that the fact that the marriage was conducted under duress has been established. The problem is that if a respondent later claims that (s)he was not served properly, or that there was some other procedural unfairness in the way proceedings were conducted, the matter would have to be restored and consideration would need to be given to whether the Queen's Proctor should be brought in to assist the court.[7] This could result in the nullity declaration being rescinded.

It worth noting that the test when attempting to prove duress is a subjective one: namely, whether the victim can prove that she did not consent to her marriage. When a petitioner is confronted by evidence (such as a video of the wedding in which she seems to be a smiling, willing participant) that would lead most outsiders to believe that the marriage was consensual, often the victim's testimony about her experiences of these events and her reasons for appearing to consent is the only available evidence of duress. Similarly, when actions can be interpreted in different ways, the victim's testimony is vital for establishing their meaning; for example, only a bride can say whether her tears on her wedding day were ones of sorrow or of joy. As much of the evidence presented in forced marriage cases is contradictory and/or subjective, any corroborative evidence of non-consent can prove crucial. Evidence of the exact circumstances that led to the victim 'consenting' to the wedding should take precedence in these circumstances, as these may be more revealing of the true nature of the situation.

Lack of consent on the grounds of unsoundness of mind

Lack of consent on the grounds of 'unsoundness of mind' is a further factor which has been coming to the fore in recent years, following a number of cases in which there is a suspicion that parents have 'married off' adult children with severe learning disabilities in order to receive assistance in caring for them (Valios 2008). In other countries this is a common and accepted way of dealing with the problem of arranging care for adult males with learning disabilities. The crucial issues in such cases are the domicile of the parties to the marriage, the place where the marriage took place, and the issue of whether or not the alleged victim is able to understand the marital contract. Examples of the fast-evolving restatement of the law in this area can be found in the case of *City Of Westminster v IC (By His Friend The Official Solicitor) and KC and NN* [2008]. The latter involved the 'telephonic marriage' (IC was married over the telephone: he was in England and his bride [NK] was in Bangladesh during the ceremony) of an incapable adult (in this case a male). An excerpt (paragraph 32) from the judgment handed down by Lord Justice Thorpe provides a snapshot of the key issues in the case:

> In the present case it is common ground that IC lacks the capacity to marry in English law ... There is much expert evidence to suggest that the marriage which his parents have arranged for him is potentially highly injurious. He has not the capacity to understand the introduction of NK into his life and that introduction would be likely to destroy his equilibrium or destabilise his emotional state. Physical intimacy is an ordinary consequence of the celebration of a marriage. Were IC's parents to permit or encourage sexual intercourse between IC and NK, NK would be guilty of the crime of rape under the provisions of the Sexual Offences Act 2003. Physical intimacy that stops short of penetrative sex would constitute the crime of indecent assault under that statute.

The court exercised its duty to protect IC, a vulnerable adult, through refusing to recognise the marriage in this and through similar means in other cases involving the marriage of vulnerable adults with learning difficulties. [8]

A judicial assessment of whether an individual understands the marital contract must include a test of the individual's capacity to enter into sexual relations in view of the Sexual Offences Act 2003. If a victim is incapable of understanding what sexual intercourse is and what it is likely to result in, then it is likely that the person will not understand what a marriage is and, thus, any 'consent' would be void under Section 12(c) of the MCA. Moving forwards, there is a pressing need to identify a mechanism that will ensure that all (potential) victims come to the attention of the courts in the first place; in these cases, it will rarely be the victims who make the necessary legal applications as it is likely that their functioning will be too impaired for them to be able to litigate on the subject. Local authorities may initiate proceedings, but, in practice, it is often down to the victim's Official Solicitor to decide whether an application is necessary.

Recommendations

Before the Forced Marriage (Civil Protection) Act was enacted, a central difficulty in nullity applications revolved around the fact that, as set out in Section 13(2)(a) of the MCA, the petition either had be issued within three years of the marriage being conducted or permission for a 'late' petition had to be granted. In relation to the latter, a petitioner could only apply for late permission on the grounds that he or she suffered from a formally diagnosed mental disorder and, thus, that the circumstances of the case justified the lateness of the petition. This meant that, prior to the enactment of the Forced Marriage (Civil Protection) Act, victims were unable to seek a nullity if they had allowed three years to elapse before they sought the decree. The fact that a marriage, however legally void, continues until it has been *declared* void (i.e. it cannot declared void *ab initio* but only from the date of the declaration of nullity) was raised in the recent case of *SH v NB* (2009). As discussed above, the judge held that the first marriage of the victim, who was aged 16 and one day at the time and had been forced into a marriage against her will, was not recognised because the same rules of consent apply in both the UK and Pakistan: in both countries, the marriage could be construed as a forced marriage. After hearing extensive oral evidence, Mr Justice Moylan found that the victim's second civil marriage, which took place in England a few years later and involved a different man, was not bigamous:

The declaration made in [City of Westminster v. IC [2008] 2 FLR 267] was simply that the marriage was not recognised as a valid marriage in this jurisdiction. Although the facts of that case were very different to the facts in the present case, in my judgment a declaration to that effect provides a far more appropriate and just remedy in the circumstances of the present case to that potentially provided by a decree pursuant to the Matrimonial Causes Act 1973 … On my findings, a lawful marriage did not take place under Pakistani law. It was invalid. In my view, in the circumstances of this case, there is no justification for the marriage being invested under English law with any greater status than it would be accorded under Pakistani law. Accordingly, to answer the issues referred to above:

(i)   the effect of the lack of consent is that the marriage is invalid;
(ii) the appropriate remedy is to grant a declaration that there is no marriage between the Petitioner and the Respondent which is entitled to recognition as a valid marriage in England and Wales.

The procedural route by which this is to be achieved is for the Respondent to issue an originating summons seeking a declaration to that effect.

This case established a precedent and procedure for seeking a judicial declaration, three or more years on, that a forced marriage conducted outside the UK is not recognised as a valid marriage in the UK. Prior to this, nullity on the grounds of duress (issued within three years of the marriage) was the only relief available and it did not result in a decision that the marriage had never legitimately taken place but, rather, that it would be void only from the date of the nullity declaration.

Special measures and guidelines for change

The insertion of the Forced Marriage (Civil Protection) Act into existing legislation to tackle domestic violence firmly placed forced marriage within the scope of the family justice system. Our involvement in discussions during the pivotal second reading of the Private Member's Bill in the House of Lords, when the decision was made to insert the Forced Marriage (Civil Protection) Act into the Family Law Act, provided us with a number of insights into the process that led to the enactment of the Forced Marriage (Civil Protection) Act. Previously, when we responded on behalf of the Family Law Bar Association to the 2005 consultation on the possible criminalisation of forced marriage, we suggested that the flexibility afforded by the family courts to provide remedies tailored to individual cases was invaluable and would afford greater protection to victims than criminalisation, as cases would then need to be heard in the criminal courts. As we argued, protection would be made more attainable as a result of applying the standard of proof required in the family courts (i.e. 'the balance of probabilities'), which is less onerous than the criminal standard of 'beyond reasonable doubt'.

We also suggested that, in our experience, the overwhelming majority of victims were reluctant litigants who did not want their families prosecuted in the criminal courts and possibly even imprisoned. Instead, while they wanted protection against being forced into marriage and the option to dissolve/ nullify a forced marriage that had already taken place, they also wanted to retain or rebuild relations with their families. It is widely recognised that fear of estrangement from family and social isolation as a result of transgressing against accepted social norms prevents many young people from disclosing abuse or taking legal action against their families. The Forced Marriage (Civil Protection) Act contains specific provisions that take these concerns into account; it therefore enables victims to obtain protection when they might otherwise have been unwilling to do so.

As with other domestic violence legislation, the Forced Marriage (Civil Protection) Act enables the family courts to accept undertakings from respondents, where appropriate. Undertakings can be drafted in the same terms as Forced Marriage Protection Orders; they require respondents to carry out, or refrain from carrying out, certain acts. Breach of undertakings and breach of orders invoke the same enforcement proceedings. The respondent is required to sign the undertakings on a prescribed form and is warned that if the court is satisfied of any breach to the requisite criminal standard of proof (i.e. beyond reasonable doubt), then the court has the power to impose a fine and or imprisonment for up to two years. To issue such orders, the court has to be satisfied that the risk of a forced marriage exists or that one has already taken place. Therefore, either the respondent has to make admissions in relation to this or there has to have been a finding of fact following a contested hearing. In giving an undertaking, the respondent makes no admission of any wrongdoing, but promises not to engage in the specified acts in future. This facility has particular importance in forced marriage cases. It affords the family a means of saving face/honour and minimising shame, whilst ensuring that the victim is protected. However, the added protection of a power of arrest cannot be attached to an undertaking, though it can be attached to an order.

Whilst the availability of undertakings may help some victims to avoid what they perceive as a confrontational step (i.e. taking their family to court), difficulties may arise if the victim and the legal advocate, or the family court, disagree over the level of risk involved and, thus, there are fears that an undertaking may not provide sufficient protection to the (potential) victim. In some cases, victims may be advised not to accept an undertaking and, instead, to press for an order with a power of arrest; alternatively, the court may decide that, given the circumstances of the case, it cannot accept undertakings. The court may exercise its own discretion in this regard, irrespective of the wishes of the person to be protected.

An examination of the Forced Marriage Protection Orders that were granted during the first year of the Forced Marriage (Civil Protection) Act's operation reveals that most of the orders had a power of arrest attached to them and that the court accepted only one undertaking (Ministry of Justice 2009a). As orders with a power of arrest attached provide a higher level of protection for the victims, this may indicate that the courts have a solid understanding of the substantial risks associated with forced marriage. As more women initiate proceedings of their own accord, we may well observe changes in the use of undertakings, as women exercise their agency to utilise the statute in a way that best meets their needs.

Another issue that needs to be addressed is that of special measures. These can be put in place to protect the alleged victim (who is deemed a vulnerable witness) whilst she is giving evidence (for example, through the use of a live video link or a screen in the courtroom to prevent her from having to see the alleged perpetrators). When the Forced Marriage (Civil Protection) Act was drafted, it was anticipated that there would be a greater-than-usual need for special measures in forced marriage cases. However, unlike Crown Courts, many of the family courts designated to hear forced marriage cases do not have the facilities to provide adequate protection via special measures. For instance, many of these courts do not have enough space for a victim to be seated in a separate area whilst discussing the case with her advocate or waiting for the case to be heard. In some cases, this has led to confrontations between victims and respondents, and/or intimidation of victims by respondents, in common areas of the court; the risk of such problems increases when the respondent is accompanied by a number of supporters hostile to the victim. Frequently, the victim attends court on her own or is left with a representative from her solicitor's office while her advocate engages in negotiations with the respondents or their legal representatives; therefore, confrontations of this type can be particularly unpleasant and threatening for the victim. Similarly, some court buildings do not have a separate entrance that the victim may use, so arrangements must be made to ensure that the victim's arrival and departure from court are timed so that she does not encounter the respondents.

In cases involving allegations of forced marriage, the courts have increasingly directed that evidence be filed in the form of a report from a cultural/religious expert engaged to assist in the decision-making process. However, there is no standard requirement regarding the qualifications, expertise and impartiality of some of the professionals who undertake work of this type for the family courts. A system of accreditation needs to be developed in order to ensure the evidential value of such 'expert' opinion.

It is generally recognised that passing legislation is not, in itself, sufficient to address the problem of forced marriage. Victims require holistic support, including help with matters such as securing legal assistance, welfare benefits, counselling, education (for instance, so that they can learn English), housing, and resolving issues relating to their immigration status. The services provided by community and voluntary sector agencies in co-ordinating all these services and advocating on behalf of victims are indispensible (Khanum 2008).

Looking to the future, while the law in this area is evolving rapidly, there is still some way to go. Victims need to know that they should seek a nullity or a declaration of invalidity as soon as they are practically able to so, otherwise they risk hindering their chances to free themselves from the marriages they have been forced into. Moreover, few victims are aware that the courts have started to provide a sensitive, swift approach to dealing with forced marriage cases and, thus, many who would benefit from this legislation may mistakenly believe that pursuing redress through the courts requires a clear-cut choice between their own interests and those of their family. It is therefore likely that if victims were more aware of the provisions of the Forced Marriage (Civil Protection) Act that are specifically designed to deal with such emotional conflicts, more would be willing to act in order to free themselves from forced marriages. At present, the details of the Act are known to only a few specialist practitioners, but it is hoped that, over the coming years, there will be better training for professionals (for instance, via the Judicial Studies Board programme of training in the Act for judges) and a more widespread, general awareness and utilisation of this statute. This collection aims to contribute to this process of dissemination.

Conclusion

We do not labour under any illusions that the remedies available in law for victims of forced marriage are, in themselves, sufficient to address the serious issues and challenges raised by actual or threatened forced marriage. Our experience resonates with that of other practitioners with regard to the need for

(1) the need for a holistic approach to the problem in terms of increasing awareness,

(2) the need for education and training of practitioners, the judiciary, and other professionals working in the legal arena and communities alike; and

(3) the need for funding of community and voluntary sector organisations, to whom victims often turn in the first instance for advice, support and assistance.

However, the introduction of the Forced Marriage (Civil Protection) Act and the development of the law relating to forced marriage by the family courts have produced positive results. There are now a number of effective measures for addressing the problems faced by victims and providing them with protection and redress.

Notes

1   See The Marriage (Prohibited Degrees of Relationship) Act 1986 and the Matrimonial Causes Act 1973, Section 11.

2   The procedure for petitioning for nullity is set out in the Family Proceedings Rules 2.1–2.51. On 21 October 2008, *The Times* reported on an application of this type: 'A woman who went to India for the funeral of her husband was kidnapped by his family and forced to marry her father-in-law's nephew, a High Court judge was told today. The 29-year-old Sikh was allegedly told she would be killed if she didn't wed the 27-year-old groom, whom she eventually fled from and returned to the UK. Today Mrs Justice Parker ordered that the marriage – which came two-and-a-half weeks after the death of the first husband – should be annulled because it was forced on the woman. [The judge] said the wife had told her that in the Punjab she had been given sedative pills by her husband's family and then injected with drugs when they believed she was not taking them. Her father-in-law continued to put pressure on her with implied and direct threats.'

3   Note that children born of a marriage before it has been rendered void are treated as legitimate for all purposes, and the first spouse is presumed to be their natural

parent: this is because the marriage is not void *ab initio*, but only after the decree is made (Legitimacy Act 1976 Section 1 [1]-[2]). This is why nullity provisions are of significant concern to victims who have survived a forced marriage and also why a nullity application may only be issued many years after the marriage.

4   This route was recommended by Mr Justice Coleridge in *P v R (Forced Marriage: Annulment: Procedure)* [2003].

5   The Family Proceedings Rules 1991, Rule 2.3.

6   See the dicta of Mrs Justice Macur in *RE S (Practice: Muslim Women Giving Evidence)* [2007] 2 FLR 461 and the case *SH v NB*, where screens and a separate room were used in order to ensure that the judge was able to obtain oral evidence from a reluctant witness.

7   For an example, please see *Kaur v Singh (CA)* 1972. The Queen's Proctor is a barrister who is instructed by the state to assist the court in certain, rare types of family cases.

8   Similar issues were addressed in the following cases: *Sheffield City Council v E and S* (2005) and *Re: M and B and A and S* (2005).

Cases cited

NS v MI (Nullity) (2006) EWHC 1646 (Fam) [2007] 1 FLR 444

International Family Law [2006] IFL 20.

SH v NB (MARRIAGE: CONSENT) [2009] EWHC 3274 (Fam) [2010] 1 FLR 1927

City of Westminster v IC (By His Friend The Official Solicitor) and KC and NN [2008] 2 FLR 267).

P v R (Forced Marriage: Annulment: Procedure) [2003] 1 FLR 661.

Re S (Practice: Muslim Women Giving Evidence) [2007] 2 FLR 461

Kaur v Singh (CA) 1972 1WLR 105

Re E (An Alleged Patient); Sheffield City Council v E and S [2004] EWHC 2808 (Fam) [2005] 1 FLR 965

Re M and B and A and S (By The Official Solicitor) [2005] EWHC 1681 (Fam) [2006] 1 FLR 117

References

Anitha, S., and Gill, A. (2009) 'Consent, Coercion and the Forced Marriage Debate in the UK'. *Feminist Legal Studies*, vol. 19, no. 2.

Baig, A. (2008) 'When having it all isn't asking a lot'. Accessed 20 June 2010: http://www.thesun.co.uk/sol/homepage/woman/article2040899.ece

Ferstman, C. (2010) 'Reparation as Prevention: Considering the law and practice of orders for cessation and guarantees of non-repetition in torture cases', *Essex Human Rights Review*, vol. 6, no. 2: special issue 2010: *Preventing Torture in the 21st Century – Part II*.

Ellison, L., and Munro, V. (2010) 'Jury Deliberation and Complainant Credibility in Rape Trials', in McGlynn, C., Munro, V., eds. *Rethinking Rape Law: International and Comparative Perspectives*, Ashgate, London.

Gill, A. (2004) 'Voicing the Silent Fear: South Asian Women's Experiences of Domestic Violence', *Howard Journal of Criminal Justice*, vol. 43, no. 5.

Gill, A. (2009) '"Honour" Killings and the Quest for Justice in Black and Minority Ethnic Communities in the UK', *Criminal Justice Policy Review*, vol. 20, no. 4, 475–94.

Home Affairs Committee (2010) 'Follow up to the Committee's Report on Domestic Violence, Forced Marriage and Honour-Based Violence – Home Affairs Committee: Examination of Witnesses (Questions 37–57)', 9 March 2010. Accessed 1 July 2010: http://www.publications.parliament.uk/pa/cm200910/ cmselect/ cmhaff/429/10030903.htm.

Khanum, N. (2008) *Forced marriage, family cohesion and community engagement: national learning through a case study of Luton*, Equality in Diversity, London.

Ministry of Justice (2008) *Forced Marriage (Civil Protection) Act 2007 – Relevant Third Party.* : Ministry of Justice, London. Accessed 1 July 2010: http://www. justice.gov.uk/consultations/docs/forced-marriage-third-party-response.pdf .

Ministry of Justice (2009a) *One Year On: The Initial Impact of the Forced Marriage (Civil Protection) Act 2007 in its first year of operation.* Ministry of Justice, London. Accessed 22 June 2010: http://www.justice.gov.uk/one-year-on-forced-marriage-act.pdf.

Ministry of Justice (2009b) *Forced Marriage (Civil Protection) Act 2007: Guidance for local authorities as relevant third party and information relevant to multi-agency partnership working.* Ministry of Justice, London. Accessed 22 June 2010: http://www.justice.gov.uk/guidance/docs/forced-marriage.pdf.

Razack, S. (2004) 'Imperilled Muslim women, dangerous Muslim men and civilised Europeans: Legal and social responses to forced marriages', *Feminist Legal Studies*, vol. 12, 129–74.

Stobart, E. (2009) *Multi-agency practice guidelines: Handling cases of forced marriage.* London: Forced Marriage Unit. Accessed 20 June 2010: http://www.fco.gov.uk/ resources/en/pdf/3849543/forced-marriage-guidelines09.pdf.

Sweeney, J. (2009) 'Credibility, proof and refugee law', *International Journal of Refugee Law*, vol. 21 no. 4.

Valios, N. (2008) 'Forced Marriage of people with learning disabilities', *Community Care*, 22 August 2008. Accessed 22 June 2010: http://www.community care. co.uk/Articles/2008/08/22/109193/Forced-marriage-of-people-with-learning-disabilities.htm.

8

The practice of law making and the problem of forced marriage: what is the role of the Muslim Arbitration Tribunal?

Samia Bano

Today, the changing methods of resolving disputes in matters of commercial, civil and family law generate much discussion and debate. Questions regarding the emergence and type of new methods of dispute resolution have led to an unprecedented rise in the number of scholarly and policy-orientated initiatives that seek both to promote and to critique such developments (see Genn 1999). Such debates fall within the wider discussions on promoting access to justice for all citizens and on how better to understand the relationships between cultural and social norms that may underpin such forms of dispute resolution. Indeed the contemporary landscape of civil and family justice is part of a renewed recognition by the state of the need to build upon mechanisms of Alternate Dispute Resolution (herein referred to as ADR), mechanisms that are evidenced by the increasing use of arbitration, mediation, conciliation and initiatives developed by practitioners such as collaborative law. Issues such as cultural diversity and need to accommodate community needs also underpin such contemporary initiatives. We have therefore seen the rise of cross-cultural mediation mechanisms which have come to the fore in determining both the use and the delivery of services and in the desire to accommodate the needs of all users. In essence, then, what we see is not only the emergence of new forms of legal cultures but also the ways in which new forms of informal and formal adjudication in all its complexity emerge and develop within groups, communities and networks. This increasing privatisation of disputes takes shape outside the traditional adversarial framework of family law but also seeks to resolve matrimonial disputes in conjunction with state law process and practice.

More importantly, it raises a number of fundamental questions relating to citizenship, personhood and agency and the extent to which the privatisation of ADR mechanisms may undermine traditional conceptions of justice, 'equality before the law', and 'common citizenship'. A further question relates to the ways in which ADR mechanisms may in fact increase citizen participation in civil society and the effect of this upon changing patterns of state governance in resolving family law disputes. Over the years academics and practitioners have recognised the roles played by culture and more recently religion in the ways in which matrimonial and family law disputes are resolved.

In Britain we have seen the emergence of community and family mediation mechanisms that seek to resolve matrimonial disputes both outside the framework of state law and in conjunction with state law mechanisms. For example, the work of Shah-Kazemi (2001) and Bano (2007) illustrates the emergence of Sharia councils within diasporic Muslim communities that act as mechanisms to resolve matrimonial disputes within the family, home and local communities. This development has been followed by the emergence of the Muslim Arbitration Tribunal which operates as a civil law mechanism under the auspices of the 1996 Arbitration Act to produce decisions that may be enforced and relied upon in the civil courts. Within British Muslim communities we therefore currently have a three-tier approach to resolving matrimonial disputes: state law, unofficial community mediation (Sharia Councils) and the new Muslim Arbitration Tribunal.

This chapter draws upon this material and considers how the newly established Muslim Arbitration Tribunal tackles the issue of forced marriage. The Muslim Arbitration Tribunal was set up in June 2007 and aims to settle disputes in accordance with religious Sharia law. The authority of this tribunal rests with the Arbitration Act 1996 which permits civil matters to be resolved in accordance with Muslim personal law and within the ambit of state law. For many, this process of resolving disputes provides the ideal fora that allow the arbitrating parties to resolve disputes according to English law while fulfilling any obligations under Islamic law. The advantages of arbitration, it is argued, allow the parties to achieve some level of autonomy in the decision-making process. This, coupled with the informal setting, lower costs, flexibility and time efficiency, means that for some it may prove a more attractive alternative to the adversarial courts system in England and Wales. However there remain real concerns about whether this process can restrict women's equality and affect issues of fairness and justice in areas of family law. This chapter analyses how the problem of forced marriage is tackled by the Muslim Arbitration Tribunal and provides a critical reflection on how this new form of 'dialogical dispute resolution' is accessed, used and serviced by the disputants.

178

Religion and access to justice

Recently, the scholar Ayelet Shachar declared that 'The vision of privatized diversity in its fully-fledged "unregulated islands of jurisdiction" variant poses a challenge to the superiority of secular family law by its old adversary: religion' (2008, 573). This vision of privatised diversity can be applied to the new Muslim Arbitration Tribunal if we understand privatised diversity as a model in which to achieve and possibly separate the secular from the religious in the public space, in effect encouraging individuals to contract out of state involvement and into a traditional nonstate forum when resolving family disputes. This vision would include religious tribunals arbitrating according to a different set of principles than those enshrined in English law. This approach has been advocated by the Archbishop of Canterbury, Dr Rowan Williams, who in a speech to the Royal Courts of Justice stated, 'there are ways at looking at marital disputes, for example, which provide an alternative to the divorce courts as we understand them. In some cultural and religious settings they would seem more appropriate' (Williams 2008, 2). He also suggested that the recognition of Sharia in Britain seems 'unavoidable' and advised that we need to find a 'constructive accommodation' of Sharia in the law. Although he was careful not to restrict his general argument to Muslims *per se*, but more broadly to encompass all those belonging to religious communities, the focal point was Muslims and the recognition of Sharia in English law. Lord Phillips, the Chief Justice at the time, added further weight to the argument when he stated, 'there is no reason why principles of Sharia law, or any other religious code, should not be the basis for mediation or other forms of alternative dispute resolution' (Phillips 2008, 4). Both speakers suggested that Islamic mechanisms of family disputes could perform a function not dissimilar to that of the Jewish Beth Din courts which deal with matters relating to marriage and divorce.

For Ayelet Shachar there are real concerns over individuals being expected to live 'as undifferentiated citizens in the public sphere, but remain free to express our distinct cultural or religious identities in the private domain of family and communal life' (2008, 580). For her and many other liberal scholars, the issue surrounds the contentious question of where private identity and private life end and public identity begins. She rightly points out that if we are expected to express personal identities in the private sphere, at which point in the public sphere do they cease to be so? Shachar also discusses the fact that the vision of privatised diversity will evoke different feelings for different people: for those who want to establish a pluralistic system of law recognising claims of culture and religion, this vision would not be so terrifying but those who are 'blind' to these needs will see it as challenging the superiority of universal laws that apply to all, 'for others who endorse a strict separationist approach, or 'blindness' towards religious or cultural affiliation, the idea that we might find unregulated 'religious islands of binding jurisdiction' mushrooming on the terrain of state law is seen as evidence of the dangers of accommodating diversity, potentially chipping away, however slightly, at the foundational, modernist citizenship formula of 'one law for all' (2008, 580).

Such arguments are echoed by Parkinson (1996, 24), who points out that '[a]cceptance of cultural diversity, and recognition of cultural issues in the application of the law, are especially important in relation to family law, for families play such an important role in the development of a person's cultural identity.' Therefore the intimate relations between the individual, family and community must to some extent be recognised by a legal system that increasingly serves plural and multicultural Western societies.

The issue of forced marriage raises questions about the extent to which the state, together with state law mechanisms, supports community-driven initiatives to challenge its practice. Today we have a number of legislative and policy initiatives which seek to eradicate state practice and at the heart of these policy and legal initiatives lies the experience of women as victims of forced marriage – within the wider framework of dealing with violence against women. It is interesting to note that strategies to challenge forced marriages also include initiatives designed to explore the psychological motivations of the offenders' behaviour; to understand the complex ways in which forced marriage manifests in the family, home and community; and to understand the relationship of forced marriage to cultural practice and religious ideology (in this case principally Islam). Yet the wider debates on conceptualising a generic definition of a forced marriage and its articulation within different communities have proved both contentious and problematic. Perhaps more important, the culturalist approach adopted by the state has led many to argue that the debate on forced marriage has led to the stigmatising of Islam and of Muslim communities as *key* perpetrators of forced marriages, giving rise to the logic that there is an irreconcilable clash between Islam and the West. For Muslim diasporic communities living in the West, such understandings are deeply troubling as they raise fundamental questions of loyalty to the state and the failure of Muslims to integrate within

Western democratic societies; these discourses have become closely linked to debates on immigration and border controls.

There have been a number of UK initiatives on forced marriage, most recently culminating in the introduction of the Forced Marriage (Civil Protection) Act 2007. In 1999 a working group on forced marriage was set up by the Home Secretary to investigate the extent to which forced marriage was practised in England and Wales. In the same year the Community Liaison Unit was set up by the Foreign and Commonwealth Office (FCO) which was given responsibility for dealing with the international dimension of forced marriages (see below). In 2000 the report *A Choice by Right*, was published by the working group: this report focused on clarifying the distinction between arranged and forced marriage and on providing clear guidelines to public bodies such as the police, schools and social services on what can be deemed a forced marriage (Home Office 2000). In 2002, police guidelines were issued by the Association of Chief Police Officers to better equip members of the police force in dealing with forced marriage (see Phillips and Dustin 2004, 535). Each of these initiatives has focused on the option of exit for vulnerable women forced into marriage. Moreover, community attempts to persuade the state to adopt a dialogue-centred approach via the use of mediation services has been met with resistance from women's organisations.[1] It is argued that in practice women's attempts to reconcile with families can lead to undue levels of social pressure to reconcile with families in the face of a continued threat.

Arbitration and mediation: the historical context

Since the early 1960s, the practice of resolving matrimonial disputes outside the sphere of formal legal adjudication has gained renewed impetus among practitioners, researchers and legal academics. We have seen the emergence of different forms of ADR mechanisms that act both as oppositional to and work as part of the state law processes in resolving civil, commercial and family law disputes (see Roberts 2008).

ADR occupies an interesting and contested arena in legal practice whereby competing legal discourses interact and overlap to produce a wide array of disputing mechanisms. As a process of resolving disputes it is deemed to be oppositional to state law, but it can equally be initiated, supervised and be supported by the state. Working in tandem with individuals, state law and local communities, it has for many years been perceived as the natural space in which conflicts arising from formal and informal legal systems can be amicably resolved. This increase in 'informalism' has generally been perceived as a positive development against the overarching power of state law, a development which in turn can have a social transformative role on 'law' and 'legal relations'.

In this context the literature on ADR and its relationship to community raises a number of interesting issues. For example in Britain the emergence of local organisations that provide ADR/mediation services that are specifically catered to the needs of local minority communities has flourished since the mid 1980s. In the US, San Francisco Community Boards were the first such organisations to be based around notions of 'civic responsibility' and 'local self governance' in order to encourage settlements away from state law (Harrington 1992, 32)

For many scholars, therefore, the issue remains the extent to which the state retains control in the resolution of disputes and whether this control underpins the relationship between ADR and the community. For example, Abel points out that although ADR works under the guise of reducing state control and is often presented as being less coercive and oppressive in intervening in the lives of private individuals, it can in fact demand greater forms of state control and intervention. For many ADR scholars the question therefore arises of whether ADR embodies a socially transformative role in law and in the lives of the parties. Abel concludes that it remains a part of the existing legal system and cannot in itself instigate any real change. Nevertheless he accepts too that state law mediation can also offer protection against forms of abuse which informal mediation may fail to protect against. 'Formality,' he states, 'can frequently be a useful weapon for the powerless. It can justify the demand for equality across lines of race, religion, gender and even class' (Abel 1992, 10).

The legal context of family mediation in Britain

This international growth of ADR had an early impact on the development of mediation in Britain. The moves towards informalism coupled with critiques of formalism were also part of a wider movement exploring the limits of law and legal action. For example, much of the ADR literature emerged as part of the critical legal studies movement which aimed to counter the dominant prevailing systems of law as rule-centred and positivist.

It is generally accepted that the era of mediation in Britain began in the

1970s with the disputing parties seeking to resolve disputes outside the formal adversarial system of the law. Yet what we understand as mediation can vary according to which context and place it is applied. For example, family mediation may vary enormously from neighbourhood disputes and the resolution of commercial disputes. The most important issues in relation to mediation are the norms and values that underpin this approach but not that of the adversarial approach. For example it is generally accepted that mediation cannot take place without being underpinned by norms of fairness, voluntary participation, equity and mutual respect. The underlying norms seek to provide 'fora' that take into account the often emotionally charged issues addressed by mediation and seek to create a level playing field in terms of seeking a full and fair resolution for both parties.

A number of writers point to the inherent definitional problems associated with mediation. Terms such as conciliation, reconciliation and arbitration have often been used interchangeably, and this has led to a confusing situation. Mediation in English family law has been presented as a dilemma for the liberal state which grapples with regulating 'family life' on the one hand and with preserving 'family privacy' on the other. This relationship between the state and the family is epitomised through family law legislation. As Kurczewski explains, 'the duty of the State is to support and protect the authentic institution of the family, respecting its natural shape and natural and inalienable rights' (1997, 5). Most commentators accept that the 'authentic' shape of the family is based on the idea of the 'sacred character' of the family and the centrality of gender relations.[2]

The term 'mediation', in general, covers a number of current ADR trends which share in the ideological aims of resolving disputes outside the formal civil system of court-based adjudication but which also share in promoting a sense of equity and fair practice for all the parties involved. The issue of creating specialist mediation services to deal with matrimonial disputes has been extensively discussed. In 1971 the Finer Committee advocated the use of conciliation for parties seeking to settle issues arising from separation and divorce (including arrangements for children and financial and property matters). Such a conciliation service was set up in Bristol in 1978, and others followed suit in the 1980s.

A key principle of the mediation process is the autonomy of the parties involved and issues such as the role of decision making and authority. But what do we understand as the mediation process? How does the decision-making process take place? Arguably the key participant in the mediation process is the mediator who acts as the third party assisting the parties involved. It is precisely this role which generates questions relating to fair practice, equity, and the justice of the mediation process. For example the capacity for a mediator to enter this process on a neutral basis has been both questioned and extensively discussed. As Roberts points out, 'the mediator has no stake in the dispute and is not identified with any of the competing interests involved. The mediator has no power to impose a settlement on the parties who retain authority making their own decision' (2008, 9). Statutory recognition of mediation was provided for in the Family Law Act 1996 which provided public funding for approved mediation services. Part III of the Family Law Act 1996 (re-enacted in the Access to Justice Act 1999) requires all those seeking legal aid to seek mediation, although exemptions apply to cases of domestic violence and/or child protection or where the other party has already commences court proceedings. As Parkinson (1996, 56) points out, 'Early settlement of family matters is encouraged by the legal requirement for advising lawyers to refer clients seeking legal aid for family proceedings to a mediator, to receive information and consider mediation, before legal aid can be obtained for court proceedings.'[3]

The practice of mediation is enshrined in English law. Part 1 of the Civil Procedure Rules contains the objective of cases being resolved 'justly'. The Court of Appeal has made it explicit that the overriding objective is the duty to the parties as well as the court.[4] Mediation is extensively used in civil law disputes, especially in the fields of commercial law where the commercial nature of the relationship is often in dispute. In *R (Cowl and Others) v Plymouth City Council*,[5] Lord Woolf CJ stressed the importance of ADR 'even in disputes between public authorities and the members of the public for whom they are responsible'. The state has also expressed a preference for the use of ADR. In 2001 the Lord Chancellor encouraged the use of mediation thus: 'In future, Government departments will only go to court as a last resort. Instead government legal disputes will be settled by mediation or arbitration whenever possible.'[6] In commercial cases the emphasis on ADR has increased quite considerably. The courts have moved from gentle persuasion to orders that explicitly encourage the use of mediation.[7] This has led to interesting legal arguments on whether such orders amount to an unacceptable restraint of the right of access to court in violation of Article 6 of the European Convention of Human Rights. The Court of Appeal in Halsey rejected this argument, stating that such orders do not amount to compulsion.[8]

But in this case the Court Appeal was clear on the need to avoid direct compulsion of mediation, stating:

> It is one thing to encourage the parties to agree to mediation, even to encourage them in the strongest terms. It is another to order them to do so. It seems to us that to oblige truly unwilling parties to refer their disputes to mediation would be to impose an unacceptable obstruction on their right of access to the court. (And) even if (contrary to our view) the court does have jurisdiction to order unwilling parties to refer their disputes to mediation, we find it difficult to conceive of circumstances in which it would be appropriate to exercise it.[9]

The increasing move towards a nonadversarial approach to resolving disputes has been acknowledged as part of legal policy. In 1974 the Finer Report emphasised the importance of ADR in resolving family breakdown and conflict, and this emphasis was strengthened with the Booth Report in 1985. ADR is now a recognised part of legal policy and is embedded in the legal framework: the Access to Justice Act 1999 (incorporating section 11 of the Family Law Act 1986), the Adoption and Children Act 2002 and the Children Act 2004. It must be noted that the majority of divorce cases are settled outside the adjudication process; only a tiny percentage come before the courts. So agreements are made within the shadow of the law. In August 2008 the Legal Services Commission (LSC) published its paper entitled 'Publicly Funded Family Mediation: the Way Forward' which set out its objectives for publicly funded family mediation.[10]

The remit of religious courts under the Arbitration Act 1996

The debate on the emergence of new forms of governance in Britain has recently centred on the establishment of Sharia courts under the heading of the Muslim Arbitration Tribunal under the auspices of the 1996 Arbitration Act. The establishment of the Muslim Arbitration Tribunal has been controversial for a number of reasons: it has been claimed, first, that Sharia courts have been allowed in through the back door, and, second, that they directly challenge the superiority of the English legal system and undermine the principles upon which English family law are based.

As Blackett (2009, 13) observes, 'it is important to point out that the Muslim Arbitration Tribunal does not resemble or operate as a court but is an arbitration tribunal that must have the consent of the parties to rule on an issue. The Muslim Arbitration Tribunal has no power of enforcement but decisions can be enforced by the English county or high courts. This process therefore means that the decisions made by these arbitration bodies have to be in line with principles of English law or judges will not enforce them under sovereign rule.' The authority within the law of these courts was outlined by the Parliamentary Undersecretary of State Bridget Prentice in the House of Commons in October 2008:

> If, in a family dispute dealing with money or children, the parties to a judgement in a Sharia council wish to have this recognized by English authorities, they are at liberty to draft a consent order embodying the terms of the agreement and submit it to an English court. This allows English judges to scrutinize it to ensure that it complies with English legal tenets.[11]

Under English law, parties cannot agree that a court should apply Sharia law but in arbitration the position is different. Section 46 of the Arbitration Act 1996 provides that:

> The arbitral tribunal shall decide the disputes in accordance with the law chosen by the parties as applicable to the substance of the dispute; or b) if the parties so agree, in accordance with such other considerations as are agreed by them or determined by the tribunal 2) For this purpose the choice of laws of a country shall be understood to refer to the substantive laws of that country and not its conflict of laws rules.

Hence the parties can agree that the arbitrators will decide their dispute according to Sharia law. The Arbitration Act 1996 contains a number of safeguards. An agreement to arbitrate is, in a sense, just like any other contract, and so it is necessary to show a genuine agreement to arbitrate by both parties. Contracts obtained by duress will not be enforced; neither will contracts with minors or the incompetent. Agreements to arbitrate must be evidenced in writing. An arbitration award is, in itself, of no effect. It is of value only to the extent that a court is prepared to enforce it. Courts may refuse to enforce awards on various grounds, including: (a) that a party was under some incapacity, (b) that the agreement was not valid under the applicable law, (c) that a party did not have proper notice of the arbitrator's appointment or of the proceedings or was unable to present their case, (d) if the award deals with a matter which it was not agreed would be submitted to arbitration, (e) if the award relates to a matter which is not capable of being settled by arbitration, or if it would be contrary to public policy to enforce the award. An arbitration award which is given under some law other than

English law cannot be appealed on the grounds that the arbitrators got that law wrong, but it can be challenged and set aside by an English court under Article 68 of the Arbitration Act 1996 on various grounds, including failure by the tribunal to comply with its general duty to act fairly and impartially. [12]

The Muslim Arbitration Tribunal and forced marriage

At present, there are five tribunals operating as part of the Muslim Arbitration Tribunal across Britain. In addition to addressing issues of religious divorce and other Muslim family law matters (including marriage contracts, wills and inheritance disputes) these tribunals also arbitrate on matters relating to forced marriage and domestic violence. [13] The Muslim Arbitration Tribunal states all agreements are settled in accordance with Qur'anic Injunctions and Prophetic practice as determined by the recognised schools of Islamic sacred law, and as fairly, quickly and efficiently as possible. It also states that, where appropriate, members of the Tribunal have responsibility for ensuring this in the interests of the parties to the proceedings and in the wider public interest.

It is held that Islamic decisions can be reached quickly and cheaply, and can be used as evidence before the civil court when seeking other remedies. The tribunal does not deal with criminal offences but states that 'where there are criminal charges such as assault within the context of domestic violence, the parties will be able ask the Muslim Arbitration Tribunal to assist in reaching reconciliation which is observed and approved by the Muslim Arbitration Tribunal as an independent organisation. The terms of such reconciliation can then be passed by the Muslim Arbitration Tribunal on to the Crown Prosecution Service (CPS) through the local Police Domestic Violence Liaison Officers with a view to reconsidering the criminal charges. Note that the final decision to prosecute always remains with the CPS.' In 2008, the *Sunday Times* reported that the tribunal had 'divided the estate of a Muslim man between his two sons and three daughters. Keeping with Islamic religious law, the sons were awarded twice as much money as the daughters. In six domestic violence cases on which the tribunal deliberated last year, the rulings required no further punishment for the husbands than anger management classes and community mentoring. After these rulings were issued, all six women withdrew their complaints to the UK police' (Madeira 2010, 3).

The authority of the tribunal rests with the Arbitration Act 1996 which permits civil matters to be resolved in accordance with Muslim personal law and within the ambit of state law. For many, this process of resolving disputes provides the ideal forum which allows the arbitrating parties to resolve disputes according to English law while fulfilling any obligations under Islamic law. The advantages of arbitration, it is argued, are that it allows the parties to achieve some level of autonomy in the decision-making process. This, coupled with the informal setting, lower costs, flexibility and time efficiency, means that for many arbitration may prove a more attractive alternative to the adversarial courts system in England and Wales. However there remain real concerns about whether this process could seek to restrict women's equality and compromise issues of fairness and justice in areas of family law including domestic violence, child custody, divorce, financial support, and inheritance.

In 2008, the Muslim Arbitration Tribunal produced a report entitled *Liberation from Forced Marriages* which stated that the Tribunal was the most appropriate forum for the Muslim community to resolve problems such as forced marriage. It put forward the following proposals to combat the practice of forced marriage as a community-driven initiative with emphasis placed upon protecting British citizens marrying abroad who are victims of forced marriage. First, this includes requiring the foreign spouse to voluntarily submit 'an oral deposition to the Judges of MAT, satisfying them that the marriage he/she entered into was neither forced nor coerced'. As a voluntary deposition by the British citizen rather than a legal requirement, the judges of the Muslim Arbitration Tribunal would then produce a written declaration that they were satisfied that the marriage was entered into without any force or coercion. The proposal further states that 'the British citizen can then use this declaration to support the application of the foreign spouse to settle in the UK. If however, the foreign spouse fails to produce such a declaration from MAT or any other appropriate evidence, then it would be open for the ECO [Entry Clearing Organisation] at the entry clearance point, to draw such inferences deemed appropriate as to the status of the marriage' (Muslim Arbitration Tribunal 2008, 25).

The Muslim Arbitration Tribunal claims that voluntary submission is the key factor in the challenging of forced marriages with foreign spouses and that 'a community based court would be better placed to deal with the intricacies of the community issues' as the community would be intolerant of state intervention. The report further states:

> Assessment by professionals and scholars of the Muslim Community within the Muslim Arbitration Tribunal organisation will enable this process to be

carried out responsibly. When Muslim professionals and scholars who are from the UK, live in our multi-cultural, multi-ethnic and diverse society review a case before them then they will do so with the scrutiny and compassion it deserves. The team that is recruited by the Muslim Arbitration Tribunal to carry out this service will have extensive experience of dealing with forced marriages because they have been surrounded by examples of this in their families, communities and localities. The Muslim Arbitration Tribunal provides that environment which will give British Muslims the confidence to come forward to utilise the process to its fullest potential.

The decisions of Muslim Arbitration Tribunal judges are recorded on tape and hearings recorded on camera.

All hearings before the judges will be in camera. Evidence may include speaking to family members 'to highlight the wider consequences of participating or being complicit in a coerced or forced marriage'. The use of community elders as a source of social scrutiny to embarrass perpetrators is also proposed as a source of action. So the proposal envisages a scenario where they hope to work closely with both perpetrators and victims of forced marriage.

One of the primary objections of the Muslim Arbitration Tribunal report is to what it describes as the limited nature of the Forced Marriage Protection Orders.[14] It cites the following reasons: there is no clear support infrastructure for the victim of the marriage; the imposition of the protection order upon the wider family will be resented by them and held against the victim, adding to his/her perils; there will be greater reluctance of victims to approach the English court system for assistance; the reference by the third parties to the English courts can easily be obfuscated by the efforts of the wider family; and, finally, there is no clear pathway for the victim to seek annulment of the marriage directly as a consequence of the protection order. As to the Forced Marriage (Civil Protection) Act, it can be argued that it is too early to examine the impact of the forced marriage legislation as it has only been implemented for one year. Nevertheless, the legislation has been a catalyst for a number of changes within the public sector (e.g. government, the judiciary, the police, social services, education, health and immigration) and these can be examined.

A 2009 policy paper by the Ministry of Justice (MOJ) reported on research into the effectiveness of the statute.[15] The results indicated that there has been a need for the statute as it has been used widely. Analysed as a whole, the figures in the MOJ report appear to indicate that more orders were made by the courts than there were actual applications. This in itself has shown the responsibility the courts have taken on in attempting to prevent potential forced marriages from taking place. The report also points to the fact that judges are working hard to learn more about the procedures in order to make just decisions.[16] For example, judges themselves have noted that there does need to be more judicial training in this area; this reinforces the view that the Act is still at an early stage of interpretation.[17] Furthermore, there appears to be a relatively proportionate number of orders attached with powers of arrest; this suggests that the theoretical argument about the risks faced by forced marriage victims is in fact about realities that are being addressed through legal means. The report states that significantly more children were victims of forced marriage in the first year than adults. Now, forced marriages can to an extent be quantified can lead to appropriate methods of dealing with them. Perhaps more awareness and resources should be invested into local authorities as there has been a suggestion that some local authorities have 'been slow to get involved' and there is 'lack of clarity between boundaries between care proceedings under the Children Act, Court of Protection cases, and forced marriage cases. The Act does not sit well with social services working methods.'[18] These issues are results of the Forced Marriage (Civil Protection) Act being legislated and therefore need to be addressed. Without proper training within social services, education and health agencies, for example, or sufficient 'practical and mainstream support', the Act may become 'a symbolic outlawing of forced marriage' rather than serving to eradicate it.[19] Nevertheless, the police appear to have taken on a more active and dedicated role since the Act's implementation by promoting awareness as well as being able to take action at any sign of a potential case of forced marriage. Government guidelines distributed in schools and across the National Health Service have also had a positive impact in promoting awareness and encouraging preventative actions. Research has indicated that both schools and GPs have referred suspected cases of forced marriage to the police.[20] In addition, it has been possible to make applications for FMPOs outside of the England and Wales jurisdiction; this has helped a number of individuals who have been taken abroad to be married against their will to obtain legal protection. For example, in December 2008, Mr Justice Coleridge granted an FMPO to prevent Dr Humayra Abedin[21] from undertaking a wedding ceremony in Bangladesh, where she was being held against her wishes, and to secure her return to Britain. This was an important case, which encapsulated the importance of having a specific Act that tackled forced marriages; this means the courts are now better equipped than when they were trying to mould the laws as they had done previously. Coleridge's view is also supported in the MoJ policy paper which indicates that judges have found it relatively easy to grasp the new law on forced marriage, so that court procedures have been able to be fast enough to provide efficient remedies.

The Muslim Arbitration Tribunal report on forced marriage concludes that amongst other things this community initiative can avoid expensive legal battles in the High Court over Forced Marriage Protection Orders. In addition to tackling forced marriage, the Muslim Arbitration Tribunal deals with issues of domestic violence within Muslim communities. The Tribunal's website states:

> It is not only the victims of domestic abuse who remain silent on the issue, but also certain Imams. It is said that the practice of domestic abuse derives legitimacy from the Islamic scriptures and therefore is a matter which all Muslims believe in and accept. For an Imam to preach contrary to this would be sacrilege. However, is this actually factually correct and how far is this legitimacy derived from a distorted interpretation of the scriptures? Furthermore, is the silence of the Imams more to do with preserving their own position within their communities than preserving the supposed practices of the Islamic faith?

So what does formal arbitration entail, and how does the Muslim Arbitration Tribunal fall under the ambit of arbitration? The Muslim Arbitration Tribunal is modelled on the Jewish Beth Din which has operated under the auspices of arbitration legislation for many decades. The Beth Din tribunals are used to resolve private disputes raging from religious divorce to business transactions. It is interesting to note that these tribunals have been operating in Britain for many years with little if any of the publicity and hostility that have been directed towards the Muslim Arbitration Tribunal. A report on the Beth Din observed that 'civil courts ... retain the right to intervene in any case where the award of the Beth Din is considered unreasonable or contrary to public policy'. The report also stressed that 'in neither arbitration cases nor religious judgments is the Beth Din recognized as a legal court nor does it offer a parallel legal system: Beth Din rulings or advice can only be reflected in UK law if both parties freely agree and the decision is approved by the civil courts' (Centre for Social Cohesion 2009, 8).

In her work, Andrea Jarman (2008) points out that arbitration is a jurisdictional hybrid of private and public law. Redfern and Hunter point out that 'it begins as a private agreement between the parties. It continues by way of private proceedings, in which the wishes of the parties are of great importance. Yet it ends with an award which has binding legal force and effect and which, on appropriate conditions being met … the courts … will be prepared to recognize and enforce' (2004, 3). More recently the relationship between arbitration and the Human Rights Act has been explored in three judgments.[22] The question in these cases involved whether it was possible during the course of the arbitration agreement to forgo one of the European Convention of Human Rights rights, namely Article 6 and the right to a fair trial. It was found that the terms of the 1996 Arbitration Act did fulfil the requirements of Article 6 so long as the arbitration agreement was entered into 'freely' or was 'agreed without constraint' and the agreement itself 'did not run counter to any important public interest'. Central to all this was the need for the tribunal to be impartial and to follow procedural fairness. So how does the Muslim Arbitration Tribunal run as an arbitration body and does it fulfil key requirements of the Arbitration Act? At present there is no body of case law with which to analyse its effectiveness, but we can see that its institutional structure is paralleled by state law mechanisms but also emanates from social and cultural postulates. In this way the overlap of jurisdictions, the choice of forums and the personal behaviours and decision-making focus attention on new forms of interlegality and multicultural interlegality. The legitimacy of various legal and social domains mixes up our understandings of law and decision-making. But to what extent does this approach challenge liberal conceptions of equality, human rights, and individual choice, and undermine gender equality?

Should we mediate in cases of forced marriage?

The approach taken by the Muslim Arbitration Tribunal raises the question of whether we should ever mediate in cases of forced marriage. Forced marriage has been described as 'a marriage without the full and free consent of both parties' and 'where people are coerced into a marriage against their will and under duress' (FCO 2005, 3), and it falls under the spectrum of domestic violence according to English law. For many practitioners, therefore, the idea of mediating on the issue of violence is one to be approached with extreme caution. The Muslim Arbitration Tribunal emphasises the community initiative on the basis that it encourages and promotes family and community cohesion and individual personal autonomy and empowerment for all individuals who wish to resolve such issues within the framework of family, home and local community.

However the Muslim Arbitration Tribunal does not sufficiently address the issue of power and power relations within the context of family and home. The issue of control and powerlessness for many female victims of forced marriage has long remained a central issue in the challenge to eradicate its practice. Concepts such as dialogue, discussion, compromise and cooperation may in fact adversely affect the safety of female victims of forced marriage. Research indicates that many women who are victims of forced marriage do not occupy an equal position in the family and home in terms of the bargaining power, respect and prestige that are often accorded to male members of the same household. The mediation process can increase rather then reduce the level of harm and possible violence directed to women. Penny Booth argues that such tribunals can create a system of coercive control of women, 'The danger is in the development of a parallel system of [...] law where the choice as to which system or principle is used is determined not by the individual or the issue but by the group bullies. In family law this danger could arise where the determination of system and approach is not made by the woman but the men; not through females but through the male dominated system' (Booth 2008, 936).

Feminist criticisms of arbitration and mediation therefore relate to issues of unequal power relations between men and women that can result in unfair bargaining practices and outcomes for women. The issue of the fairness and equity of agreements effected via the mediation approach underpins any feminist criticisms of mediation. Feminist scholars (Smart and Brophy 1985; Fineman 1988; Menkel-Meadow 1985) argue that family law statutes and practices are implicitly biased against women. As Irving and Benjamin (1995) sum up, 'Patriarchal bias inheres in the adversarial system, with male judges and lawyers tending to advance characteristically "male" solutions to the problem of divorce, emphasising conflict, competition and "winning"; and women are consequently typically rendered passive, dependent observers in their own cases' (1995, 203).

For some feminists, therefore, the alternative to an adversarial system with its inherent male bias can only provide a better situation for vulnerable women. Rifkin argues that mediation reflects what she understands as a feminist analysis, one that stresses cooperation, negotiation, equity, and especially participation and ownership. In short, mediation would appear to provide one basis for resolving divorce disputes that gives women back their voice (Rifkin [1984], cited in Irving and Benjamin 1995, 203). However, the 'feminist' position on mediation is largely critical, and as a result the debates have largely stagnated as being in either in favour of mediation or against. Irving and Benjamin (1995) suggest that the feminist critique of family mediation involves four general arguments – concerning neutrality, equality, rights and practice standards – and that these can be translated into five specific assertions:

1 Neutrality has failed. In practice mediation can never be a process that is objective and value-free, and the mediator inevitably brings to the mediation process a set of values and beliefs which influence his role as the mediator. In this way the mediator may replicate existing patriarchal forms of social ordering.
2 Mediation merely reflects patriarchal power and inequality, and the subordinate position that women occupy in wider society.
3 Mediation as a process does not empower women to make better settlements for themselves.
4 Mediation can pose considerable risks to women who have experienced violence. The courts provide better safeguards and protection for women.
5 Mediation is a lesser forum.

Davis and Roberts (1989, 306) note that perhaps the main challenge to the feminist critique of mediation as perpetuating a power imbalance between men and women lies in the control over the mediation process (by) controlling the ebb and flow of negotiation; in some cases, the 'weaker' party (does) indeed feel empowered. Davis and Roberts also note an important gender difference: 'what the man sees as unnecessary interference and control, the woman may have experienced as protection and support' (1989, 305). Irving and Benjamin point out that feminist-informed mediation would require two modifications in terms of empowerment (1995, 216): (a) to expand its assessment procedures to routinely explore the spousal power balance and (b) to expand current techniques to include measures expressly designed with power balancing in mind.

There are other problems with organisations such as the Muslim Arbitration Tribunal mediating on the issue of forced marriage. For example, an enormous amount of trust is placed in Muslim Arbitration Tribunal judges, and they may provide a safe framework that cannot be extended to the family context once the victim returns. As Marianne Hester et al. (1997,

45) point out, 'While mediation appears to be a safe, humanitarian, non-adversarial, inexpensive way to intervene in many situations, the best way to protect the rights of victims who are in unequal and dangerous relationships to their abusers is to engage in adversarial proceedings which can punish or deter criminal conduct.' In relation to the Muslim Arbitration Tribunal, despite the recording of mediation sessions, the process is conducted in private and there is little if any accountability either of mediators or concerning the way in which cases are handled. Also, the intervention of family members may hinder the capacity for the female victim to make an informed decision. In these ways the principles of mediation may not suit the tackling of the issue of forced marriage.

Conclusion

In his report for the think tank Civitas, Denis MacEoin (2009) remains critical of the Muslim Arbitration Tribunal, arguing that 'it is a challenge to what we believe to be the rights and freedoms of the individual to our concept of a legal system based on what Parliament enacts, and to the right of all of us to live in a society as free as possible from ethnic–religious division or communal claims to superiority and a special status that puts them in some respects above the law to which we are all bound' (2009, 76). This argument is flawed in multiple ways, not least because it fails to recognise the plural nature of ADR and law and to understand how in practice law evolves, develops and seeks to accommodate the needs of all its citizens from multiple and diverse backgrounds. Therefore, instead of promoting an exclusive move back towards state law (the state, as we know, has never been a neutral arbiter of disputes), we need instead to understand better the experiences of Muslim women as primary users of the Muslim Arbitration Tribunal and to understand *why* they may choose to use it. As Anitha and Gill point out, 'Women exercise their agency in complex and often contradictory ways, as they assess the options that are open to them, weigh the costs and benefits of their actions, and seek to balance their often competing needs with the expectations and desires. While there remains a need to recognise gendered power imbalances, at the same time there also remains a need to respect women's exercise of agency … We need to give more support to those women who wish to express their subjectivity within the framework of the communities of which they perceive themselves to be such a fundamental part' (2010, 34).

At present, little if any data exists documenting the experiences of Muslim women using ADR mechanisms to challenge the practice of forced marriage. Feminist scholars have, however, pointed to the problems associated with the exit-centred approach and the high emotional and psychological costs this may involve (see Anitha and Gill 2009). However, as discussed in this chapter, the mediating of issues such as forced marriage with vulnerable female victims can be both dangerous and ineffective as relationships between abusers and victims are full of power imbalances that are not sufficiently addressed by the Muslim Arbitration Tribunal. Currently we know very little about how this process actually takes shape, and we must therefore remain cautious of believing that we yet understand both the motivations and the experiences of Muslim women using this forum to challenge the practice of forced marriage.

Notes

1   For example, the women's organisation Southall Black Sisters resigned from the working group on forced marriage in protest against the recommendation of mediation to reconcile victims of forced marriage with their families.

2   In her work, Mackinnon argues that as the law itself is patriarchal, family law therefore merely reflects this reality (1983, 447).

3   The Green Paper 'Parental Separation: Children's Needs and Parents' Responsibilities' published in July 2004 emphasised the importance of parties using mediation and other forms of ADR resolution mechanisms to avoid court proceedings. The Lord Chancellor's White Paper *Looking to the future: mediation and the ground for divorce* is often cited by legal commentators as the shift in legal policy towards mediation.

4   Per Brooke LJ, *Dunnett v Railtrack* (2002) 1 WLR 2434 (2002) 2 All ER 850, 853.

5   (2002) 1 WLR 803.

6   Statement by the Lord Chancellor Lord Irvine, 23 March 2001 which can be found at www.dca.gov.uk/civil/adr/adr/adrmon.htm/part2.

7   *Halsey v Milton Keynes General NHS Trust* (2004) EWCA Civ 576, at paragraph 30.

8   *Halsey v Milton Keynes General NHS Trust* (2004) EWCA Civ 576, at paragraph 32.

9   At paragraph 9.

10   See Walsh (2008).

11   Hansard (HC) 23 October 2008, written answers, column 562W.

12   See Blackett (2009).

13 The Muslim Arbitration Tribunal has stated that 'MAT will operate within the legal framework of England and Wales thereby ensuring that any determination reached by MAT can be enforced through existing means of enforcement open to normal litigants. Although MAT must operate within the legal framework of England and Wales, this does not prevent or impede MAT from ensuring that all determinations reached by it are in accordance with one of the recognized Schools of Islamic Sacred Law. MAT will therefore, for the first time, offer the Muslim community a real and true opportunity to settle disputes in accordance with Islamic Sacred Law with the knowledge that the outcome as determined by MAT will be binding and enforceable.' For a summary of its aims and objectives see www.muslim_arbitration_tribunal.com.

14 The Forced Marriage (Civil) Protection Act 2007 s63B(1); Family Law Act 1966 Part 4A.

15 See Prentice (2009).

16 Ibid., p.22, para 40.

17 Ibid, p. 22, para 40.

18 Ibid., p. 33.

19 *Hansard, Lords Debates*, vol. 688, col. 1326 (26 January 2007).

20 Prentice (2009) at paragraph 56.

21 Judge Coleridge granted further orders to continue her protection and to prevent her being removed from the UK without her consent. See Walsh (2009).

22 *Stretford v Football Association* (2007) All ER (D) 346; *Sumukan Ltd v The Commonwealth Secretariat* (2007) EWCA Civ 243 and *Shuttari v The Solicitors Indemnity Fund* (2007).

Cases cited

Dunnett v Railtrack (2002) 1 WLR 2434 (2002) 2 All ER 850, 853
Halsey v Milton Keynes General NHS Trust (2004) EWCA Civ 576
R (Cowl and Others) v Plymouth City Council (2002) 1 WLR 803
Shuttari v The Solicitors Indemnity Fund (2007)
Stretford v Football Association (2007) All ER (D) 346
Sumukan Ltd v The Commonwealth Secretariat (2007) EWCA Civ 243

References

Abel, R. (1992) 'Popular Justice, Populist Politics: Law in Community Organizing', in *Social and Legal Studies*, vol. 1, no. 2, June.

Anitha, S. and A. Gill (2009) 'Coercion, Consent and the Forced Marriage Debate in the UK', *Feminist Legal Studies*, vol. 17, no. 2, June.

Bano, S. (2007) 'Muslim Family Justice and Human Rights: The Experience of

British Muslim Women', *Journal of Comparative Law*, Volume 2, Issue 2.

Blackett, R. (2009) 'The Status of "Religious Courts" in English Law', *Decisions, Decisions: Dispute Resolution & International Arbitration Newsletter*, pp. 11–22.

Booth, P. (2008) 'Judging Sharia', *Family Law*, vol. 38, September.

Centre for Social Cohesion, (2009) *Beth Din: Jewish Law in the UK*, London.

Davis. A. and Roberts, M. (1989) *Mediating Family Law Disputes*, Ashgate, Aldershot.

FCO (2005) 'Forced Marriage: A Wrong Not a Right', Foreign and Commonwealth Office, London.

Fineman, M. (1988). 'Dominant discourse, professional language, and legal change in child custody decisionmaking', *Harvard Law Review*, vol. 101, no. 4, 727–74.

Genn, H. (1999) *What People Do and Think about Going to Law*, Hart Publishing, Oxford.

Harrington, C. B. (1992) 'Popular Justice, Populist Politics: Law in Community Organizing', *Social and Legal Studies* 1, 177-98.

Hester, M., Pearson, C. and Radford, L. (1997) *Domestic Violence: a National Survey of Court Welfare and Voluntary Sector Mediation Practice*, Policy Press, Bristol.

Home Office (2000). *A Choice by Right: The Report of the Working Group on Forced Marriage*. London: Home Office Communications Directorate. Available at http://www.fco.gov.uk/Files/KFile/AChoiceByRightJune2000.pdf.

Irving, H. and Benjamin, M (1995) *Family Mediation: Contemporary Issues*, Sage, Thousand Oaks, CA

Jarman, A. (2008) 'Plural Jurisdiction: Lawyers Reflect on the Archbishop of Canterbury's Speech', unpublished paper, presented to IALS, 15 April 2008.

Kurczewski, J. (1997) *Family Law and Family Policy in the New Europe*, Dartmouth, Aldershot.

MacEoin, D. (2009) *Sharia Law or 'One Law for All'?* Civitas: Institute for the Study of Civil Society, London.

Mackinnon, C. (1983) 'Feminism, Marxism, Method and the State: Toward Feminist Jurisprudence', *Signs: Journal of Women in Culture and Society*, 635: 8.

Maclean, M. and Kurczewski, J. (eds.) (1997) *Family Law and Family Policy in the New Europe*, Dartmouth, Aldershot.

Madeira, M. (2010) 'Shari'a or the State?: Islamic Law Tribunals in Western Democracies', unpublished paper for ISA Conference, 12 February 2010.

Menkel-Meadow, C. (1985) 'The Transformation of Disputes by Lawyers. What the Dispute Paradigm Does and Does Not Tell Us', *Missouri Journal of Dispute Resolution*, 25–44.

Muslim Arbitration Tribunal (2008) *Liberation from Forced Marriages*, MAT, London.

Parkinson, P. (1996) 'Multiculturalism and the Recognition of Marital Status in Australia', in Douglas, G. and Lowe, N. (eds.) *Families Across Frontiers*, Kluwer, London.

Phillips, A. and Dustin, M. (2004) 'UK Initiatives on Forced Marriage: Regulation,

Dialogue and Exit', *Political Studies,* vol. 52, no. 3, October.

Phillips, Lord Chief Justice (2008) 'Equality Before the Law', East London Muslim Centre, 3 July 2008.

Prentice, B. (2009) *One Year On: The Initial Impact of the Forced Marriage (Civil Protection) Act 2007 in Its First Year of Operation,* Ministry of Justice, London.

Redfern, A. and Hunter, M. (2004) *Law and Practice of International Commercial Arbitration,* 4th edn, Sweet & Maxwell, London.

Roberts, M. (2008) *Mediation in Family Disputes, Principles of Practice,* Ashgate, Aldershot.

Shachar, A. (2008) 'Privatizing Diversity: A Cautionary Tale from Religious Arbitration in Family Law', *Theoretical Inquiries in Law,* vol. 9, no. 2, June.

Shah-Kazemi, N. (2001) *Untying the Knot: Muslim Women, Divorce and the Shariah,* Nuffield Foundation, London.

Smart, C. and Brophy, J. (1985) *Women in Law: Explorations in Law, Family and Sexuality,* Routledge, London

Walsh, E. (2008) 'Publicly Funded Family Mediation: the Way Forward', *Family Law,* November.

Walsh, E. (2009) Forced Marriage Action, *Family Law,* vol. 81, no. 2.

Williams, Dr Rowan, Archbishop of Canterbury (2008) *UK law needs to find accommodation with religious law codes,* 7 February. www.archbishopofcanterbury.org/1580.

9

Constructing victims, construing credibility: forced marriage, Pakistani women and the UK asylum process

Marzia Balzani

> Building a safe, just and tolerant society
> (statement on every page of the Home Office's Reason for Refusal Letters)

A successful asylum-seeker granted refugee status in the UK is not only someone who can demonstrate past persecution but also someone who can demonstrate to the satisfaction of the United Kingdom Border Agency, and probably also to the Asylum and Immigration Tribunal, a likelihood of future persecution if returned to the country where the persecution took place. Here 'persecution' is understood within the terms of the United Nations Refugee Convention (UNHCR 1992) definition of a refugee as someone who, 'owing to a well-founded fear of being persecuted for reasons of race, religion, nationality, membership of a particular social group or political opinion, is outside the country of his nationality and is unable or, owing to such fear, is unwilling to avail himself of the protection of that country.' However, for would-be refugees there are obstacles to demonstrating persecution already suffered and the probability of future persecution. Obstacles can be structural, cultural, political, legal and financial and they can combine to militate against asylum applicants, so that the outcomes of any case may be far from predictable, consistent and equally fair to all (Amnesty International 2004; Tsangarides 2009).[1]

After negotiating flight from a country of origin, something most victims of persecution never manage, an asylum-seeker needs to claim asylum at the port of entry or the UK Border Agency office in Croydon and to put on record basic details, including her or his name and nationality.[2] The applicant later attends a full asylum interview where she sets out her case. She may at this stage be detained in the fast-track system as are perhaps one third of asylum seekers. The fast-track system was established in 2005 to speed up asylum decisions and deportations (Travis 2006; UK Government 2005).[3] Since 2007, asylum claims have been processed through the New Asylum Model designed to speed up further the processing of claims and to enhance the consistency of decision making.[4] Human Rights Watch has described the fast-track system as one that fails women with complex gender-related cases (Human Rights Watch 2010, 38; Travis 2006).[5] Similarly, a report by Cutler concluded that the chances of female asylum seekers securing refugee status or humanitarian protection is dramatically reduced if claims are decided while they are detained (Cutler 2007; Smith 2007).[6]

A considerable body of literature now exists setting out the failings of the system and raising doubts about the evaluation of claims that guidelines are applied in a consistent manner (Amnesty International 2004; Thomas 2008; UNHCR 2006). As Tsangarides states: 'Given the huge variance in the quality of individual actors within each of the stakeholder groups, namely legal representatives, UK Border Agency staff, IJs [Immigration Judges] and experts, the RSD [refugee status determination] process can almost be seen as a lottery in terms of the predicted and actual outcome of any individual case' (2010, 82).

This chapter considers some obstacles that all asylum seekers face but with reference to one particular group: Pakistani women seeking refugee status on the basis of persecution as members of a particular social group[7] because of the threat of, or an escape from, forced marriage. For these women to succeed in gaining refugee status the narratives of their experiences for the UK Border Agency and the Asylum and Immigration Tribunal must be 'credible' and the women themselves must also be constructed and presented as 'credible'. Credibility is central to any successful asylum application, but for women persecuted by non-state agents there may be additional difficulties in demonstrating persecution within the terms of the convention.[8]

Primary data comes from consultancy as an expert witness producing 'culture' reports to help the Asylum and Immigration Tribunal understand the social, legal, and religious contexts from which the asylum seekers have come and to which they risk return when applications fail. To understand this data we need also to understand the stages through which an asylum application passes, the roles of those who process it, and the data used to evaluate and judge the application. How knowledge is constructed in the assessment of asylum applications is crucial to understanding what works and what goes wrong for applicants in the decision-making process. How asylum caseowners are trained,[9] how solicitors and barristers are taught to construct 'facts' to argue their cases in adversarial contests, and the political necessities of an age in which global migrant flows from the South are portrayed as threats to the social cohesion strategies of the UK government, all play a role in the construction of such knowledge. And for the particular social group under consideration here, we also add the need to understand forced marriage as a gendered form of persecution (Gangoli and Chantler 2009; Dauvergne and Millbank, 2010). The conflictual nature of the practices and modes of understanding that define the asylum process reflects the complex ways in which groups construct their own strategically beneficial definitions and positions on forced marriage and gender persecution as well as contesting those of others. Below I demonstrate how current Home Office constructions of a 'typical' victim of forced marriage serve to deny asylum to most women who claim asylum on this basis.

Constructing victims

The freedom to choose a spouse and not to be forced into an unwanted marriage is a human right. The failure to protect this right may result in a form of modern enslavement. The 1962 UN Convention on Consent to Marriage, Minimum Age for Marriage and Registration of Marriages reaffirms that 'all States' should work to abolish 'such customs ... and practices' relating to marriage as restrict 'complete freedom in the choice of a spouse', to eliminate 'completely child marriages and the betrothal of ... girls before the age of puberty' and to establish 'penalties where necessary' and 'a civil or other register in which all marriages will be recorded' (UNHCR 2008, 195). In addition, Article 1 of the 1956 Supplementary Convention on the Abolition of Slavery obliges state parties to abolish any institution or practice whereby a woman has no right to refuse a match or is sold into marriage, where a woman may be transferred by a husband or family to another person in exchange for value received, or where widows can be inherited (UNHCR 2008, 195).

In the UK, forced marriage became a public issue in the late 1990s when three high-profile cases made an official study and response to the matter necessary (Phillips and Dustin 2004). Following consultation, the UK government decided not to criminalise forced marriage but to provide for a civil response within the Family Law Act 1996. The Forced Marriage (Civil Protection) Act came into force in the UK in 2007 (Anitha and Gill 2009, 168–9). Official definitions of forced marriage make careful distinctions between arranged marriages, considered as the acceptable cultural practice of some minority communities within the UK, and forced marriages, which are not acceptable and not a part of any community's sanctioned practices (Phillips and Dustin 2004, 533). This formulation was agreed so as not to alienate minority communities or to risk any increase in racial unrest in the UK.

However, the institutionalisation of forced marriage as a matter of policy development and implementation has, across Europe, been presented more as a matter of immigration regulation than a problem occurring between those who reside and marry within the EU (Phillips and Dustin 2004). This is evident in the UK with the location of the Forced Marriage Unit (FMU) within the Foreign and Commonwealth Office and the recent increase in the age at which a UK citizen can sponsor a spouse's visa (Yeo 2009). Similar changes in regulation have occurred across Europe, for example in Denmark, where the increased age required of spouses applying for visas in immigration matters has been presented as a means of protecting young women considered at risk of forced marriage and not as a method for curbing immigration from the subcontinent (Gangoli and Chantler 2009; Yeo 2009). Inevitably such a position infantilises minority women, assuming a generalised incapacity for any decision making. Such a position also implies that a young woman is *de facto* incapable of agreeing to an arranged marriage with a foreign spouse. In such cases the assumption in the official literature is that pressure has been applied to gain consent or, more extremely, that the young woman has been coerced.

In the UK no systematic records are kept of forced marriages occurring between individuals already residing in the UK, making it impossible to gauge the extent of the problem. Nor it is possible to estimate the numbers of forced marriages taking place within the EU between those already resident in the EU. The invisibility of 'home-grown' forced marriage is only one part of the problem; another is the stereotypical construction of the victim of a forced marriage as a young, dependent female who is whisked out of the UK to marry against her will. Such victims do, of course, exist and the Forced Marriage Unit assists several hundred people in this situation each year.[10] The real problem is that these are not the *only* victims of forced marriage and the UK Border Agency is decidedly unhelpful in acknowledging that women can be forced into marriage even if they are not stereotypically young, dependent, uneducated and British.

This is not entirely the fault of the UK Border Agency since 'parliamentary debates and government documents' repeatedly 'suggest that forced marriage predominantly affects young people' (Gangoli and Chantler 2009,

268). So, for example, a concern for the well-being of the young was given as a key reason by the Labour government for raising the age at which a person can apply for a spouse-and-partner visa from 18 to 21 in 2008 (Yeo 2009, 365). But, as Yeo demonstrates, this rationalisation is disingenuous at best because the Home Office was fully aware that the reasons it gave for the new legislation were contradicted by research it commissioned in 2006. This report concluded 'there was no evidence to suggest the previous rise from 16 to 18 had done anything to prevent forced marriages, there was no reason to think that a further increase would assist prevent[ion of] forced marriages in future and in fact a further rise might well harm the best interests of vulnerable young women and men' (Yeo 2009, 365). It is perhaps not surprising that the Home Office made limited reference to this report.[11] But if the UK Border Agency has accepted the stereotype of the forced marriage victim as a vulnerable youth, it has dealt with forced marriage in relation to asylum-seeking women very differently to the way in which the matter is dealt with for a UK citizen. In asylum cases, even the acceptance that forced marriage happens and where it does, that this is a harm amounting to persecution, is avoided. In part this is done through the production of the materials that the UK Border Agency uses to assess asylum cases.

The Home Office produces its own 'objective' information such as Country of Origin Information (COI) reports on the main refugee-producing countries which is used by caseowners to gain an overall sense of the country from which asylum seekers come. The COI reports are compilations of data from a variety of sources. In the report for Pakistan (Home Office 2010), 'Underage/forced marriage' is a subdivision in the section on 'Childcare and Protection'. This reflects the fact that the report considers forced marriage mainly as a form of underage marriage and even in this context the topic is treated in very general terms. Elsewhere in the report, forced marriage receives only passing mention as one item in a list of harms. For example, forced marriage is mentioned in relation to women's issues in general (section 23), lesbian, gay, bisexual and transgender persons (LGBT) (section 21) and trafficking (section 25). Though the report notes a recent, unenforced, law making forced marriage illegal in Pakistan, forced marriage is not highlighted as a significant issue and, in a document 239 pages long, 'forced marriage' appears only a handful of times. What happens in cases of forced marriage is never discussed and appears to be treated as self-evident and unproblematic.

Nonetheless, even these perfunctory references to forced marriage are a slight improvement over previous COI reports on Pakistan, as these make no mention of forced marriage at all (e.g. Home Office 2005). At least the issue is now one that has a name. Other reports that caseowners use to evaluate asylum applications such as the most recent Home Office *Operational Guidance Note* for Pakistan dated February 2009 (Home Office 2009), which includes a section on women asylum claimants, makes no mention of forced marriage although it includes subsections on domestic violence, rape and honour crimes. Given the limited time that caseowners have to decide on a claim, this lack of consideration of what forced marriages entail may increase the numbers of unsatisfactory initial decisions in cases of forced marriage.[12] This is particularly so as caseowners have been shown to work with an 'information hierarchy', in effect preferring to use Home Office COI and assuming that other COI produced by nongovernmental organisations and others are biased and less reliable (Tsangarides 2010, 94-5).

This brief survey of Home Office documentation suggests that as the British public from the late 1990s onwards discovered 'forced marriage', the Home Office was minimising references to forced marriage in some of its own literature. For example, the Immigration Appellate Authority's *Gender Guidelines* (2000) produced to facilitate decision making in asylum cases, and which did include explicit reference to forced marriage as a gender-specific form of harm, were revised and cut by the new tribunal in 2005 which held that it was not compelled to follow previous guidelines (see Home Office API 2009a: Berkowitz 2000). Again, it is difficult to avoid concluding that as forced marriage became an issue that the public viewed as persecution, so asylum as a consequence of forced marriage was being limited by the reduction of references to this as a form of persecution in Home Office documentation relating to asylum seekers.

Furthermore, despite the fact that forced marriage is now mentioned in some UK COI, the Home Office does not provide a publicly available official breakdown of reasons why women claim asylum, and so the extent to which forced marriage figures in asylum applications remains unknown. However, 'organizations and solicitors working with women' consistently report forced marriage as one of the issues 'behind [asylum] claims' (Human Rights Watch 2010, 16). This suggests that forced marriage is not an uncommon issue for women asylum seekers. To fail, therefore, explicitly to treat forced marriage as a form of gendered violence means that such violence can be downplayed and the possible consequences of this can be minimised by caseowners and IJs.[13]

A further complication is that forced marriage, in cases I have prepared reports for, is rarely a stand-alone issue. In most cases forced marriage is one element in a case where property, debt, business deals, inheritance, religion, child custody, and sexual orientation, for example, are interwoven. Forced marriage cannot therefore be isolated other than analytically and still hold good as a credible asylum narrative where a simple forced marriage scenario of child kidnapped and married against her will is the predominant model that caseowners work with.

Two brief examples make this clear. In the first case, a Christian woman and orphaned daughter of a Muslim father and Christian mother had been raised from childhood by her Muslim uncle. The uncle managed his deceased brother's property which was technically now that of the daughter. The uncle avoided arranging a suitable marriage for his niece so that he could profit from his late brother's property. However, when the possibility arose of a marriage with a Muslim man who could be of assistance to the uncle in business, the uncle attempted to force his niece into an unwanted marriage as the third wife to a man who would make her convert, against her will, to Islam. The niece fled to the UK where her case was fast-tracked on the grounds that she was a mature woman and therefore, simply by virtue of this, could avoid a forced marriage; that her faith was not an issue as she could practise this in Pakistan without being forced to convert to Islam; and that her level of education – the woman had a degree by correspondence course but lived in seclusion and had never been employed – meant that she could fend for herself in Pakistan as a lone woman from a minority faith, with no family, no resources, no social network for support, while living in fear of being tracked down by her uncle. The woman's claim that she was at risk of forced marriage was dismissed as 'not credible' and, although not stated explicitly, it was clear from the Reasons for Refusal Letter (RFRL) that this was because the caseowner was unable to imagine a social context in which anyone other than a child could be compelled to marry against her will. The caseowner was also unable both adequately to assess the significance of the woman's inheritance as a factor in the strategies of men to control wealth and to evaluate the place of Christianity in modern Pakistan and the future risk of harm to this woman.

Here, religion and property claims made sense of why forced marriage was credible. Unfortunately, these latter issues were not discussed as relevant to the claim and were treated in isolation from each other so that it was not possible for, or perhaps not in the interest of, the caseowner to connect them to realise how they fitted together to explain how and why the narrative the woman presented was plausible. The strategy of the caseowner, as in many

RFRLs, was to take each element in isolation and seek to dismiss it as a problem rather than to work to understand how gender, faith, past experiences of domestic violence et cetera in combination lead to increased risk of harm for particular women with specific sets of issues. Worryingly, on the use of COI Tsangarides notes: 'in response to a question asking in what cases would one not use country information, a UK Border Agency caseowner wrote: "when the information would be damaging to our stance in refusing a claim"' (2010, 42). Extrapolating from this to RFRLs it almost seems that for each point raised by a claimant some caseowners scour the COI to find 'objective evidence' to dispute it.

In the second case, a lesbian mother, who had been forced into a marriage by family and societal pressure to conform to gender norms, sought asylum in the UK because her husband had discovered her sexual orientation. Again, the credibility of the woman was questioned, and this time not only was the issue of forced marriage not taken seriously by the caseowner but a normalised and Western construction of a stereotypical and culture-bound lesbian life history was generalised and universalised to dispute the possibility that the life this woman described could ever have existed. There are, however, many examples of lesbians forced into marriage but who have been denied asylum on the grounds that LGBT persons do not enter into heterosexual marriages, thus consigning such cases to the 'lacking credibility' category (Laviolette 2007, 188; Berg and Millbank 2009). The gendered implications of marriage are rarely considered: both lesbians and gay men may be forced into marriage but the consequences are harsher for women living in patriarchal societies.

Other examples of forced marriage involve attempts by women to choose their own spouses or the discovery by family that a woman has been 'dating'.[14] This sometimes leads families hastily to arrange a marriage according to family wishes. In these cases it is clear that women have found ways of evading family restrictions and making choices for themselves even in highly sexsegregated social contexts. The Reason for Refusal letters in these cases usually revolve around disbelief that it is possible for a woman to date in Pakistan for any length of time without discovery by the family and then to the arguement, apparently accepting that such dating is possible, that if she has managed this then she can return to Pakistan and live there in safety on her own as she is clearly capable of acting on her own initiative. The contradictory assertions made to justify the rejection of an asylum application do not seem to trouble caseowners; again there is an overwhelming sense that any and all situations will be used to deny a claim bit by bit rather than to assess a claim on its merits in the round.

The outcome of Home Office policies is that there are two ways of dealing with forced marriage. One approach is applied to women who are British citizens or resident in the UK. For these women the reality of forced marriage is accepted and viewed as an infringement of their human rights. The FMU will intervene to protect them, even if the women are not in the UK at the time their plight becomes known to the authorities.[15] Here women are viewed as individuals with liberal post-Enlightenment rights to self-determination.

The other approach is for women seeking asylum, in part or predominantly because of forced marriage. These women are typically viewed as lacking credibility and sometimes even as failing to submit to the reasonable cultural demands that all women should be married and that families should decide who a woman marries. Here culture dominates over individual rights and it is not considered unduly harsh to expect individuals to conform to cultural practice. Pressure to marry is seen as a universal feature of the culture and therefore is not a harm for a specific group. This limits the chances of individuals successfully claiming forced marriage constitutes persecution in its own right and *also* because of their membership of a particular social group. Further, as marriage is viewed as a social institution it is difficult to link it to religious or political forms of persecution, and so two other Convention grounds for refugee status are eliminated. At best such a marriage might infringe one's human rights but would not also necessarily amount to persecution according to Convention grounds. As marriage is perceived as an institution that all adults in some cultures are expected to submit to, there is an assumption that all members of society are similarly situated in relation to this institution. This leads to 'a failure to acknowledge that gay men and lesbians are not similarly situated in relation to marriage in comparison with heterosexual people for the very reason that marriage is a heterosexual institution' (Dauvergne and Millbank 2010, 74). These are some of the reasons why women fleeing forced marriage find the odds stacked against them in asylum applications.

Construing credibility

Though the outcome of an application for asylum may depend and falter on the UK Border Agency construction of forced marriage, it is not entirely determined by this. The asylum seeker's own testimony and statements are also taken into account when determining a claim.

Unfortunately, here too, there are hurdles that the asylum seeker needs to overcome and which are not always explicitly recognised as such, or which may not in fact have a direct bearing on whether or not persecution has taken place or would take place if a person returned to their country of origin. In a UK Border Agency interview there are many obstacles to the presentation of a full history and to explanation of the case for asylum. Aside from the difficulties of presenting often private information to a stranger in a stressful situation, there is the additional problem, for many, of working through an interpreter who, no matter how well intentioned, adds layers of cultural, class and gendered mediation that the asylum seeker has to negotiate (Berg and Millbank 2009; Rycroft 2005). In addition, the Home Office caseowner conducting the interview is trained to seek only certain types of information, the 'material evidence' deemed relevant, and to ignore or ask the 'client' to stop talking about matters that to the caseowner do not self-evidently seem relevant. Caseowners, using materials considered 'objective', evaluate the interview material and mostly reject the asylum applications in a Reason for Refusal letter which sets out, in formulaic and often literally 'cut and paste' paragraphs, why the application has failed.[16] Asylum seekers may be able to appeal against a refusal, but this depends on many factors, including access to legal advice which is increasingly difficult to obtain for those who cannot fund their appeal no matter how strong their cases (James and Killick 2010; Tsangarides 2009, 80–2).

Every step in the process is a potential pitfall, and while caseowners are required to evaluate each case in accordance with international and national laws and guidelines, there are good reasons to be concerned about the fairness of a process in which an asylum seeker's initial asylum decision is made by an official who does not need to have a degree-level education and who has no required background or training in law, yet is entrusted with decision making in a field that often requires specialist legal knowledge (Sweeney 2009, fn10, 724). Concerns have also been expressed about the hostile attitudes of some UK Border Agency staff.[17] By way of context for the unhelpful attitudes which may be held by some UK Border Agency staff, researchers have suggested that being 'presented constantly with claims of torture or persecution' may 'induce compassion fatigue and an organisational culture of disbelief towards claimants', leading to a 'refusal mindset' (Thomas 2006, 84).

Asylum cases are difficult and complex as they not only depend on an understanding of relevant laws, but also require an evaluation of subjective fear in relation to objective country situations. Getting an asylum decision wrong may have appalling consequences for an individual, which should require those making the decisions to be competent, well-trained, provided with the best possible resources and given sufficient time for each case to reach a sound decision. Unfortunately, it is clear that such training, resources and time are rarely provided.

While there are many points at which a claim may falter, here I focus specifically on one key area of an applicant's claim, that of the credibility of the narrative presented by an asylum seeker together with the credibility of the applicant herself. Credibility has been a topic of considerable discussion in refugee studies (for Australia see Coffey 2003; in relation to particular social group and sexual orientation see Millbank 2009). As Coffey has succinctly put it, credibility is 'conceptually elusive and adjudicatively influential' (Coffey 2003, 377). Recent work in the UK on asylum and credibility has highlighted many problems in the understanding and application of credibility findings made by initial bureaucratic decision-makers (Good 2007, 187–209; Thomas 2006; Sweeney 2009; UNHCR 2006. section 2.3.6–7; Amnesty International 2004, 20). Understanding how credibility is assessed is important because for the UK Asylum and Immigration Tribunal '[f]indings of credibility are one of the primary functions' of the asylum decision maker 'since they lead to the establishment of much of the factual matrix for the determination of the case. In some cases, but by no means all, the issue of credibility may be the fulcrum of the decision as to whether the claim succeeds or fails' (Blake 2001, 25, 27, cited in Thomas 2006, 79).

The UN Refugee Convention makes no mention of credibility either in relation to the refugee definition in Article 1A(2) or the prohibition on *refoulement* – deportation or expulsion of a person to a country where that person faces persecution, or risk of serious human rights violations – in Article 33(1), yet many asylum applications fail because of doubts about 'credibility'. However, despite its importance, the term 'credibility' is used in several different ways in the UK with a range of descriptive intentions and legal consequences (Sweeney 2009, 700). Sweeney (2009) has undertaken a comprehensive review of the understanding and application of credibility assessments in the UK, considering in particular the Asylum Policy Instructions (APIs) used by caseowners to make initial decisions on asylum applications.[18] I outline Sweeney's arguments and conclusions at some length because he has provided a rigorous account of the deployment of 'credibility' in the UK asylum process and because my own assessment of the limitations and effects of its application are largely in keeping with his. This chapter contributes to the discussion by bringing to it the qualitative and ethnographic dimension made available by individual case studies, although these are treated briefly here. Individual narratives of forced marriage help us understand how credibility is applied and what effect this has in particular instances; but equally, a broad and conceptual understanding of credibility provides an essential frame for understanding how forced marriage is handled in the UK asylum system.

As Sweeney notes, given the lack of higher education and legal training that caseowners may have, the 'APIs ... play a role in bridging the gap between law and practice by making complex legal and conceptual issues accessible to decision makers'. Sweeney sets out three key areas that credibility assessments are primarily concerned with: internal consistency, external consistency and plausibility. However, as Sweeney adds, 'this does not tell us *how* internally consistent, *how* externally consistent, or *how* plausible the applicant's story would need to be in order to be "credible"'. Does an asylum seeker, for example, 'need to "prove" credibility, and what is the extent of the relationship between credibility findings and the outcome of the case?' (Sweeney 2009, 704). Sweeney's close study of the API on credibility (HO API 2009b), despite his comments on the inferred good intentions of the document's writers, ends with a trenchant critique of the API on credibility and calls for its deletion as 'it is not an adequate summary of the domestic or international law on credibility' (Sweeney 2009, 726). The problems with the current API *Assessing Credibility in Asylum and Human Rights Claims* include: presenting a disparate range of materials on credibility 'as if they are consistent on the significance of credibility in the RSD process ... and its relationship ... to refugee law' (Sweeney 2009, 707–8); the misreading of UK case law and hence provision of incorrect guidance on this basis (Sweeney 2009, 720ff); a setting up of hurdles *all* of which the asylum seeker has to meet to be considered credible even when some of these have no bearing on the matter of refugee status or persecution itself (Sweeney 2009, 716–17); the omission of 'Immigration Rule (IR) 339J or Article 4(3) EC Qualification Directive (QD) – which are, in fact, the main provisions on assessing applications for asylum' (Sweeney 2009, 710); credibility used to determine the 'truth' of an asylum narrative as opposed to using this as a measure for ascertaining 'the benefit of the doubt' as set out in the UNHCR Handbook; and lastly, the API conflates credibility with proof while the UNHCR 'sees credibility as an alternative to proof, and not a synonym for it. It is about giving the benefit of the doubt to a credible account in circumstances where proof has not been possible' (Sweeney 2009: 711). This results in the failure of the Home Office to distinguish between two possible approaches to credibility which Sweeney labels 'broad and narrow' approaches.

Considering just the 'broad and narrow' approaches to credibility in more detail Sweeney notes that a broad approach to credibility is where a caseowner decides if an 'application is meritorious and, consequently, successful. On a broad interpretation of credibility, therefore, to describe a claim as "credible" is to say that the applicant's statements are true and that ... she warrants international protection' (Sweeney 2009,708). Here 'credibility' is virtually synonymous with 'proof'.

A narrow definition of credibility views 'the conclusion that a particular statement is credible as more contingent' (Sweeney 2009, 708). A contingent credibility statement 'is not certainly true, not yet proven, but because it is plausible, consistent, and reflects generally known facts, must not be dismissed from the consideration of whether the applicant has a well founded fear of persecution. The UNHCR Handbook describes admitting unsupported but credible statements as evidence as giving asylum seekers "the benefit of the doubt"' (Sweeney 2009, 710). In short, and unlike the API on credibility, the 'UNHCR sees credibility as an alternative to proof, and not a synonym for it' (Sweeney 2009, 711). Unfortunately, from the point of view of asylum seekers, caseowners appear to be working with a broad rather than a narrow approach to credibility and require asylum applicants to reach standards of 'credibility' not only relating to their claims but also by virtue of their behaviour once in the UK that go well beyond the UNHCR Handbook guidelines.

The understanding and application of credibility findings is one of a range of systems in place that limit and actively hinder the just appraisal of asylum applications. In the final section of this chapter I want to reconnect the issue of credibility to the individual case study. Here, I reflect in particular on the ways in which solicitors, in attempting to make individual claims 'credible' in Home Office terms, may in fact unwittingly reproduce the government's discourse of credibility and hence silence the very women they represent – even if the claim for asylum ultimately succeeds. Credibility is a barrier to asylum applications, in part because caseowners, guided by the COI reports and APIs, are, perhaps unwittingly, encouraged to prove what does not need to be proved, and to compel asylum seekers to meet requirements they do not have to meet under international law in order to gain refugee status.

Engineering silence

Women often find that their own stories of persecution are reworked to meet the expectations of various authorities, or questioned and undermined in order to deny their credibility and hence to reject the asylum application. Sometimes the reworking of narratives is conducted by solicitors who organise lived experience to make it conform more directly to Convention grounds, thereby increasing the likelihood of a successful asylum application. For instance, solicitors may attempt to persuade caseowners and IJs that acts of persecution carried out by individuals, including family members, constitute persecution as defined by the UN Convention by imputing a 'political view' to claimants resisting forced marriage and hence claiming for them possible membership of a particular social group (Laviolette 2007, 173-4; Ziegler and Stewart 2009, 122ff). From the Home Office side, narratives are questioned and discounted to reduce the likelihood of a successful asylum application. In both cases, however, a woman's own understanding of her experiences and persecution is at best sidelined, and sometimes elements that are key to the understanding of her experiences are erased from the record.

Here I mention one small but revealing example taken from an interview with a victim of domestic violence. During the interview the woman repeatedly returned to one incident which had caused her great psychological pain but which both interviewer and solicitor were unable to understand in context. The woman wanted to convey the abuse and insult she experienced when a shoe was used to hit her on the head. The interviewer, however, was more interested in injuries that had resulted in visits to hospitals as 'objective' evidence. In a South Asian context using a shoe to hit someone, particularly on the head, is a declaration of the abuser's contempt. For this woman the beating with a shoe was more damaging and harder to heal than bruises from other beatings. In the interview, her experience was dismissed as insignificant and irrelevant. Given the rawness of the experience which came through, with the woman's continual return to this incident, and the difficulty she had in describing this to the caseowner, the silencing of her account in this small way was one more abuse, another act where her experiences did not count. In the very interview where she was supposed to have an opportunity to give a full account of her experiences, she had been 'muted' – a term Ardener (1975) used to account for the failure to 'hear' certain categories of people who speak but whose language is not recognised as valid in the same way in which the discourse of dominant groups is.

These erasures and mutings produce accounts of victim experiences which are routinised, conform to standard expectations, and quickly become formulaic. I read many such accounts and quickly find that every report, every witness statement, every narrative covers the same or very similar ground and remains within limited confines whatever the case. Details, locations, dates and names change but it becomes harder and harder to distinguish the individuals in these accounts; I suspect that the individuals who are the ultimate sources of these narratives would also find it difficult to recognise themselves in these statements.

While I do not doubt the good intentions of solicitors who reorder client material to get the best statement to help their clients, I also wonder about the asylum seekers left with narratives which diverge markedly from any original narratives they may have started with (cf. McKinley 1997, 70). McKinley describes this process as one where 'the process of "translating" personal experience into a linguistic framework intelligible for judges and practitioners presents insuperable barriers in accommodating the "truth" of narratives with the demands of the legal process' (1997, 72). When a case goes well, such narrative violence may be accepted as a price to be paid for a greater good, but when a case fails and the asylum seeker is in effect told that her case did not fall within Convention grounds, or that she is simply not believed, then the lurking suspicion that she did not get to tell her story her way may be an added issue to deal with.

In a perhaps somewhat perverse counter-reading of the narratives of women asylum seekers one might argue that while solicitors tend to highlight the lack of options women have in their countries of origin and stress the persecutory nature of 'cultural' practices which victimise women, it is the Home Office, through caseowners, who present cultural practices as negotiable and portray women as capable of the resistance possible only when embodied in autonomous and independent agents. When witness statements ordered by solicitors succeed and women do gain refugee status it is often because representations of women as essentialised, disempowered victims have been accepted.

A different way in which narratives of persecution are erased has to do more directly with forced marriage as a harm which is not considered sufficiently persecutory in its own right in the UK to merit refugee status. Dauvergne and Millbank reviewed available tribunal and court refugee determinations from 1995 to 2008 on forced marriage and found only 11 published cases for the UK (Dauvergne and Millbank 2010, 67). However, as Dauvergne and Millbank note, this may underrepresent the actual number of cases as very few decisions from low-level tribunals are published (Dauvergne and Millbank 2010, 67–8).

My work suggests another possible way of making sense of this low number of forced marriage cases among the published UK tribunal decisions. A review of the Pakistan cases I took on from August 2007 to April 2010 includes 10 cases involving 12 women and one minor-age male where forced marriage was a significant part of the claim. In one case the solicitor explicitly asked me to consider not putting weight on the forced marriage in my report as this was not something IJs would base a decision on. The perception, probably a good one, is that in the best interest of clients, solicitors, no matter what they may think of forced marriage, cannot risk a case failing by focusing on this when other issues are more easily justified as tried-and-tested forms of 'persecution'. The strategy is to go with what is known to work. Given the current lack of general awareness and understanding in the Asylum and Immigration Tribunal of forced marriage as persecutory in its own right, a solicitor would limit a client's chances of success if this matter were to be the central part of a claim for asylum. On a case-by-case basis this may lead to more successful outcomes, but for women themselves this is another way in which their narratives of persecution are manipulated and their experiences are silenced.[19] At a more global level this strategy means forced marriage is an issue that all parties – solicitors, IJs and, by deference to the greater knowledge of their solicitors, asylum applicants – collude together to keep hidden.

Conclusion

There is a sombre irony in the realisation that a woman fleeing forced marriage is most likely to be considered a credible and therefore to become a successful asylum applicant precisely when her narrative of persecution plays down the violence of forced marriage and accommodates more thoroughly to a British perception of Asian culture as repressive of women who are rendered passive by socialisation. Hence precisely when a narrative is least authentic as a woman's own testimony of her experiences it is likely to be most convincing. The strategic essentialism employed by solicitors on behalf of clients may help individual women but ultimately will not help women as a whole who can and do negotiate relations within and across cultures in complex ways, but for whom any capacity for agentive action is construed as evidence that they do not meet the necessary threshold to demonstrate persecution in a country of origin.

Notes

1   However, someone who does not qualify as a refugee in the UK may be granted humanitarian protection or discretionary leave to remain on human rights grounds.

2   As of October 2009, Croydon is the only centre for asylum applications other than ports of entry.

3   For legislation on the fast track rules see: http://www.opsi.gov.uk/si/si2005/20050560.htm. Also http://www.guardian.co.uk/uk/2006/jan/03/immigration.immigrationandpublicservices2/print

4   The New Asylum Model was first proposed by the Home Office in 'Controlling our borders: Making migration work for Britain' (Home Office 2005). The strategy was to introduce a faster asylum process, with 'rapid and increased numbers of removals from the UK'. Human Rights Watch 2010, 10.

5   'After a woman is referred into ... [fast track], her claim is decided within [a few] days. If refused – and in 2008 96 percent of claims were refused on first instance– she has two working days to appeal ... from start to finish the whole process takes around two weeks ... Since May 2005 over 2,000 women have been detained by the UK Home Office in Yarl's Wood ... In 2008 91% of appeals were refused' (Human Rights Watch 2010, 1).

6   Smith's 2007 review of the situation for women asylum seekers described in in Cutler's *Refusal Factory* ends with key findings which include: poor representation for women; lack of time to gather reports or to disclose traumatic events; the speed of the process militating against fairness; complex cases unsuitable for fast-track systems; and a lack of statistics and monitoring making effective scrutiny virtually impossible.

7   The category of 'particular social group' was a last-minute addition to the categories of refugee in the 1951 UN Convention Relating to the Status of Refugees. Defining who may constitute a particular social group has resulted in much discussion and debate since 1951 (Good 2007, 74ff).

8   However, case law and gender guidelines produced by the UNHCR and member states have helped to remedy some difficulties women faced in the past (Canadian Immigration and Refugee Board 1999; UNHCR 2002; HO API 2009a; Laviolette 2007).

9   Since the introduction of the New Asylum Model, a single individual is now responsible for processing an asylum application. This includes interviewing and producing the Reasons for Refusal letter.

10   According to the Foreign and Commonwealth Office website, 'In 2009 FMU gave advice or support to 1682 cases.' http://www.fco.gov.uk/en/travel-and-living-abroad/when-things-go-wrong/forced-marriage (accessed 22 June 2010).

11   See the research report and Home Office reasons for non-publication at

http://www.whatdotheyknow.com/request/forced_marriage_research (accessed 15 June 2010).

12 Tsangarides (2010, 79) states that caseowners spend a total of 15 hours on a case including the time used for interview. Approximately three hours are spent on COI research. Caseowners themselves consider this to be half the time they would ideally spend on research.

13 Although men are also victims of forced marriage, most victims are women. In cases I have worked on, the men tend to be vulnerable and run the risk of forced marriage because of their sexual orientation or because they are very young, others seek to control their inheritance or other coveted social capital.

14 An interesting approach to this issue is taken by Siddiqi, who suggests that many forced marriage cases where a family suspects a woman is 'dating' an unsuitable man involve the urban, educated sectors of society (Siddiqi 2005, 297–8). Such findings are in accordance with cases I have worked on.

15 As in the case of Dr Humayra Abedin who was held captive by her family in Bangladesh and was rescued by the British and Bangladeshi authorities and returned to the UK. http://www.timesonline.co.uk/tol/news/uk/crime/article 5340058.ece.

16 Materials consulted by caseowners including the COI Service reports are themselves the subject of some debate as to their actual 'objectivity' and reliability (Houle 1994; Thomas 2008; Tsangarides 2009).

17 Taylor and Muir (2010) – Issues raised here are the subject of parliamentary questions.

18 The Home Office official site states: 'The asylum policy instructions are the Government's policy on asylum. They are followed by asylum caseowners in the UK Border Agency.' The site lists over forty APIs. http://www.ukba.homeoffice. gov.uk/sitecontent/documents/policyandlaw/asylumpolicyinstructions/.

19 On this see McKinley (1997, 75) describing the transformation over twelve weeks of a statement from one the asylum seeker first gave to one that her solicitors persuaded her to accept as in her own best interest.

References

Amnesty International (2004) *Get It Right: How Home Office Decision Making Fails Refugees*, Amnesty International, London. http://www.amnesty.org.uk/uploads/documents/doc_15239.pdf (18 June 2010).

Anitha, S. and A. Gill (2009) 'Coercion, Consent and the Forced Marriage Debate in the UK', *Feminist Legal Studies*, vol. 17, no. 2, August.

Ardener, E. (1975) 'Belief and the Problem of Women', S. Ardener (ed.), *Perceiving Women*, John Wiley & Sons, New York.

Berg, L. and J. Millbank (2009) 'Constructing the Personal Narratives of Lesbian,

Gay and Bisexual Claimants', *Journal of Refugee Studies*, vol. 22, no. 2, June.

Berkowitz, N. (2000) 'Gender Guidelines for the UK', *Forced Migration Review*, vol. 9.

Canadian Immigration and Refugee Board (1999) *Women Refugee Claimants Fearing Gender-Related Persecution: Update.* http://www.irb.gc.ca/eng/media/bckinfo/Pages/ back_women.aspx (23 June 2010).

Coffey, G. (2003) 'The Credibility of Credibility Evidence at the Refugee Review Tribunal', *International Journal of Refugee Law*, vol. 15, no. 3, July.

Cutler, S. (2007) *Refusal Factory: Women's Experiences of the Detained Fast Track Asylum Process at Yarl's Wood Immigration Removal Centre.* http://www.biduk.org/pdf/Fast%20track/BID_RefusalFactory_07.pdf (23 June 2010).

Dauvergne, C. and Millbank, J. (2010) 'Forced Marriage as a Harm in Domestic and International Law', *Modern Law Review*, vol. 73 no. 1, January.

Gangoli, G. and Chantler, K. (2009) 'Protecting Victims of Forced Marriage: Is Age a Protective Factor?' *Feminist Legal Studies*, vol. 17, no. 3, December.

Good, A. (2007) *Anthropology and Expertise in the Asylum Courts*, Routledge-Cavendish, Oxford.

Home Office (2005) *Controlling Our Borders: Making Migration Work for Britain* http://www.archive2.official-documents.co.uk/document/cm64/6472/6472.pdf (11 July 2010).

Home Office API (2009a) *Gender Issues in the Asylum Claim* http://www.ind.homeoffice.gov.uk/sitecontent/documents/policyandlaw/asylumpolicyinstructions/apis/genderissueintheasylum.pdf?view=Binary (22 June 2010).

Home Office API (2009b) *Assessing credibility in asylum and human rights claims* http://www.ukba.homeoffice.gov.uk/sitecontent/documents/policyandlaw/asylumpolicyinstructions/apis/credibility.pdf?view=Binary (23 June 2010).

Home Office (2009) *Operational Guidance Note Pakistan* http://www.ukba.homeoffice.gov.uk/sitecontent/documents/policyandlaw/countryspecificasylumpolicyogns/pakistanogn?view=Binaryhttp://www.bia.homeoffice.gov.uk/sitecontent/documents/policyandlaw/countryspecificasylumpolicyogns/pakistanogn?view=Binary (23 June 2010).

Home Office (2010) COI Report Pakistan http://rds.homeoffice.gov.uk/rds/pdfs10/pakistan-180110.doc (10 July 2010).

Houle, F. (1994) 'The Credibility and Authoritativeness of Documentary Information in Determining Refugee Status: The Canadian Experience', *International Journal of Refugee Law*, vol. 6, no. 1.

Human Rights Watch (2010) *Fast-tracked Unfairness: Detention and Denial of Women Asylum Seekers in the UK.* http://www.hrw.org/en/reports/2010/02/24/fast-tracked-unfairness (23 June 2010).

Immigration Appellate Authority (UK) (2000) *Gender Guidelines.* http://www.unhcr.org/refworld/docid/3ae6b3414.html (12 July 2010).

James, D. and Killick, E. (2010) 'Ethical Dilemmas? UK Immigration, Legal Aid

Funding Reform and Caseowners', *Anthropology Today*, vol. 26, no. 1, February.

Laviolette, N. (2007) 'Gender Related Refugee Claims: Expanding the Scope of the Canadian Guidelines', *International Journal of Refugee Law*, vol. 19, no. 2, July.

McKinley (1997) 'Life Stories, Disclosure and the Law', *Political and Legal Anthropology Review*, vol. 20, no. 2, November.

Millbank, J. (2009) '"The Ring of Truth": a Case Study of Credibility Assessment in Particular Social Group Refugee Determinations', *International Journal of Refugee Law*, vol. 21, no. 1, March.

Phillips, A. and M. Dustin (2004) 'UK Initiatives on Forced Marriage: Regulation, Dialogue, and Exit' *Political Studies*, vol. 52, no. 3, October.

Rycroft, R. (2005) 'Communicative Barriers in the Asylum Account', in P. Shah (ed.), *The Challenge of Asylum to Legal Systems*, Cavendish Publishing, London.

Siddiqi, D. (2005) 'Of Consent and Contradiction: Forced Marriages in Bangladesh', in Welchman, L. and S. Hossain (eds.), *'Honour': Crimes, Paradigms and Violence against Women*, Zed, London.

Smith, K. (2007) 'New Report Criticises "Fast Track" Asylum Claims', Institute of Race Relations, London. http://www.irr.org.uk/2007/september/ ks000011. html (June 10 2010).

Sweeney, J. (2009) 'Credibility, Proof and Refugee Law', *International Journal of Refugee Law*, vol. 21 no. 4, December.

Tayor, D. and H. Muir. (2010) 'Border Staff Humiliate and Trick Asylum Seekers – Whistleblower Louise Perrett says she was Advised at the Border Agency Office in Cardiff to Refuse Difficult Asylum Claims', *Guardian* 2 February. http://www.guardian.co.uk/uk/2010/feb/02/border-staff-asylum-seekers-whistleblower (11 July2010).

Thomas, R. (2006) 'Assessing the Credibility of Asylum Claims: EU and UK approaches examined', *European Journal of Migration and Law*, vol. 8 no. 4, July.

Thomas, R. (2008) 'Consistency in Asylum Adjudication: Country Guidance and the Asylum Process in the United Kingdom', *International Journal of Refugee Law*, vol. 20, no. 4, December.

Travis, A. (2006) 'Asylum Seekers Face Tough Controls Under New Fast-track System: Detention and Tagging for those Facing Removal, Immigration Service to Improve Claims Handling', *Guardian*, 3 January. http://www.guardian. co.uk/uk/2006/jan/03/immigration.immigrationandpublicservices2/print (28 May 2010).

Tsangarides, N. (2009) 'The Politics of Knowledge: An Examination of the Use of Country Information in the Asylum Determination Process', *Journal of Immigration Asylum and Nationality Law*, vol. 23, no. 3.

Tsangarides, N. (2010) *The Refugee Roulette: The Role of Country Information in Refugee Status Determination*, Immigration Advisory Service, London.

UK Government (2005) *The Asylum and Immigration Tribunal (Fast Track Procedure)*

Rules 2005 http://www.opsi.gov.uk/si/si2005/20050560.htm (22 June 2010).

UNCHR (1992) *Handbook on Procedures and Criteria for Determining Refugee Status under the 1951 Convention and the 1967 Protocol relating to the Status of Refugees* http://www/unhcr.org/publ/PBUL/3d58e13b4.pdf (23 June 2010).

UNHCR (2002) *Guidelines on International Protection No. 1: Gender-Related Persecution within the context of Article 1A(2) of the 1951 Convention and/or its 1967 Protocol relating to the Status of Refugees (HCR/GIP/02/01)* http://www.unhcr.org/publ/PUBL/3d58ddef4.pdf (23 June 2010).

UNHCR (2006) *Quality Initiative Report: Third Report to the Minister.* http://www.unhcr.org.uk/fileadmin/user_upload/pdf/3_QI_Key_Observations_and_Recommendations.FINAL.doc.pdf (23 June 2010).

UNHCR (2008) *Handbook for the Protection of Women and Girls* http://www.unhcr.org/refworld/docid/47cfc2962.html (23 June 2010).

Yeo, C. (2009) 'Raising the Spouse Visa Age', *Journal of Immigration Asylum and Nationality Law*, vol. 23, no. 4.

Ziegler, S. and K. Stewart (2009) 'Positioning women's rights within asylum policy' *Frontiers*, vol. 30, no. 2.

10

'Wayward girls and well-wisher parents': habeas corpus, women's rights to personal liberty, consent to marriage and the Bangladeshi courts

Sara Hossain*

Since before independence, the superior courts in Bangladesh have regularly issued directions in the nature of habeas corpus in order to release women and girls from illegal or improper detention.[1] These cases typically arise in a context where a woman or girl is alleged by her parents to be a minor, and a victim of a violent, often sexual, crime, with the police then 'rescuing' her and the courts placing her in so-called 'safe' or 'judicial' custody. In some cases the detenu is held in confinement by her own family. As the law reports reveal, the almost invariable counter-narrative made about the woman or girl herself, once she is produced before the courts, is that she is an adult and has married through her own choice, without her family's approval, or in opposition to their decisions. The Supreme Court has repeatedly affirmed that courts have no powers to hold any adult woman in 'safe' or 'judicial' custody against her will, unless she is an accused or a witness in a case. However, while consistently finding such confinement to be illegal, they have given a range of directions regarding what happens to the woman on her release. The cases of a woman aged over eighteen or under sixteen are clear-cut – with the courts setting the former at liberty to 'go where she chooses' and invariably directing the latter to be placed in her parents' custody. Where the woman is aged between sixteen and eighteen, the courts, with only a few exceptions, have been far more cautious, in some cases setting her free, in others returning her to parental custody or, at worst, compelling her to continue in judicial custody, often in prison. These decisions to leave her in custody effectively result in the success of the

* I would like to thank Dr Dina Siddiqi and Dr Hameeda Hossain for their comments, Amanda Sen for thoughtful discussions and research, and Rokeya Chowdhury for research assistance.

parents' strategy of taking recourse to the law to force not the marriage, but the breaking up of the marriage, and the denial of the woman's choice (Siddiqi 2005).[2] Most of these cases involve inter-religious, inter-community or inter-class relationships. A few have involved an international element, with Bangladeshi women living abroad facing abduction and confinement within the country.

In this chapter, I examine a series of such decisions made by the superior courts over the past forty years, since independence, in order to identify the extent to which the courts now recognise women's rights to liberty and freedom from violence, in the context of marriages of choice and/or forced marriage. First, I set out the constitutional framework for recognition and realisation of the rights to personal liberty and freedom from violence. Second, I outline how the interplay of existing laws (on marriage, custody, and violence against women and children), several of which are pre-constitutional and colonial in origin, result in violations of women's rights to personal liberty, including confinement against their will, and denials of their choices regarding marriage. Third, I examine a series of judgments to illustrate the use of habeas corpus in such cases, highlighting contrasting responses and approaches, with women's liberty rights being variously affirmed and curtailed depending primarily upon the court's determination of the age of the detainee, culminating in the Dr Shipra Chowdhury judgment, where the court for the first time expressly articulated the right to personal liberty in the context of marriage and women's rights to consent. Finally, I explore the limits and possibilities of obtaining judicial recognition of a wider definition of women's rights to personal liberty, including not just freedom from confinement, but also freedom to choose if, when and whom to marry. I argue that this broader understanding is needed to trigger the provision of more effective and systematic legal protection of the rights of women contesting forced marriage and asserting marriages of choice. I conclude by arguing that it is only such judicial recognition, refracted through broader public discourses (including the media) that can catalyse the realisation of women's decisions with respect to marriage and sexual choice.

The rights framework: constitutional and treaty norms

The Constitution of Bangladesh 1972 guarantees a range of fundamental rights, including the core rights to personal liberty and to life.[3] While it does not expressly recognise the right to choice in or consent to marriage, this can be extrapolated from the right to liberty and other guaranteed constitutional rights. These include the right to equality, to non-discrimination (including on grounds of religion, race, caste or sex), to be treated in accordance with law, to freedom of movement, expression, and protection of the home and correspondence,[4] to safeguards on arrest and detention, to speedy trial, and to protection from torture or cruel, inhuman and degrading treatment or punishment.[5]

The fundamental right to enforce any of these rights through remedies which may be sought on application to the High Court Division of the Supreme Court is also guaranteed.[6] Such remedies include directions in the nature of habeas corpus, which enable the court to determine if a person is being held in custody 'without lawful authority or in an unlawful manner'.[7]

In interpreting the ambit of rights, or in fashioning remedies, the courts may invoke the Fundamental Principles of State Policy,[8] which include the principles of economic and social justice and respect for the dignity and worth of human persons.[9] The courts may also invoke international human rights law, including the various elaborations on the right to liberty, as well as express recognition of the right to consent to marriage, which are recognised in, among others, the Convention on the Elimination of All Forms of Discrimination against Women.[10] It is particularly relevant to recall General Comment no. 21 of the United Nations Committee on the Elimination of Discrimination against Women (CEDAW Committee), which clearly delineates that Article 16 of CEDAW encompasses the right 'to choose, if, when and whom to marry' (Chowdhury, P. 2007; Welchman and Hossain 2005; AALI 2003; and IWRAW-AP 2005).

The legal framework: contradictions and concerns

Although the Constitution mandates that any existing laws inconsistent with fundamental rights shall become void,[11] a number of laws operate to contravene or constrain women's rights to personal liberty, including by permitting their confinement in certain circumstances, and also expressly limiting their rights to choice and consent with respect to marriage, as outlined below.

First, different laws provide different definitions of a 'child' for different purposes, and there is no uniform age of majority. The general provision, under the Majority Act, is that the age of majority is eighteen for all purposes other than, among others, marriage or divorce.[12] Various personal laws in turn provide for different ages of majority for the purpose of marriage; for example, Muslim law provides for the age of majority to be puberty, which is presumed to be fifteen for girls,[13] while Hindu law as applicable in Bangladesh allows for the marriage of girls at any age. A person who is an adult for the purposes of marriage (i.e. sixteen) may nevertheless still be a minor for other purposes, including, for example, guardianship and custody (if under eighteen),[14] or may be liable to be put in detention in a 'place of safety' or in 'safe custody' if considered to be at risk of becoming a victim of an offence (if under eighteen).[15]

Second, the existing confusion over the age of minority is further confounded by the inconsistency or conflict among the laws that give courts and tribunals, as well as police officers, powers to place minors, and even adults in certain cases, in 'safe custody'. This umbrella term has been used to cover detention in jails, certified institutes, government approved homes, and shelters. So for example, Special Tribunals on Violence against Women and Children may pass orders for any woman or child to be placed, during the trial of any offence under the Act, in 'safe custody' in any specified place, with the government or any person or organisation, other than a prison where they consider this to be necessary.[16] Further, any probation or police officer may place any child in a place of safety if there is reason to believe there is a risk of an offence being committed in respect of her subject to production before a court.[17] A magistrate may then make an order for care and detention of the child if he considers an offence has been or is likely to be committed, and the order of detention shall continue until proceedings against the person responsible are terminated.[18] A magistrate may also direct restoration of the custody of any girl aged less than sixteen if he finds that she had been detained for an illegal purpose.[19] In all of these cases, the woman or child whose safety is at issue is given no opportunity to be asked whether she or he consents to being placed in safe custody.

Third, religion-based personal laws may lay down restrictive criteria regarding the capacity of parties to marry, thus limiting the right 'whom to marry'. To give the example of Muslim law as applicable in Bangladesh, a Muslim woman may only marry a Muslim man, and her marriage to a person from any other religious background is void.

Fourth, such laws also permit marriages on the basis of parental consent, further restricting not only the right 'whom to marry' but also 'if and when to marry'. Under Muslim law, minors, or persons lacking mental competence, may be contracted in marriage at any time, without their knowledge, and even against their will, on the basis of the consent of their guardians.

224

Fifth, special laws on 'child marriage restraint' may also operate to limit women's right to decide 'when to marry'. A child marriage, defined as a marriage involving a groom aged under twenty-one and a bride aged under eighteen, may result in penalties being imposed on any adult party to such a marriage or on a (male) adult who solemnises or arranges such a marriage. However, paradoxically, such a marriage remains valid. While there do not appear to be any examples of individual prosecutions involving this law, these provisions have been referred to by the courts in habeas corpus cases (see below), resulting in denial of women's legal rights to marry when aged sixteen or seventeen.

Habeas corpus: release from confinement, but recognising consent?

The interplay of religion, age and gender is particularly relevant in cases of marriages of choice/forced marriage. In practice, the contradictions and inconsistencies prevailing in the laws regulating marriage, when overlaid upon existing criminal procedures for the placing in custody of women and child victims of violence, result in women and girls being denied the right to liberty and personal security in the harshest of circumstances and being confined against their will for prolonged periods. In many cases, court orders regarding safe custody, or restoration to parental custody, which fly in the face of the woman's or girl's expressed wishes, and are made without any determination of family history or consideration of the best interests of the child, end up adversely affecting her choices regarding marriage.

These situations occur when parents (usually fathers) claim that a daughter has been subject to crimes of (usually sexual) violence, for example, kidnapping or abduction for purposes of unlawful sexual intercourse or forced marriage, or rape, in cases where a woman or girl has married without her knowledge or approval. Existing criminal procedures are then applied to 'recover' the woman or girl concerned, and to place her in safe custody. As a result, paradoxically, laws intended with a protective purpose, to safeguard girls from child or early marriage, or children from abuse, not only fail to fulfil their stated purpose in large measure, but also operate to restrain young women from making their own choices regarding marriage.

Habeas corpus proceedings then become the means used both by the parents and by the women to contest or assert the choices made with regard to marriage. Parents claiming custody of a daughter tend to allege that she is a minor (i.e. below sixteen, or between sixteen and eighteen), and has been kidnapped or abducted for forced marriage, and/or raped. The detainee who seeks release from judicial custody, or to be handed over to her husband's custody, usually claims that she is a major (either over sixteen or over eighteen) and has married of her own free will. In a few cases, the detainee is confined not in safe custody, but directly by the family who she claims are threatening to force or have forced her into marriage.

In the majority of cases, both the High Court and Appellate Divisions have declared any such detention to be illegal, in the safe custody cases on the basis that no court has powers to detain a person who is neither an accused nor a witness in any case. Where the detainee is aged under sixteen, the courts invariably hand her over to her parents' custody. In the case of girls aged over eighteen, the courts are far more robust, and not only set them at liberty to 'go where they choose' but also, in some cases, articulate clearly the circumstances in which they are doing so, as well as reinforcing the elements of a right to make decisions and choices regarding marriage.

However, there is considerable confusion regarding the cases of girls aged sixteen to eighteen, with the court either handing them over to the custody of their natural guardian, or, where they refuse to go, requiring them to remain in 'safe custody' till they attain majority.

Much therefore turns on the issue of determining the age of majority, a question of law, and, in each case, determining the age of the woman or girl concerned, a question of fact. Where the superior courts have sent women aged sixteen back into their parents' custody they have referred to the Children Act, and also to the Guardians and Wards Act or the Child Marriage Restraint Act in support. Where they have allowed women aged sixteen or above to be set at liberty, they have in some cases referred to personal laws on marriage, or to the Penal Code. These judgments do not, however, refer to seeking the woman's consent or even to ascertaining her wishes as to whether she wishes to be placed in safe custody. They also do not, with one exception, discuss the woman's right to liberty in any context beyond confinement, that is, with regard to making decisions regarding her own life, and loves.

The section below discusses a series of decisions and the reasoning involved.

Under-sixteens released to parental custody

In habeas corpus petitions, whenever a detainee girl in safe custody has been found to be aged under sixteen, the court directly hands over her custody to her parents/father. It justifies such action by alluding to practical considerations, such as the lack of a neutral home,[20] and more subjective considerations about the parents being the girl's 'best well-wishers';[21] it has dismissed her adamant refusal to go with them as being 'not at all a material consideration'.[22]

In determining the detenu's age, the courts have variously relied on the parents' statements or their supporting documents, and have disregarded the girl's statements of being over eighteen and supporting medical reports and radiographer's reports.[23] In disregarding medical evidence, the court relied on precedents including medical jurisprudence texts and Privy Council decisions, holding that the court may give greater weight to evidence in conflict with expert opinion.[24]

Sixteen-plus, but still in parental custody

As in the cases of under-sixteens, the superior courts have always affirmed that holding a girl in safe custody in jail or elsewhere is illegal. However, in one strand of cases, the Appellate Division has stated that even if a girl is aged over sixteen, and therefore a major for the purposes of marriage, she will nevertheless remain a minor for purposes of custody and guardianship until she reaches eighteen. This has resulted in the court passing orders that a girl aged sixteen to eighteen should be released from judicial custody, but then handed over to her parents' custody rather than set at liberty, and that her refusal to go to her father is immaterial.

In such cases courts have preferred parents' statements supported by affidavits, school register entries, and 'admit cards' to the girl's statement, marriage registration certificates, and medical reports.[25] In setting the test for minority as being under eighteen, the High Court Division of the Supreme Court referred to the prohibition on child marriages (i.e. marriages where the woman is aged under eighteen) and the rules regarding guardianship, and refused to follow the earlier line of authorities which had established sixteen as the age of majority in such cases, taking the view that the reference to this in the relevant penal code sections on kidnapping (Sections 361 and 366) relates to whether the offence is committed, not whether the girl is *sui juris* or not.[26]

In *Sumati Begum v Rafiqullah*,[27] the court found that for the purposes of custody a female child is a minor until she reaches sixteen, referring to Section 552 of the Code of Criminal Procedure 1898, Section 361 of the Bangladesh Penal Code and Section 2(f) of Children Act. It noted that the reference to age in the Penal Code relates to the definition of kidnapping and is not relateable to custody. It held that the Children Act provides for keeping a child in custody even after sixteen on considering sections 2(f), 55, 56, 57, 58 and 61 of the Act is necessary till the proceeding is terminated in conviction, discharge or acquittal.

The bias of the court, and particularly of Bangladesh's apex, or highest court, the Appellate Division of the Supreme Court, towards the family and its refusal to give credence to the woman's statement comes through starkly in several cases.[28] In *Khairunnessa v Illy Begum* 48 DLR AD 67, the Appellate Division of the Supreme Court insisted that there was no reason to disbelieve *prima facie* the mother's allegations of her daughter's abduction, commenting acidly that to give credit to the detainee's statement regarding her age was to assume 'that the daughter must have been born before her mother', and further 'that the mother is an enemy of her daughter and so she [the mother] was falsely claiming her to be a minor, and further that the welfare of the victim girl would be safer and better in her own hands than in her parents'. The Appellate Division criticised the High Court for failing to bear in mind that 'force is being applied to settle a matrimonial and social issue' – and failing to bring to bear its 'mature experience' in judging 'the attitude of a girl in [many] such cases who are mostly guided by infatuation and flush of youthful romanticism without caring for tomorrow'.[29] It also noted with evident relief the girl's agreement to go to her mother (apparently ignoring that the only other choice she was given was to remain in jail), commenting that 'the wayward girl now seems to have turned her face towards the right direction'.[30]

The apex court appears very reluctant to recognise the extent of women's right to liberty in such cases as *Jharna Rani Saha v Khandaker Zayedul Hoque and another.*[31] The apex court criticised the High Court for dealing with this case as if '*only* the issue of detention of an adult person in jail custody' was in question. While robust in its position that she must be released from safe custody in jail, it articulated the position implicit in its earlier decisions that '[t]he girl cannot be allowed to make her own choice because, *prima facie*, it appears that she is a minor' and placed her in her mother's custody.

In *Arun Karmakar v the State*, the Appellate Division reaffirmed that where the High Court finds that the person brought before it in a habeas corpus petition is being illegally and improperly confined or detained and is a minor, it may transfer custody to their guardian according to law, but if the person is a major, the only jurisdiction which the court can exercise is to set the person at liberty, whether illegally or improperly detained in public or private custody. It reasserted its view that the age of majority for such purposes is eighteen (the detainee in this case was handed over to her father's custody).

Sixteen-plus and held in continuing judicial custody

In some extraordinary cases, where the detainee is adamant that she will not return to her parents' custody, the High Court directs that she must remain in safe custody until she reaches the age of majority.

As in the cases discussed earlier, the courts prefer to rely on the father's or family's statements over medical reports, even where the daughter's statement regarding her age is supported by her own (remarried) mother. In discussing its reasons, the court has variously referred to the importance of the woman needing to 'develop her independent opinion', it apparently being assumed that her choice to marry someone other than the person selected by her family cannot have been made on this basis.[32]

Sixteen-plus – set at liberty

In contrast to the above decisions, in a number of cases the High Court has taken a more robust position, setting at liberty girls who were aged over sixteen at the time of the offence of which they are the alleged victim.[33] In these cases, it has held that the age of majority for determination of the issue of custody in a habeas corpus is sixteen not eighteen, and, further, that the father's isolated statement must be corroborated.[34]

It has also been willing to release a detainee, found to be aged over seventeen, on her own bond, subject to her appearances before the trial court.[35] In these cases, it has also given more priority to examining the detainee in person and taking her statement, and has clarified that her age at the time of deciding the question of custody is what is relevant.[36] In a pre-independence case, the then Dhaka High Court had directed the release of Jahanara Begum, aged sixteen, on bail pending disposal of the criminal case in which she was allegedly a victim. It observed that no court had any power to detain a woman aged over sixteen against her will, given that she is not an accused and is at most a witness, although it could do so for minors exercising its inherent discretion. It described safe custody as having the 'complexion of guardianship' and being intended to isolate the person from 'certain influences'.[37] In a few cases, the courts have freed detained women/girls in recognition of the changed realities in their lives, such as the detainee being pregnant, while nevertheless decrying her 'being more guided by her heart than her head' and noting that her statements were unreliable as she remained in the 'romantic world of love'.[38]

In other cases, the court, in issuing its orders to set a girl aged sixteen-plus at liberty, may have considered the context, of the woman being a British Bangladeshi, and also of her ill-treatment in custody, which included being chained when brought to court.[39]

Eighteen and over, set at liberty

Where the detainee is aged over eighteen, the choice before the court is clear. In all such cases, the court finds that if the detainee is found to be above eighteen and *sui juris*, her detention in judicial custody amounts to illegal detention.

Disturbingly, despite the clarity of the issue, cases of women aged eighteen and over (between twenty and thirty-three) being confined against their will by their families continue to come to light, over half a decade after the Supreme Court established that the courts have no authority to hold an adult who is a victim or witness of an offence in so-called judicial custody. In one recent case, the woman was detained for over six years in a safe custody home,[40] and in another the woman was held for four months in a psychiatric clinic, in each case with little action taken by the authorities concerned, and the women would likely have remained forgotten if a close friend or relative had not intervened, with the support of *pro bono* lawyers and legal services organisations.

In the most recent case, that of *Dr Shipra Chowdhury v Joynal Abedin and others*, the detainee, Dr Humayra Abedin, a 33-year-old Bangladeshi trainee doctor based in Britain, was drugged, confined in a psychiatric clinic for three months and then forced into a marriage by her parents. After she gave her testimony in a closed courtroom, the court pronounced its order, categorically denouncing her parents' 'barbaric actions' and directing that Dr Abedin be taken immediately to the British High Commission accompanied by a court officer and a police officer, and that no one be permitted to speak to her. On Dr Abedin's return to the UK, the story broke in national and international news media of her 'rescue', ascribing this to the intervention of the English courts.[41] In its judgment, the High Court in Bangladesh un-equivocally asserted a woman's right to consent to marriage, and elaborated on her right to choose her partner and decide whether or not she would marry. Dr Abedin's age, the very serious allegations regarding the nature of her confinement, the fact of the UK court order, and the request it contained for judicial cooperation, but most of all the extreme intransigence of her family and their persistent efforts to avoid subjecting themselves to the Court, until the final issuance of a contempt order, all appear to have contributed to the robustness of the decision.

For the media in Bangladesh, Humayra's case was initially not a story – because there was nothing out of the ordinary about it. In contrast, for the British, and then the international media, Humayra's case became a *cause célèbre*. It had everything needed for a dream tabloid story – sex, violence, drugs and religion – and, most important, a perfect peg – being the very first use of the new UK law on forced marriages (the Forced Marriage [Civil] Protection Act 2007). The intense and highly visible media interest catalysed a response in the Bangladesh press.

The stories that broke worldwide the next day made reference to the role of the Bangladesh court, and its fashioning of a set of orders which would not only ensure Dr Abedin's immediate protection from her family, but also enable her safe return to the UK. They emphasised the intervention of the English High Court, perhaps attributing a disproportionate significance to it as the sole trigger for her release from captivity. They also all flagged Dr Abedin's alleged relationship with a Hindu man in order, it seemed, to provide some kind of justification for the family's actions (although, interestingly, the family never cited this issue in any of their pleas). Thus they depicted Humayra's confinement as having been precipitated by religious differences, rather than by sexual choices or patriarchal controls.

Towards recognising women's right to personal liberty in decisions on marriage?

The cases discussed represent a very small proportion of the actual incidents in which women and girls are prevented from making their own decisions about if, when and whom to marry. The majority of cases are unlikely to reach the superior courts, given that most individuals caught up in these situations will not have the resources to access legal remedies, or to pursue them to the final stage, being inhibited by the costs and delays involved, or more optimistically perhaps, having reached some kind of amicable resolution along the way.

The one consistent position that emerges from all the cases, concerning women of all ages from under-sixteens to over-eighteens, is of clear judicial disapproval of the practice of safe custody. In case after case, the principle articulated in the 1950s in Jahanara Begum's case is reaffirmed: that the courts do not have any legal authority to detain a person in safe custody if she is neither an accused nor a witness, but only the victim in a case.

Unfortunately, the court's rulings have not been translated into practice, and the incarceration of women against their will and ostensibly for their own protection in safe custody homes, and, shockingly, even in prisons, continues today. In many cases, despite the categorical terms not only of judgments but also of the law on violence against women, women are still held in safe custody in prison cells, ostensibly for lack of any alternative arrangements.[42]

Further, despite the courts' categorical affirmation of women's right to liberty – in terms of freedom from being detained against their will in judicial custody – their actual decisions with regard to the women and girls involved has been more equivocal. So, in a number of cases impossible to square with their condemnation of the practice, the courts have themselves required that girls who refused to go to their parents must remain in judicial custody until they reached the age of majority, even where this meant that they would have to remain in jail for up to three or four years. In others, they have consistently preferred the parental narrative of 'violated minor/victim/daughter' to the woman or girl's own claims of adulthood and agency, insisting that she return to parents who were the cause of her incarceration and ill-treatment.

In doing so, the courts have disregarded both explicitly articulated pleas by women regarding their fears of 'mental torture' and implicit threats that they may face violent repercussions, either physical or psychological, if returned to their parents. They have never commented adversely on the nature of such parental relationships, even where the facts recited in each judgment clearly show that the parents' narratives wholly contradict those of their daughters, and where it appears that the parents' need to control their daughters' lives has gone to the extent that they are willing for them to be taken into police custody, subjected to invasive medical tests, and then imprisoned, in some cases for years, rather than be permitted to pursue their own marriage and life choices. In all these cases, instead of questioning the parents' motivations or actions, the courts have almost invariably affirmed that the parents are 'well-wishers' of their children, even where all the evidence before them is to the contrary.

These decisions – and the lengths to which the courts appear to go in some cases to identify women at best as minors lacking all agency or ability to decide for themselves, and at worst as 'wayward' and 'infatuated' – are an outcome of ambivalence, or, perhaps more accurately, their reluctance to acknowledge young women as being capable of sexual lives and their refusal to secure their rights to make sexual choices. Thus, they have repeatedly given greater evidential weight to the supporting documents produced by parents to back up their claims regarding their daughter's minority, even when such documents are widely known to be easily 'managed' (e.g. school certificates, birth certificates, passports), or to be unreliable (horoscopes), over expert medical reports or supporting documents provided by the women themselves (e.g. marriage certificates). The courts have done so even after directing that medical reports be issued following invasive medical examinations, which ironically often spell out in painstaking detail the extent of bodily growth and development of the woman or girl in question, clearly demonstrating that she is not a minor incapable of any sexual life. They have also preferred their own superficial and fleeting examination of the woman/girl during a court hearing to detailed medical reports which support the women's claim to majority.

The court's convoluted approach to assessing evidence of age is mirrored in its legal justifications for why women's choices regarding marriage must be denied. In one series of judgments, discussed above, which accorded pre-eminence to women's rights to liberty, the courts have been clear that the only issue before them concerns the powers of the lower courts to restrain women against their will. But in others, where the outcomes have been either to retain women into safe custody or to send them to parental custody, the courts have referred to, amongst others, the Children Act, the Child Marriage Restraint Act, the Guardianship Act and the definition of offences under the Penal Code to justify their decisions. While the last three of these appear irrelevant to the issue of determining the age of majority for purposes of securing the woman's release from detention, the invoking of the Children Act, noted by a commentator, appears to fly in the face of the approach mandated by the statute itself, that of protection of children (Malik 2004).

The courts' reluctance to intervene may also reflect the prevailing social reality of disapproval of inter-religious and inter-community (and inter-class) marriages.[43] Existing personal laws, as noted above, do not facilitate such relationships, and in some cases bar them outright.[44] Even where couples overcome these hurdles by one of them converting and adopting the other's religion, their choices are not accepted, and they face social ostracism and exclusion from their families, as well as the harassment that follows on the institution of criminal cases.

The courts remain unwilling to give much credence to women's statements except where they are over eighteen, but reluctantly concede that they may remain with the chosen husband/accused once it is established that the woman has become pregnant or had a child, an indication that it will be particularly difficult to restore the *status quo ante*, of simply returning her to her parents' home. The courts' disapproval also comes through in their reference to 'neutral homes', and in the view that women/girls who seek to take decisions or make choices regarding marriage that are not family-sanctioned somehow need an opportunity simply to 'clear their heads' and find the right path.

Since 1960, some clear and more positive trends have emerged. The involvement of women's rights organisations and human rights lawyers, and media spotlights on the practice of holding women in safe custody have contributed to the identification of safe custody as an issue which clearly invokes human rights concerns. At least at the level of the superior courts, it is clear that women cannot be held in judicial custody against their will, and that this practice involves denials of basic rights to equality, to be treated in accordance with law, and to personal liberty. Courts have also given more latitude to women to speak directly about their own situation and wishes, and have also established good practices in terms of providing a more enabling environment for women, clearing courtrooms or taking statements in judges' chambers. Again, this is in contrast to earlier approaches that minors should be 'seen but not heard', as their statements could not conceivably be considered credible if in contradiction to those of their parents. Much remains to be done to ensure effective trickle-down of these decisions, but there is at least a recognition of the issues. The highlighting of cases involving women, such as Dr Abedin, who are clearly adults, and competent professionals, has served to catalyse public debate on the issue. Paradoxically, however, the allegations of extreme violence in Dr Abedin's case, as well as the international element, also made it easier to 'exoticise' this case and to inhibit a much-needed debate about how and why routine, quotidian denials of such continue without comment across and within diverse communities within Bangladesh.

Conclusion

In this chapter I have examined the discrepancies between the constitutional rights framework – which recognises women's rights to equality, treatment in accordance with the law, and personal liberty – and its routine denials in cases where women make choices regarding marriage and sexuality. I have discussed gaps and inconsistencies in laws, and their misapplication, which permit such routine violations to take place. I have also focused attention on the tensions apparent in judicial responses to such cases, and the trend in decisions of the Supreme Court being inflected not only with gender bias but with an implicit familial/patriarchal ideology, always according pre-eminence to parental/paternal narratives over those of young women asserting their own marital and sexual choices. In doing so I have sought to place in context, and thus to underscore, the importance of the recent Dr Shipra Chowdhury judgment, which appears to break new ground in expressly articulating the right to liberty together with the right to consent to marriage.

The importance of this judgment in linking the issues of liberty and marriage choices is highlighted by a review of the earlier cases, all of which failed to do that. The question arises of whether the judicial recognition and interpretation of the ambit of the right to personal liberty in this context will have any broader impact. The cases show that in Bangladesh, while safe custody has been highlighted as an issue of concern, the right to choose if, when and whom to marry is not fully recognised or protected. Beyond the courts, similarly, safe custody has been identified as a human rights concern, with documentaries, articles, and even sporadic public interest litigation,[45] but this issue of the right to choice and consent in marriage has not been incorporated into ongoing campaigns by an otherwise very active and vocal women's rights movement.

The challenge before us is to find a greater fit between activism on the ground and the process in the courts, to take forward the wider interpretation of rights made available through some of these decisions, and to catalyse a discussion that engages with and demands women's rights to personal liberty in the fullest sense, including not only freedom from confinement but also a woman's right to make decisions regarding her own life, including marriage and sexuality.

Notes

1   The term 'superior courts' refers here to the High Court Division (HCD) and Appellate Division (AD) of the Supreme Court of Bangladesh. The cases discussed refer to decisions of both Divisions in respect of applications under either Section 491 of the Code of Criminal Procedure 1898 (CrPC), or, more exceptionally, Article 102 of the Constitution.

2   These cases highlight both how marriage and related kinship ties, as well as prevailing controls on women's sexuality, are central to maintaining the 'status

quo' or the social order of things, and the role the courts play in this regard (personal communication with Dr Dina Siddiqi).

3   See the Constitution of Bangladesh, 1972, articles 31 and 32, which provide as follows: 'To enjoy the protection of law, and to be treated in accordance with law, and only in accordance with law, is the inalienable right of every citizen, wherever he may be, and of every other person for the time being within Bangladesh, and in particular no action detrimental to the life, liberty, body, reputation or property of any person shall be taken except in accordance with law' (Article 31); 'No person shall be deprived of life or personal liberty save in accordance with law' (Article 32).

4   See Chapter III of the Constitution of Bangladesh, in particular articles 27 (equality), 28 (non-discrimination), 31 (treatment in accordance with law), 36 (movement), 39 (expression) and 43 (home and correspondence).

5   See the Constitution of Bangladesh, articles 33 and 35 respectively.

6   See the Constitution of Bangladesh, Article 44(1), read with Article 102.

7   See the Constitution of Bangladesh, Article 102(2) (b). Similar remedies for production of a person before the court to determine whether they are being held in an 'illegal or improper manner' may be sought under Section 491 of the CrPC.

8   While the Fundamental Principles of State Policy were earlier considered non-justiciable, the courts have subsequently held that they may serve as a guide to the interpretation of particular rights: see the Constitution of Bangladesh, Article 8; *Kudrat-E- Elahi v Bangladesh* 44 DLR (AD) 319.

9   See the Constitution of Bangladesh, Articles 8 and 11.

10   The relevant treaties which Bangladesh has ratified to date include the Convention on Consent to Marriage, Minimum Age for Marriage and Registration of Marriage 1964; the International Covenant on Civil and Political Rights 1966 (ICCPR); the International Covenant on Economic, Social and Cultural Rights 1966 (ICESCR); the Convention on the Elimination of All Forms of Discrimination against Women 1981 (CEDAW); and the Convention on the Rights of the Child 1990 (CRC). International human rights treaties are not directly executable in Bangladesh, unless incorporated into domestic law: see the Constitution of Bangladesh, Article 145A. However, the courts may apply their provisions in interpreting the scope and ambit of fundamental rights to the extent that there is no direct contradiction with national laws: *HM Ershad v Bangladesh*, 21 BLD (AD) (2001) 69.

11   The Constitution of Bangladesh, Article 26.

12   Section 2 of the Majority Act 1875 provides that 'Nothing herein contained shall affect: (a) the capacity of any person in any of the following matters (namely) marriage, dower, divorce and adoption'.

13   See Mullah, para 251, and *Bakshi v Bashir Ahmed PLD 1970* SC 323 at 324 ff.

14 See the Guardians and Wards Act 1861.

15 See Section 2(f) Children Act 1974 which provides that a child is defined as any person aged under sixteen, unless s/he has been placed in custody, whether with a relative or in an institution/home, and in which case it means any such person for the whole period of such detention even if s/he attains sixteen years during that period. Under Section 2(a) of the Suppression of Violence against Women and Children Act 2000, a child is any person not exceeding sixteen years.

16 Section 31 of the Suppression of Violence against Women and Children Act, 2000, as amended in 2003. The Act provides for the trial of offences including acid attacks, abduction, kidnapping, trafficking and rape.

17 Section 55 of the Children Act, 1974.

18 Section 56 of the Children Act, 1974. See also in relation to provisions on safe custody that appear rarely to be applied: sections 57–66 (regarding sending the victimised child to juvenile court, orders for committal, supervision, breach thereof, search warrants, and parental contributions, among others), in particular Section 66 (presumption and determination of age) of the Children Act 1974.

19 Section 552, Code of Criminal Procedure, 1898.

20 See *Bashu Dev Chatterjee v Umme Salma and others 51 DLR (1999)* AD 238 per Chief Justice ATM Afzal: the Appellate Division released Umme Salma Suma Chatterjee from 'safe custody' in jail to her father's custody, on finding her to be *prima facie* a minor (13 at the time of the offence).

21 *Abdul Majid Sarkar (Md) v State* 55 DLR AD 2003 per Chief Justice Mahmudul Amin Choudhury: here the Appellate Division held illegal the detention of Masuda Khanam (Hasi) in safe custody. and on finding she was aged 15 at the date of occurrence (based on an entry in the municipal birth register). See also Prafullah Kumar's case.

22 In contrast, in the much earlier Jahanara Begum case, 15 DLR, the High Court had noted, obiter, that Section 27 of the Bengal Children Act (since repealed, and replaced with the Children Act 1974) authorised detention in custody of minors (aged under fourteen) who were not accused of any offence, but also *required consideration of the minor girl's interests* as the most important factor.

23 See Bashu Dev Chatterjee's case, cited in note 20.

24 *Prafulla Kamal v Government of Bangladesh* 28 DLR (1976) 123, per Justice Shahahabuddin Ahmed: here the court handed over custody of Shipra Rani to her father, after disregarding medical reports showing her to be 19, and personally examining her and finding that she looked 'very tender aged' and 'appears to be below 16 years and as such she is minor'.

25 Sukhendra's case, *Arun Karmakar v The State*, 7 BLC (AD) 61.

26 Sukhendra 42 DLR (1990)79; Krishna Pada Datta 42 DLR (1990) 297; Khairunnessa v Illy Begum; Arun Karmaker.

27 44 DLR (1992) 500.

28 See *Sree Mongal Chandra Nandy* 17 BLD AD (1997) 33, in which the Appellate Division described the father (whose allegation regarding his daughter's abduction had resulted in her being held in safe custody for over twenty months) as her 'best well wisher' and his actions as being prompted by 'filial love, affection and welfare of the minor daughter', even where the daughter preferred to remain in judicial custody rather than go to him.

29 *Khairunnessa v Illy Begum*, at paragraphs 12 and 13.

30 See also discussion of this case by Dina M. Siddiqi in Lynn Welchman and Sara Hossain (eds.), *'Honour': Crimes, Paradigms and Violence against Women*, Zed Books, London, 2005.

31 52 DLR (AD) 2000 66, per Justice ATM Afzal.

32 *Dr Kazi Mozammel Hoque v State* 45 DLR (1995) 197 where the detainee was put into judicial custody after she refused to return to 'mental torture' in her father's custody. The court referred to section 552 of the Code of Criminal Procedure as prohibiting the handing over of custody of a woman aged sixteen plus to any person. Also, in *Babul Miah v State 30* DLR (1978) 187, the court refused to hand over custody of the detainee to her mother on the basis that the latter had remarried, consigning her to remain in safe custody instead.

33 In addition to those discussed below, see 17 DLR 544; 1 BLD 469 (over 16 *sui juris*); 1990 BLD 85 (girl over 16 *sui juris*).

34 *Manindra Kumar v Ministry of Home* 48 DLR (1991) 71.

35 *Sunil Kumar Chakrabarty v State* 2 BCR (1982) 41.

36 Ananda Mohan Bannerjee on behalf of *Priti Mohan Bannerjee v State*, 35 DLR (1983) 315 and also *Sree Tarapada Sarkar v The State*, 49 DLR (1997) 360.

37 *Jahanara Begum alias Jotsna Rani Saha v State and Snandra Nath Saha*, 15 DLR (1963) 39.

38 See *Badiur Rahman Chowdhury v Nazrul Islam* 16 BLD AD (1996) 263. The father claimed that Nasrin Chowdhury, then aged 15, was kidnapped by her class friend, Zahir. Nasrin refused to go to her father, who she claimed, in an unusually frank statement, had thrown her out after he found out about her 'love affair'. The Appellate Division held that the High Court Division had wrongly made findings (regarding the girl's age, and her having married of her own accord) which could prejudice Zahir's trial, and that it should have paid more attention to the 'words of the parents than to those of a wayward daughter who is currently enamoured'.

39 See *Rehana Begum v. Bangladesh* 50 DLR (1998) 557 In one of the few cases filed directly by way of a constitutional writ petition, Rehana, aged 16, a British/Bangladeshi national, was set at liberty from safe custody after the court heard her statement that her father brought her to Bangladesh from the UK on the pretext of a holiday; that he took away her passport; that when she married

someone locally without his knowledge, her father started a criminal case for rape against the husband, claiming she was a minor and mentally unstable.

40 *Jatio Mohila Ainjibi Samity v Bangladesh* 59 DLR 2007 448: the High Court released Najma, on questioning her along with her husband, Uttam, and discovering that he had converted to Islam, renamed himself Jashim and was now an imam, that she was now aged twenty, and that they had married and were anxious to begin 'to lead a conjugal life'.

41 Once in England, Dr Abedin applied in the English courts for annulment of her Bangladesh forced marriage. In the meantime, her father filed a petition in the apex court in Bangladesh, seeking leave to appeal against the High Court's judgment, but ultimately did not pursue it.

42 'Rangpur DC Asked to Shift Rape Victim to Safe Custody', *Daily Star*, 9 June 2010. The courts have not built upon earlier precedents, from Jahanara Begum's case onwards, which have reiterated the need for 'neutral homes'. Currently there are twenty-one shelter homes, seven of which are run by the government and fourteen by NGOs, situated across Bangladesh, a number clearly grossly inadequate for providing safe custody to survivors of violence (personal communicaton with Nina Goswami, lawyer, Ain o Salish Kendra).

43 The majority of cases concerned women from Hindu families claiming to have converted to Islam and married of their own free will. The few exceptions include Sukhendra Chandra's case (see notes 25 and 26) where a Hindu girl, Ranjana Rani, married Shahidul, a worker at her uncle's handloom, and son of a sharecropper on her father's land; the Jatio Mohila Ainjibi case where a Muslim woman detainee was married under Muslim law to a Hindu who converted to Islam and became an imam; and Dr Shipra Chowdhury's case and that of Aberystwyth Women's Aid which involved threats of or actual forced marriage carried out by the parents.

44 The Special Marriage Act 1872 permits inter-community marriages only for certain groups (Buddhists, Jains, Hindus and Sikhs) and can only be used by Muslims and Christians if they first affirm that they have abandoned their respective faiths.

45 In *Rokeya Kabir v. Government of Bangladesh*, 52 DLR (2000) 234, Rokeya Kabir filed a public interest petition against the practice of safe custody, claiming there was no statutory basis for the practice. The High Court determined, 'The legality of the system of safe custody has already been decided by a long line of decisions by our courts (...) [S]afe custody is a judicial custody for the definite purpose of ensuring the welfare of a victim girl devised by our courts and sanctioned by the Appellate Division (...) It does not matter that there is no statutory basis for safe custody as there is a law laid down by the highest court of the country.' Very recently, in a public interest litigation, *Mahbub Shafique and others v Bangladesh* Writ Petition No. 48543 of 2010, the court directed the

government to show cause why the practice of holding persons in jails in the name of safe custody should not be held unconstitutional. In compliance with the court's directions, the prisons authority has identified some 59 women and girls held in prisons across the country in safe custody, and the National Human Rights Commission has been directed to review these cases and report to the court.

References

AALI (Association for Advocacy and Legal Initiatives), (2003) *Against the Forces: Report and Recommendations of National Consultation on Women's Right to Choose If, When and Whom to Marry*, AALI, Lucknow.

Chowdhury, P. (2007) *Contentious Marriages, Eloping Couples*, Oxford University Press, New Delhi.

IWRAW-AP (International Women's Rights Action Watch-Asia Pacific) (2005) *The Right to Decide If, When and Whom to Marry*, IWRAW-AP Occasional Papers Series No. 6, Kuala Lumpur.

Malik, S. (2004) 'The Children Act, 1974: A Critical Commentary', Save the Children UK (SCUK), Dhaka.

Siddiqi, D. (2005) 'Of Consent and Contradiction: Forced Marriage in Bangladesh', in Welchman and Hossain (eds.), *'Honour': Crimes, Paradigms, and Violence against Women*, Zed Books, London.

Welchman, L. and S. Hossain (eds.) (2005) *'Honour': Crimes, Paradigms and Violence against Women*, Zed Books, London.

About the contributors

Dr Sundari Anitha is Lecturer in Criminology in the School of Social Sciences, University of Lincoln. Her research interests lie in two broad fields: (1) violence against black, minority ethnic and refugee women in the UK, and health, social policy and criminal justice responses to this problem; and (2) migration, 'race', ethnicity, gender and working lives among the South Asian diasporas in the UK. She has published articles in journals including *Violence Against Women*, the *British Journal of Social Work* and *Feminist Legal Studies*. In between academic jobs, Anitha has managed a Women's Aid refuge and worked as an advice worker for Asha Projects, a specialist refuge for survivors of domestic violence. She has been active in campaigns and policy making on violence against women, including forced marriage, and is currently a trustee of Asha Projects.

Dr Marzia Balzani is a reader in social anthropology at Roehampton University, the Chief Examiner for the Assessment and Qualifications Alliance A-level in Anthropology and an associate lecturer with the Open University. She also prepares expert reports for asylum seekers from South Asia with a focus on religious persecution and gendered violence. Her monograph *Modern Indian Kingship* (2003) is an examination of tradition and politics in a high-caste Hindu community in Rajasthan, India. She is currently researching a book on the Ahmadi Muslims of London, a diasporic South Asian community on which she has published several articles.

Dr Samia Bano is a lecturer in family law in the School of Law, University of Reading. She obtained her PhD in 2005 at the University of Warwick, where her doctoral thesis explored the practice of Muslim family law in the UK and the experiences of Muslim women. Her research interests include

Islamic family law in the UK and Europe, Islamic jurisprudence and human rights, and issues concerning the rights of Muslim women. Her current work explores the relationship between informal systems of dispute resolution within Muslim communities, state law and gender relations in the UK and is due to be published in 2011.

Dr Anja Bredal is a senior researcher at the Institute for Social Research in Oslo. She holds a PhD in sociology and her research interests have centred on forced/arranged marriage, autonomy, gender and generation, as well as state policies and welfare provision in the fields of immigration, social services and domestic violence. She has done commissioned research for the Norwegian Ministry for Children and Equality and the Nordic Ministerial Council. Her career includes a period at the Centre for Gender Studies University of Oslo, and at the Ministry of Foreign Affairs.

Dr Khatidja Chantler is a lecturer and researcher in social work at the University of Manchester. She has undertaken research projects on subjects including attempted suicide and self-harm among South Asian women; domestic violence and minoritisation; forced marriage; and domestic and sexual violence in male, black, lesbian, gay and transgendered communities, and published widely on these topics. She is also a counsellor and has worked in health and social care settings for over twenty-five years.

Shazia Choudhry is a Senior Lecturer at Queen Mary, University of London, where she joined the Department of Law in September 2005. Previously, she was lecturer in law at the University of Newcastle (2002–5) and prior to that a practising solicitor. Her areas of expertise and research interests are in family law, the impact of the European Convention on Human Rights on family law, and the issue of 'rights' within family law in general. She has published a number of articles on this subject and has recently co-authored a monograph on the issue entitled *European Human Rights and Family Law* with Jonathan Herring.

Dr Geetanjali Gangoli works at the Centre for Gender and Violence Research, in the School for Policy Studies, University of Bristol. She has previously taught at the University of Delhi, been a Sir Ratan Tata Visiting Fellow at the London School of Economics and Political Science and a Research Fellow at the International Centre for the Study of Violence Against

Women Research Group. She has researched and published in the areas of forced marriage, honour-based violence and domestic violence in ethnic minority communities in the UK; comparing domestic violence experiences amongst university students in the UK and China; on prostitution and trafficking in South Asia; Indian feminisms and the law and perpetrators of domestic violence. She edits the journal *Policy and Politics*.

Dr Aisha Gill is a Senior Lecturer in Criminology at Roehampton University. Her main areas of interest and research are health and criminal justice responses to violence against black, minority ethnic and refugee women in the UK. She has been involved in addressing violence against women at the grassroots and activist levels for many years. She is a member of the End Violence Against Women group and the WNC United Nations Advisory Group; an invited advisor to the Independent Police Complaints Commission (IPCC) strategic support group on investigations and complaints involving gendered forms of violence against women in the UK; a member of Liberty's Project Advisory Group; Chair of Newham Asian Women's Project (2004–9); and a member of Imkaan. She has extensive experience of providing expert advice to government and the voluntary sector on legal policy issues related to so-called honour killings and forced marriage, and has challenged politicians to be more inclusive of black minority ethnic and refugee women's voices in policy making on issues of gender-based violence and human rights. Her current research interests include rights, law and forced marriage; gendered crimes related to patriarchy; so-called 'honour' killings and 'honour'-based violence in the South Asian/Kurdish diaspora and femicide in Iraqi Kurdistan; missing women; acid violence; post-separation violence and child contact; trafficking; and sexual violence. She has published widely in peer-reviewed journals and is currently co-authoring a monograph entitled 'Crimes of "Honour" against Women: Experiences and Counter Strategies in Iraqi Kurdistan and the UK Kurdish Diaspora' with Nazand Begikhani and Gill Hague (Bristol University).

Teertha Gupta is a family law practitioner with particular experience in public and private international child abduction, stranded spouses and forced marriage matters and cases involving jurisdictional complications, e.g. international surrogacy and adoption and media interest. He represents adults and children as well as institutions in the High Court (Family Division) on a daily basis. He has made oral submissions in the European Court of Justice, and several times in the Court of Appeal. In 2007 he represented the intervening children in the second of his three recent successful cases in the House of Lords; in 2009 he also appeared in the UK Supreme Court in its first international family law case. Teertha was one of the lawyers who assisted in drafting the Forced Marriage (Civil Protection) Act 2007.

Professor Marianne Hester holds the Chair in Gender, Violence and International Policy, and is Head of the Centre for Gender and Violence Research at the School for Policy Studies, University of Bristol, as well as being NSPCC Professor of Child Sexual Exploitation. Since 1980 she has carried out research into many aspects of violence against women and children, including comparative research on child contact and domestic violence in Denmark and the UK, and a comparison of domestic violence and child maltreatment in China and the UK. She has acted as Expert Advisor to the Home Affairs Select Committee on Forced Marriage, 'Honour'-based Violence and Female Genital Mutilation. Her current work includes a longitudinal study of domestic violence and the criminal justice system; research on 'domestic violence perpetrators in the health sector' (with Gene Feder, Emma Williamson et al.); and the first study in the UK 'comparing domestic violence in same-sex and heterosexual relationships' (with Catherine Donovan, University of Sunderland). She was for a long period involved in the Rape Crisis Movement in the UK and has worked in close collaboration with organisations such as Women's Aid that provide services to women and children experiencing domestic violence. She is Patron of South Tyneside Women's Aid.

Sara Hossain is a barrister practising at the Supreme Court of Bangladesh and a Partner at the law firm of Dr Kamal Hossain and Associates. Her publications include (co-edited with Lynn Welchman) '*Honour': Crimes, Paradigms and Violence against Women* (2005, Zed Books); (with Iain Byrne) 'Socio-Economic Rights in South Asia', in Malcolm Smart (ed.) *Social Rights Jurisprudence: Emerging Trends in International and Comparative Law* (2009); and *Remedies for Forced Marriage in South Asia and the UK* (forthcoming). Her main areas of research and activism are public interest litigation, access to justice, and women's rights. She was educated at Oxford University and called to the Bar from Middle Temple. She is an active member of Ain o Salish Kendra, a national human rights organisation, and works closely with the Bangladesh Legal Aid and Services Trust (www.blast.org.bd).

Khatun Sapnara read law at the London School of Economics. She was called to the Bar in 1990 and has practised as a barrister since 1990 from chambers in London. She also sits as a judge (a Recorder of the Crown) in both family and criminal cases in the county and crown courts in London and the South East. She has served on the Family Law Bar Association Committee since 2003. Khatun was directly involved in drafting the Forced Marriage (Civil Protection) Act 2007 and advising on its passage through Parliament as well as its implementation. She regularly undertakes training of the judiciary in family law on behalf of the Judicial Studies Board. She has trained all tiers of the judiciary on the provisions of the Forced Marriage (Civil Protection) Act. She has served on the Family Justice Council since it was formed in 2004 as a multidisciplinary body of experts to advise Government on all aspects of the family justice system. Khatun is also the Chair of Ashiana Network, the only dedicated forced marriage refuge in the UK which also provides refuge and support for women from South East Asian, Turkish and Iranian backgrounds experiencing domestic violence.

Ann Singleton is a Senior Research Fellow in the School for Policy Studies, University of Bristol. Her work focuses on the production of knowledge on migration and the use of international migration data in the development of policy. She has published and spoken widely on asylum and international migration policy and statistics in the UK and the European Union. She has advised the European Commission, the European Parliament, the Council of Ministers and EU Presidencies, and has collaborated with the UNHCR, United Nations Economic Commission for Europe, the United Nations Economic and Social Commission for Western Asia, and many nongovernmental organisations and international organisations. She is co-chair of the Statewatch Trustees.

Index

A Choice by Right, working group report 2000, 158, 181

A v the United Kingdom 1999, 75-6

Abedin, Dr Humayra, case of, 17, 139, 151, 190, 230, 234; British media response, 231

Abel, R., 182

'abuses of culture', 153

Access to Justice Act, UK 1999, 184-5

Adoption and Children Act, UK 2002, 185

Afghanistan, 49, 71; bride-price, 10

age of majority, Bangladesh determination of, 226, 229

agency, women's, 177; concepts of, 103; -passivity binary, 56, 103

Ahmed, Bipasha, 1, 41

Akpinar, A., 10

Albania, forced marriage criminalized, 9

Algeria, 10, 71

Alternate Dispute Resolution (ADR), 184-5, 196; local authority involvement lack, 190; mechanisms, 178, 181; plural nature of, 195; privatization, 177; trends, 183; UK, 182

Amnesty International, 76

Anitha, Sundari, 14-16, 102-4, 195

Annan, Kofi, 70, 84

Arbitration Act, UK 1996, 178, 185-7, 192

arbitration, potential adverse effects, 193

Ardener, E., 213

Armenia, 49

arranged marriage, 54, 91, 125; as South Asian exoticism, 126; -forced marriage conflation, 28, 50, 93, 97-8, 100, 106, 123-4; -forced counterposed, 26, 32; -forced misleading binary, 59; 'inbreeding' risk, 122; non-autonomous decision presumption, 101-3

Arun Karmaker v the State, 228

Asha Projects, 140

Ashiana, women's group, 140

Association of chief Police Officers, UK, 69, 84, 181

asylum applications system, UK; Asylum and Immigration Tribunal, 200; Asylum Policy Instructions (APIs), 210-12; 'credibility' exclusive focus, 205-9, 212; forced marriage downplayed, 205; judgement 'information hierarchy', 205; knowledge constructed, 201;

orientalist tropes, 11; Pakistani women, UK, 16; -seekers narratives, 206, 213

asylum solicitors: personal experienced sidelined, 213; strategic essentialism use, 215

Australia, 11; forced marriage law, 9

Austria, 71; forced marriage criminalised, 8

'backward' communities, honour labeled, 33

Balzani, Marzia, 16-17

Bangladesh, 10, 168, 190; British High Commission, 230; Constitution 1972, 222-3; habeas corpus, 17; routine Constitutional denials, 234; 'safe custody' use, 221

Bano, S., 16, 178

Begum, Jahanara, 229, 232

Beijing Declaration and Platform for Action, 70

Belarus, 71

Benedict. H., 113

Benjamin, M., 193-4

Berlant, Lauren, 124

Bevacqua and another v. Bulgaria, 82, 84

black ethnic minority women, 153; agency, 56; empowerment, 150; hyper visibility, 120; specialist refugees, 137; violence against, 117

black minority ethnic cultures, colonial attitude towards, 60

Blackett, R., 185

Blair, Ian, 116

Blunkett, David, 124

Booth report, 1985, 185

Booth, Penny, 193

Bredal, A., 15

bride price, 10, 26, 33

Briggs, Jack, 138

Briggs, Zena, 138

Bristol UK, 1978 conciliation service, 183

'Britishness', 117, 119, 123

Byrne, Liam, 121

Canada, 11, 71; Department of Justice, 6; forced marriage, 18

Cantle Report, UK, 124

'case owners', asylum cases, 207; education lack, 211

CEDAW (Convention on the Elimination of All Forms of Discrimination Against Women), 16, 223

Chantler, Khatidja, 1, 14, 26, 33, 37, 41

Chesney-Lind, M., 69

'child', Bangladesh legal definition, 223

child marriage, 29-30, 33, 35

Child Marriage Restraint Act, Bangladesh, 225-6, 233

children: FMPO applications, 159; state protection responsibilities, 75

Children Act, Bangladesh, 226-8, 233

Children Act, UK 1989: 68, 147, 160, 190; Section 31, 161; UK 2004, 185

China, bride-price, 10

Choudry, Shazia, 15`

Chowdhury, Dr Shipra, case judgment importance, 222, 235

citizenship, 117, 177-8; 'privatisation' of, 124

City Of Westminster v IC...and KC and NN, 168, 170

civil law, recourse to, 151

Civil procedure Rules, Part 1, 184

Civitas, 195

'clash of culture', immigrant

generations, 30-1

coercion: conceptions of, 14, 41, 91; consent boundary, 13, 27; definitions of, 54, 92; family members, 39, 52; gender neutral law, 145; pressure distinction, 167; restricted legal range of forms, 61; total burden of, 55; types, 46; UK legal definition, 50

Coffey, G., 210

Coleridge, Mr Justice Paul, 190-1

Colombia, 71

community blame, violence against ethnic women, 117

community male leaders, foregrounded, 118

compulsory heterosexuality, 27-8

compulsory interviews, immigrant sponsors Norway, 98

consanguineous marriage, issue of, 57, 122-4

consent, 93; -coercion binary conception, 59, 104, 107, 152; -coercion boundaries, 13, 27; -coercion grey area, 53, 102, 103; issue of, 26; lack of grounds, 168; Pakistan rules, 170; parental, 52; quasi, 91; rules, 169

Conservative/Liberal Democratic government UK, 48

continuum concept, gender-based violence, 38-9, 46, 58-60, 103-4

Convention on the Rights of the Child, Article 1, 7

Council of Europe, 5, 15, 67; Committee of Ministers, 82

Country of Origin Information reports, UK Home Office, 204-7, 210

Court of Protection, UK, 147; cases, 190

cousin marriages, 122

'credibility' findings: asylum decision makers, 210-11; 'broad and narrow' approaches, 212

crime: media obsession with, 114; reduction policy, 47

Crime Disorder Reduction Partnerships, 47

criminal justice system, intersectional approach, 58

Crown Courts, UK, 172

Crown Prosecution Service (CPS), UK, 46, 187

Cryer, Anne, 121-3

'culture clash' approach, 30-1

Cutler, S., 201

Cyprus, forced marriage criminalized, 8

Daily Mail, 118

Dauvergne, C., 214

Declaration on the Elimination of Violence against Women, 69

Deech, Ruth, 122-3

Denmark, 15; 'Action Plan on Forced, Quasi-Forced and Arranged Marriages', 93; Aliens Act 2002, 12, 92; arranged-forced marriage conflation, 97; forced marriage discourse, 91, 101; general preventive approach, 99; immigration policies, 90-2; spouse visa age increase, 37, 95, 106, 203; 'suspect marriage' construct, 104, 106; women's agency lack presumption, 107

deterministic culture, 117

Devgon, Jasvinder, 1, 41

Dhaka High Court, 229

diasporas, gendered processes, 57

dispute resolution: new methods, 170,

177-8; non-adversarial, 184-5
divorce, 27, 138
domestic violence, 34, 36, 83, 192;
    abuse, 77, 80; community silence
    pressure 166; Domestic Violence
    Crime and Victims Act, UK, 47;
    individualised, 119; legal funding,
    162; 'lottery', 47; media trivialised,
    120; partner, 35; specialist services,
    48, 57, 153; specific forms, 139;
    Turkey, 76; UK debates, 3; under-
    reported everyday, 116; women
    complicit, 4
dowries, 139
*Dr Shipra Chowdhury v Joynal Abedin
    and others*, 230
Duluth model, 'power and control', 35
Dupont, I., 58
duress, 165; claims of, 50; emotional
    pressure, 51, 53, 140; proof
    difficulties, 167
Dustin, M., 40, 50

EC Qualification Directive, 211
emotional abuse, degradation, 74, 77
English law, 178
Entry Clearing Organisation, UK, 188
equivalence chains, 104
Eritrea, 49
essentialist stereotypes, anti-immigration
    discourse, 153; forced marriage, 11
Estonia, 71
Europe, right-wing populist parties, 90
European Convention of Human Rights
    (ECHR), 7, 67, 71, 82, 184, 192;
    Article 12, 138; Article 3, 72-8, 84;
    Article 8, 80-3; positive and negative
    obligations, 79
European Court of Human Rights, 7
European Economic Area, 93; spouse

visa age rules, 12, 37, 121
European Union, 29, 93; CEDAW
    ratification, 7; forced marriage
    statistics lack, 5, 203
extended families, South Asian, 35

family(ies) coercion within, 39; power
    relations in, 4; 'reconciliation', 143
family courts, UK, 47; Division judges,
    165; professionals, 161; standard of
    proof, 171
family law, 177, 183; 1996 Act, 141-2,
    158, 160, 170, 184, 202; Bar
    Association UK, 170
'family life', 29; respect for, 78, 82
fast-track system asylum-seekers,
    critique of, 200-1
Feinberg, J., 55
female genital mutilation, 35, 38
femininity, gendered scripts, 150
feminism/feminists, 3; activist, 34;
    adversarial legal system preference,
    195; Black, 152; critique of
    mediation, 193; law reform, 151;
    scholars, 11
Finer Committee, 183; 1974 Report,
    185
Finland, 71
forced marriage: agency lack narrative,
    117; anti-immigration rhetoric use,
    97; -arranged marriage conflation/
    binary, *see above*; asylum-seeking/
    obstacles, 204, 215; civil remedies,
    142; close kin spouses presumption,
    94; control and powerlessness issue,
    193; criminal offences by-products,
    68; criminalisation, 9, 11, 140;
    culturalist discourse, 15, 48, 55, 59,
    119, 126, 141, 180; 'degrading
    treatment', 73; disabled victims, 17;

domestic violence, *see above*; EU incidence, 5; ex-UK, 170; exit-centred approach, 27, 40, 196; 'expert opinion' accreditation need, 173; gendered nature, 34, 146, 150, 202; human rights violations, 26; immigration control use, 29, 37, 99, 125, 203; inheritance factor, 206; injunctive relief, 143; intersectional approach, 56-7; lesbian mother case, 207; media discourse, 114, 128; men as victims, 145; minority communities, 10; moral outrage narratives, 115; multiple inequalities context, 13; narratives of persecution, 214; non-specific ECHR cases, 76; nullity applications/proceedings, 102, 158, 167, 169; offenders' behaviour exploration, 180; 'othered' culture discourse, 49; proactive measures, 161, 164-5; 'problem of the 'knower', 101; safe interview space needed, 165; Sierra Leone convictions, 8; state border violation discourse, 92; statistical unreliability, 50; traditional Asian construct, 118; UK citizens/asylum-seeker contrast, 208; UK discourses, 12, 15, 26, 29, 33, 36, 46, 54, 61, 137, 144; UL legal responses, 16; UN definition, 70; victim credibility perceptions, 162-3; victim family estrangement fear, 171; 'young woman issue, 206

Forced marriage (Civil Protection) Act 2007, 16-17, 51, 138-9, 143, 145-8, 151, 158, 161, 163, 169-70, 171-4, 181, 189, 202, 231; protective intention, 159; Relevant Third Parties, 149; third party applications, 160, 162

Forced Marriage Protection Orders (FMPOs), 118, 142, 146, 190-1; applications, 147; breaches of undertakings, 171; child protection, 162; limited nature of, 189; numbers of, 148, 159; undertakings, 172

Forced Marriage: The Risk Factors...' UK 2006, 1, 41, 61, 112

Forced Marriage Unit, Joint FCO and Home Office, 32, 119, 121, 140, 203, 208

Forced Marriages in Council of Europe Member State, 5

FCO (Foreign and Commonwealth Office UK), 144; Community Liaison Unit, 181

foreign spouses, European rules, 12; forced marriage, *see above*

Foucault, M., problematisation concept, 112-13

France, 10, 12

Fundamental Principles of State Policy, Bangladesh, 223

Gangoli, Geetanjali, 1, 14, 37, 41

gender: -based violence, 38-9, 46, 58-60; relations legal means of transformation, 149; Western equality claims, 118

Germany, 71; forced marriage criminalised, 8-9

Ghana, 71

'ghettoisation', 121

Gill, Aisha K., 14-16, 102-4, 195

global migrant flows, 202

Goldstone, Clement QC, 119

Gough, Kathleen, 27

Guardians and Wards Act, Bangladesh, 226

Guardianship Act, Bangladesh, 233
Guatemala, 71
Gupta, Teertha, 17, 166

habeas corpus, Bangladesh use of, 221-6
'harmful cultural/traditional practices',
13, 30, 120, 128
Hester, Marianne, 1, 14, 28, 33, 39, 41,
194
heterosexuality, normative status, 46
High Court and Appellate Divisions,
Bangladesh, 226, 230
Hindu law, 224
Hirani v. Hirani 1983, 50, 140
Home Affairs Select Committee on
Immigration Control, UK, 121
Home Office UK, 144; COIs, 204-7,
210; forced marriage definition, 40;
forced marriage report, 1, 41, 51,
61, 112; Operational Guidance
Note for Pakistan, 205
'honour' (*izzat*), 25, 53; -based crime,
115, 137; codes of, 32;
particularized, 33; white British
positive concept, 33
honour violence, contested statistics, 4;
racist criminal justice system
obstacle, 10
Hossain, Sara, 17
House of Commons Home Affairs
Committee, UK, 127
human rights: activists, 3; discourse, 15,
18, 28, 67, 69; integrated approach
need, 68
Human Rights Act, UK 1998, 71-2, 85,
192
Human Rights Watch, 201
Hunter, M., 191
Hussein (Otherwise Blitz) v Hussein, 50,
140

Imkaan women's group, 35
immigration politics: anti- 57, 152-3;
control emphasis on, 68, 122; policy
debates, 12, 103-4, 181; UK, 146;
unequal gender relations, 31;
women's oppression use, 90
Immigration Appellate Authority UK,
Gender Guidelines, 205
Immigration Rule 339, UK, 211
Independent Domestic Violence
Advisers, UK, 149
India, 10
'informalism', legal systems, 182
intercontinental marriages, 122
International Convention on Civil and
Political Rights, 6
International Criminal Tribunal for
Rwanda, forced marriage
unconsidered, 8
international family law, 166
internet dating, South Asian use, 126
interpreters, asylum cases, 209
intersectionality, 58; meaning of, 56
Iran, 49
Iraq, bride price, 10
Irving, H., 193, 194
Islam, 31; society stigmatized, 180
*Islam (AP) v. Secretary of State for the
Home Department*, 83
Islamic/Muslim law, 16, 176-9, 185-6,
224; -English law relationship, 188
Israel, 71
Italy, 71
Ives, Wayne, 119

Jarman, Andrea, 191
Jewish Beth Din tribunals, 179, 191
*Jharna Rani Saha v Khanandaker
Zayedul Hoque and another*, 228
Judicial Studies Board, UK, 164, 173

Justice Singer, 53

Karma Nirvana, Women's Rights
    Organization, 9
Kazimirski, A., 148
Keighley, UK, 121
Kelly, Liz, 38
Khairunnessa v Illy Begum, 228
Khandelwal, M., 126
Kurczewski, J., 183

labeling, linguistic, 2
Labour government UK Blair/Brown,
    11, 48, 143, 149, 151; 'community
    cohesion' focus, 144; domestic
    violence legal funding, 162; forced
    marriage culturalist viewpoint, 144;
    legal solutions focus, 150; spouse
    visa age increase, 204
law(s), 9 2; limits to, 152; Muslim
    family, 187; Trojan horse use, 150
legal discourses, gendered stereotypes,
    11
legal diversity, privatised, 179
Legal Service Commission, UK, 162,
    185
Lester, Lord Anthony of Herne Hill,
    141
LGBT (lesbian, gay, bisexual and
    transgender)persons, 27, 204, 207
Lithuania, 71
LOKK, Danish women's shelter
    organisation, 96
Luton, UK, forced marriage research,
    119

Macedonia, forced marriage
    criminalized, 9
MacEoin, Denis, 195
Mahmood v Mahmood 1993, 51

Mahmud v Mahmud 1994, 51-2
Majority Act, Bangladesh, 223
Malaysia, 10
marriage(s): arranged, *see above*;
    consanguineous, *see above*; control of
    women mechanism, 27; forced, *see
    above*; 'for love' Western norm, 12;
    gender surveillance after, 27; inter-
    religious/class, 222, 233; 'migration',
    94; minimum age demands, 10;
    normality frame, 144, 208; nullity
    declaration, 140; 'of convenience',
    105, 121; pressure to, 52, 55;
    'telephonic', 168; women's restraints,
    152
Marriage Act, UK 1949, 138
mass media: domestic violence
    trivialised, 120; forced marriage
    discourse, 15, 49, 55, 60;
    'institutional racism', 116; news
    story selection, 114; social policy
    and crime representation, 113;
    victim images, 115
Matrimonial Causes Act, UK 1973,
    138, 170; Section 1, 165
Mauritius, 71
McCarry, Melanie, 1, 41
McKinley, M., 214
mediation, marital: cross-cultural
    mechanisms, 177; dangers of, 193;
    definitional problems, 183; mediator
    role, 184; neutrality illusion, 194
Metropolitan Police, UK, 116
migration, 'marriage', 94
Millbank, J., 214
Minimum Age for Marriage Act 1964, 5
Ministry for Refugee, Immigration and
    Integration, 93
minority communities, 34; dominant
    moral codes, 52; 'unchanging'

characterization, 30; violence against, 36

minority ethnic women: hypervisibility, 120; specialist refuges, 137; violence against, 117

Moldova, 71

Morocco, 10

mother-in-law violence, 35

Moylan, Mr Justice, 169

Multi-agency Practice Guidelines: Handling Cases of Forced Marriage, 164

multiculturalism, 25, 34, 118; ideological debates, 17; interlegality, 192; Western societies, 180

Munby, Mr Justice James, 165, 167

Muslim Arbitration Tribunal (MAT), UK, 16, 178-9, 185, 187, 191-5; enforcement power lack, 186; in camera hearings, 189; *Liberation from Forced Marriages*, 188

National Action Plan on Domestic Violence, UK 2006, 84

National Health Service, UK, 123, 190

Naz, Rukhsana, 138

'neutral homes', Bangladesh legal notion, 234

Newham Asian Women's Project, 140

Nielsen, F., 12

Nikkah ceremony, Muslim, 164

Norway, 12, 15, 71, 96; arranged marriage discrediting, 98; Directorate of Immigration, 100, 105; family reunification law, 125; forced marriage discourse, 8-9, 91, 97, 99, 101; forced marriage national plan 1998, 94; immigration restriction laws, 90, 92, 107; refugee women, 56; spouse age limit

strategy, 95; *suspect marriage* construct, 104, 106

NS v MI (Nullity), 165, 167

nullity (of marriage) proceedings, 165, 173; applications, 167; burden of proof, 166

O'Brien, Mike, 30

Observer newspaper, 117

Opuz v. Turkey, 76-7, 84

organisational culture of disbelief, UK Border Agency, 209

Orientalism, 11, 126; narratives of, 117

outmoded traditions, narrative of, 137

Pakistan, 207, 215; Christianity position, 206; consent rules, 169-70; Home Office COI on, 204-5

parental custody and consent power, Bangladesh, 224-9; 'mental torture', 232; evidential weight given to, 233

Parkinson, P., 180, 184

patriarchal bias, adversarial legal system, 193

people trafficking, forced marriage method, 70

personal laws, religious-based, 224

Phillips, A., 40, 50

Phillips, Lord Nicolas, 179

Police Domestic Violence Liaison Officers, UK, 187

police intervention, likely counter-productive, 141

poverty, forced marriage context, 33

power, cross cutting hierarchies, 57

Prentice, Bridget, 186

private life, respect for, 80

problematisation, concept of, 112

proportionality, issue of, 81

Public Law Online, 161

Queen's Proctor, UK, 167
Qur'anic Injunctions, 187

R(Cowl and Others) v Plymouth City Council, 184
Rabinow, Paul, 113
racism, forced marriage concept potential, 37; normalized racist policies, 112
Rasmussen, Andre Fogh, 12
Razack, S,, 37
Reasons for Refusal Letter, UK asylum, 206; assumptions of, 207-9
Redfern, A., 191
Reese, S., 113
Refugees, 48, 152; minoritised women, 36; passive victim preference, 17; - status decision-makers, 11
refuges, 48, 152; minoritised women, 36
Reitman, O., 54
religious weddings, UK, 166
Renaissance legal chambers, UK, 127
Revolutionary United Front, Sierra leone, forced marriage convictions, 8
Rhose, D., 151
Rich, Adrienne, 27
Rifkin, Janet, 193-4
Right of Women orgainisation, 140
Roberts, M., 184
Roberts, Rochelle, 124
romantic love, as crucial marker, 125-6
Romkens, R., 150
Royal Courts of Justice, UK, 179

'safe custody', Bangladesh involuntary, 224-6, 230-1, 234; prison, 232
Sahindal, Fadime, 95
San Francisco Community Boards, USA, 182

sanctuary schemes, 47
Sanghera, Jasvinder, 30
Sapnara, Khatun, 17, 164
Secure Borders, Safe Haven, 124
Sen, Purna, 60
Serbia, 71; forced marriuage criminalized, 9
sexual minorities, 17, 27, 204, 207
Sexual Offences Act 2003, UK, 169
SH v NB (MARRIAGE: CONSENT) 2009, UK, 166
Shachar, Ayelet, 179
Shah-Kazemi, N., 178
shame (*sharam*), 53
Sharia law, 16; 'constructive accommodation' of, 179; courts, 185; -English law relationship, 186; matrimonial disputes, 178
Sharma, Sandhya, 1, 41
Shoemaker, P., 113
Singh v Singh 1971, 52
Singleton, Ann, 1, 14, 41
'slave brides', 115
social constructionism, 114
socio-psychological 'costs of exit', 54
Soham UK, murders reported, 116
Sohrab v Khan 2002, 51
Sokoloff, N., 58
Somalia, 49
South Asian communities: marriage age norms, 29; shoe-hitting significance, 213
South Asian women; passivity presumption, 112; UK self-harm rates, 74
Southall Black Sisters, 35, 140-1
Special Court for Sierra Leone, 7, 28
Special Tribunals on Violence against Women and Children, Bangladesh, 224

Specialist Domestic Violence Court (SDVC) system, UK, 147, 149

spouses immigration/visas: age limit increases, 31, 92, 95-102, 106, 121-2, 125-6, 203; domestic violence use of, 36; UK rationalization, 204

Stanko, E., 151

Stark, E., 41

State, the, protection responsibilities, 3, 72-3, 75, 77, 83

Storhaug, Hege, 95

Sub-Saharan Africa, bride-price, 10

Sudan, 49

Sumati Begum v Rafiqullah, 227

Sunday Times, 187

Supplementary Convention on the Abolition of Slavery, 202

Supreme Court Bangladesh, 221; Appellate Division, 228; gender bias, 235; High Court Division, 223, 227

suspect marriage construct, 104, 106

Sweden, 9, 15; honour killings focus, 95

Sweeney, J., 210-12

third-party provision, FMPOs, 148

Thorpe, Lord Justice, 168

'traditional'/'modern' cultures binary, 38

traveler communities Irish, 49

Tsnagarides, N., 201, 207

Turkey, 14, 49; domestic violence, 76; Kurdish women, 10

UK (United Kingdom), 9, 11, 71; Asylum and Immigration Tribunal, 210; asylum seekers, 200; British policy, 146; Border Agency, *see below*; consent rules, 169; Country of Origin (COI) reports, 204; crime policy, 120; designated county courts, 160; Domestic Violence Crime and Victim's Act 2004, 137; forced marriage annulments, 102;; forced marriage criminalisation debate, 10; forced marriage discourses, 12, 15, 26, 29, 33, 36, 46, 54, 74; forced marriage 1999 working group, 181; forced marriage legal responses, 16, 49, 61; forced marriage statistics lack, 203; Forced Marriage Unit, 32, 38; gender-neutral law, 145; High Court judges, 33; high profile forced marriage cases, 202; Home Office Working Group, 1, 31, 139; Human Rights Act 1990, 67, 69; immigration policies, 11, 37, 57; Immigration Tribunal decisions, 215; judge training, 164; marriage laws, 138; mass media homicide reporting, 115-16; Ministry of Justice, 147, 189, 191; minority ethnic women, 55; New Asylum Model, 201; normalised female oppression, 144; refugee status obstacles, 214; religious weddings status, 166; 'right to exit' approach, 40; South Asian women, 52, 54; specialist domestic violence services, 143; 'what works' approach, 47; women as 'victims' *and* 'autonomous', 214

UN (United Nations), 15, 67; CEDAW, *see above*; Convention on Consent to Marriage, 1962, 202; Conventions on the Rights of the Child, 29; Declaration on the Elimination of Violence Against Women, 83; Division for the Advancement of Women, 71; 'harmful traditional practices' category, 120; Refugee

Convention, 200, 210; Secretary General's Report on Violence Against Women, 39; Security Council, 8; UNHCR Handbook, 211-12; violence against women definition, 2, 38

United Kingdom Border Agency, 200-1, 203; asylum 'caseowners', 207 force marriage stereotypes, 204, 208-9

Universal Declaration of Human Rights, Article 12, 6

universal laws/seperationist approach binary, 180

'unregulated islands of jurisdiction', 179

USA (United States of America), 5, 11

victim protection, courtroom situations, 172-3

'violence', etymology of, 3

violence against women: common experience of, 59; dowry-related, 38; estimates of, 4; 'honour'-based, 32, 74; legal remedies, 143; literature, 2; movement against, 25, 36; press coverage, 114; support groups, 152; UN definition, 2-3, 38

Wallis, Adam, 124

wardship proceedings, 68

Westmarland, Nicole, 1, 41

Williams, Rowan, 179

women: agency, 56-9, 91, 107, 139, 195; anti-immigration women's rights use, 90, 96, 120; asylum seekers 'muted', 213-14; Bangladeshi abroad, 222; complex dependencies, 54; detained asylum seekers, 116; 'honour'-bearers, 53; international movement, 69; minoritised refuges, 36; Pakistani asylum-seekers, 201; passive narrative, 137; South Asian UK organizations, 31; victims narratives formularized, 214; young South Asian, 52

Woolas, Phil, 122

Woolf, Lord, 184

World Conference on Human Rights in Vienna 1993, 69-70

World trade Centre 9/11 attacks, 55-6, 123

X and Others v. Bedfordshire County Council 199, 75

Yeo, Colin, 127, 204

Yüksel, M., 10

Z and Others v. the United Kingdom 2001, 75